The Book of Daily Prayer

The Book of Daily Prayer

Kim Martin Sadler
Editor

United Church Press
Cleveland, Ohio

United Church Press, Cleveland, Ohio 44115
© 1996 by United Church Press

Biblical quotations are from the New Revised Standard Version of the Bible, © 1989 by the Division of Christian Education of the National Council of the Churches of Christ in the U.S.A., and are used by permission

All rights reserved. Published 1996

Printed in the United States of America on acid-free paper

01 00 99 98 97 96   5 4 3 2 1

Library of Congress Cataloging-in-Publication Data

The book of daily prayer : morning and evening, 1997 / Kim Martin Sadler, editor.
p. cm.
ISBN 0-8298-1122-2 (alk. paper)
1. Prayers.   2. Devotional calendars.   I. Sadler, Kim Martin.
BV245.B586   1996
248'.8—dc20   95-51065
                          CIP

Contents

Introduction	vii		
January 1–5 Kathleen Gallas	1	May 5–11 G. Charles Satterwhite	125
January 6–12 John Biegert	6	May 12–18 LaTaunya M. Bynum	132
January 13–19 Barbara J. Essex	13	May 19–25 John E. Biersdorf	139
January 20–26 Elizabeth Francis Caldwell	20	May 26–June 1 Barbara Brown Zikmund	146
January 27–February 2 Anthony B. Robinson	27	June 2–8 George Polk	153
February 3–9 Charles Shelby Rooks	34	June 9–15 Lisa Shoenwetter	160
February 10–16 Margrethe B. J. Brown	41	June 16–22 Don C. Skinner	167
February 17–23 James A. Todhunter	48	June 23–29 Melbalenia D. Evans	174
February 24–March 2 Donna E. Schaper	55	June 30–July 6 Howard Stearns	181
March 3–9 Jack Sullivan Jr.	62	July 7–13 Susan M. Sanders	188
March 10–16 David T. Lyon	69	July 14–20 Barbara Dumke	195
March 17–23 Mary Susan Gast	76	July 21–27 Martha McMane	202
March 24–30 Lavon Bayler	83	July 28–August 3 F. Allison Phillips	209
March 31–April 6 Grant K. Sontag	90	August 4–10 Dorothy Ashman Fackre	216
April 7–13 Morgan Ponder	97	August 11–17 Martin Copenhaver	223
April 14–20 Frederick Trost	104	August 18–24 Leslie Carole Taylor	230
April 21–27 Bernice Powell Jackson	111	August 25–31 James Richard Lahman	237
April 28–May 4 Mary Ann Neevel	118	September 1–7 Nell M. Payne	244

September 8–14	251	November 3–9	307
Dorothy M. Lester		Lydia Waring Meyer	
September 15–21	258	November 10–16	314
Hilda R. Davis		Felix Carrion	
September 22–28	265	November 17–23	321
Alan Weatherly		Susan K. Smith	
September 29–October 5	272	November 24–30	328
Gennifer Benjamin Brooks		Thomas Dipko	
October 6–12	279	December 1–7	335
Paul H. Sadler Sr.		Jan Richardson	
October 13–19	286	December 8–14	342
Carole Keim		Kenneth A. Corr	
October 20–26	293	December 15–21	349
Sidney D. Fowler		Melva Costen	
October 27–November 2	300	December 22–28	356
Norval I. Brown		J. Denise Honeycutt	

Introduction

Prayer is the spiritual pathway to God's divine presence. It is through prayer that we are enabled to articulate our praise, our petitions, and our gratefulness to our Creator.

Daily prayer is the foundation of Christianity. Our foreparents in the faith, Martin Luther, Charles Wesley, and others, prayed several hours a day. Today, even with the demands of modern society, more and more Christians are finding time for prayer in their lives. If we would be faithful to the mandate of Jesus, "to pray without ceasing," then we too must find ourselves in consistent daily prayer. The spiritual discipline enriches the quality of our lives, empowering us to pray more effectively and with greater confidence.

The Book of Daily Prayer, Morning and Evening, 1997 is intended to provide a meaningful avenue for morning and evening devotion. With contributions from a broad spectrum of writers, the guide opens each day with a reference to a scriptural passage for consideration, then moves to a meditative prayer focusing on that scripture, a period for intercessory prayer, and a closing prayer. The opening, intercessory, and closing prayers include selections for both morning and evening.

We hope this new devotional guide will help you to strengthen your daily discipline and to renew your personal spiritual life. It is our fervent wish that this book will challenge you to delve more deeply into the sacred scriptures and to explore the unlimited possibilities of prayer.

WEDNESDAY, JANUARY 1
(Read Ecclesiastes 3:1–13)

(Morning)
O Blessed One, it is the first day of a new year. A new beginning fills me with the anticipation of new possibilities and opportunities. I lift up my voice in gratitude for all that the past year has held for me as I turn my memory to its gifts.
(Recall blessings and gifts.)

(Evening)
O Blessed One, this first day is coming to a close. I thank you for all it has held for me, joy and sorrow, each moment a lesson toward growth.

At the beginning of this new year, give me a beginner's mind, fresh and open, to listen and to explore the countless ways you are with me. God, you remind me that life means change. As a human being, I change and am changed by life's ebb and flow, by the alternating fortunes and seasons of human life. I am changed without being consulted and at a moment's notice. I long for certainty, but I am not in control. You have made everything suitable for its time within my human history. My only certainty is that you are with me. Only faith and discernment can make the difference in how I live within your design for me.

(Morning)
As I anticipate a new year, I pray for these personal needs and the needs of those who will be instruments of change for me.
(Prayers of Intercession)

(Evening)
Be with me as I recall my day. Grant me the grace to live in faith during adverse times.
(Prayers of Intercession)

**How can I make myself and others aware that you are always with us?
With confidence, I pray.**
(Pray the Prayer of Our Savior.)

(Morning)
May this day and this new year lead me to trust more fully in your great care. In your name. Amen.

(Evening)
When I awake tomorrow, I will need the gift of flexibility to flow with any given changes, but for now I close my eyes in sleep. In your name. Amen.

THURSDAY, JANUARY 2
(Read Psalm 8)

(Morning)
O Beloved Source of my life, from whom I have come and to whom I return, awaken me to your presence in my heart. You are here with me and in me and all around me; I sing your name. Eternal voice of my existence, I join the psalmist in praising your name.

(Evening)
O Beloved Source of my life, from whom I have come and to whom I return, at the end of this day I sing a song of thanksgiving for the wonder of life expressed in all of creation.

My name is precious to me. It says who I am; it is not a title that says what I do. When my name is spoken with care by someone who takes time to look directly at me, it can have the effect of being a blessing. I become animated with a warmth and love that enlivens whatever may follow. Christ Jesus, I reflect on the mystery and the power of your name. Yours is a name I can trust, and through it I can experience your saving love. Truly, your name is honey to my mouth, music to my ears, and joy to my heart.

(Morning)
May this day be a continuous prayer of praise to your name. By name I pray for those who live in my heart, my family and my friends.
(Prayers of Intercession)

(Evening)
Be with me as I recall where I missed the opportunities to praise your name and thus give you glory.
(Prayers of Intercession)

Am I mindful of the need in others to be respected as human beings in the simple unspoken request: Call me by my name. With confidence in the name of Jesus, I pray.
(Pray the Prayer of Our Savior.)

(Morning)
You call me by name. May I treat all others with the respect due their names. In your name. Amen.

(Evening)
O Sacred Source of all life, I rest in the confidence of your faithful love. In your holy name. Amen.

FRIDAY, JANUARY 3
(Read Revelations 21:1–6a)

(Morning)
Eternal God, maker of heaven and earth, I arise to this new day to sing of my love for you. I celebrate your glorious promise and fidelity to being with me always. Open my heart to your Word.

(Evening)
Eternal God, maker of heaven and earth, I thank you for being at my side every minute of this day that is now concluding.

God, you are the beginning and end of all life and existence. You chose to live among us. Each of us is a dwelling place. You fashioned within me an inner sanctuary, the heart, to be the place of intimacy wherein you dwell. You who shaped my heart also shaped the hearts of all who dwell on earth. Union with you brings me into union with all life, making everywhere one place. Christ Jesus, nothing stands apart from you. There is the wonderful promise that poverty, pain, death, and grief will pass away. But in the meantime, you are already within us and among us. Open the door of my heart to serve those in need in the present moment.

(Morning)
As I rejoice in your promises I pray for those in need of your love and care.
(Prayers of Intercession)

(Evening)
I pray that my life this day has enriched and given life to all with whom I came into contact. If I have failed in this, I ask your pardon.
(Prayers of Intercession)

How can I bring to realization our solidarity with all creation and through your Spirit renew the world? Sacred Source of all life, I pray.
(Pray the Prayer of Our Savior.)

(Morning)
Beloved Source of all life, help me to grow in the capacity to love and care as you do. In your name. Amen.

(Evening)
With a full heart and my soul at peace, I surrender to the sleep of this night. In your name. Amen.

SATURDAY, JANUARY 4
(Read Psalm 147 and Matthew 25:31–46)

(Morning)
Eternal God, I greet you with affection as this new winter day begins. May this morning awaken me to the needs of others.

(Evening)
Eternal God, this day is ending and with it a week of seven days. With gratitude, I remember the history of this week.

Christ Jesus, ruler of all hearts, you claim each person as a member of your family—even those that society deems as least. You dwell within each member and often in the disguise of the least of my brothers and sisters. You set before me awesome responsibilities. I can't declare my love for you if I fail to see you in my neighbor. Mother Teresa of Calcutta once reminded me that my neighbor is not the one across the sea from me but the one sitting next to me. Members of one's household can often be the most difficult. You once said, "As you did it to one of the least of these who are members of my family, you did it to me." Your words imply a mysterious identity between yourself and every human being.

(Morning)
Aware of how easy it is to be blind and deaf to the needs of others,
I pray for the needs of all the earthly family to which I belong.
(Prayers of Intercession)

(Evening)
Wrapped in gratitude, I now place before you my personal needs as well as the needs of others.
(Prayers of Intercession)

In these first few days of the new year, are there any resolutions that would be loving deeds for neighbors? United with Jesus, our brother, I pray.
(Pray the Prayer of Our Savior.)

(Morning)
O Holy Parent, guide my heart as I journey to you and with you this day. In your name. Amen.

(Evening)
Ruler of Night, I rest in you who watch over me while I sleep. In your name. Amen.

SUNDAY, JANUARY 5
(Read Psalm 72 and Matthew 2:1–12)
(Readings from Isaiah 60:1–6 and Ephesians 3:1–12)

(Morning)
My God, creator of the stars, I arise to the joy of a renewed life in you.

(Evening)
My God, creator of the stars, in oneness with you, I prepare to conclude the journey of this day. Even in sleep may my heart journey ceaselessly toward you.

The Christmas story portrays two paths leading to the manger. The shepherds were given precise information. The Magi had only a guiding star. To set out on a journey without any details takes courage. They must have been a little frightened. Is there not a star in the firmament of my heart? Am I afraid to leave the safe and known in my journey to God? How do I want my heart to be engaged? Set forth, my heart; take up the journey. The star shines. I can't take much with me, and I will lose much on the way. Hopefully, what I will have with me is the gold of love, the incense of yearning, and the myrrh of suffering.

(Morning)
As I journey this day, I pray for light to guide me in these personal needs.
(Prayers of Intercession)

(Evening)
Grant me the light to search this day and pray for those who,
by my thoughtlessness, I left in the shadows.
(Prayers of Intercession)

How can I lead others to see God in all people, not only those of my tradition? With trust and faith in the Star of Bethlehem, I pray.
(Pray the Prayer of Our Savior.)

(Morning)
Christ Jesus, you are the star inviting me to fullness of life. Give me the wisdom to follow you and to lead others to walk in your light. In your name. Amen.

(Evening)
May I surrender to sleep, confident in your love and compassion. In your name. Amen.

MONDAY, JANUARY 6
(Read Isaiah 60:1–6)

(Morning)
Illuminating One, Light of the World, as a moth is attracted to a flame, so I desire to make conscious contact with you, the light of life, at the beginning of this day.

(Evening)
Illuminating One, Light of the World, God of the day and of the night, as the shades of evening fall around me and I assess the day that is coming to a close, I once again turn to you in the spirit of prayer.

Your prophet of old reminds me that you are the creator of all nations and all people; so I know that you are my God. You desire to dispel the gloom that sometimes creeps into the world with the radiance of your love. You desire to enrich life with the gifts of your Spirit—love, joy, peace, patience, kindness, generosity, faithfulness, gentleness, self-control. You also call me to brighten the lives of others with your love.

(Morning)
May what I say and do in the hours to come emulate the example I have experienced in Jesus, who taught his followers to pray.
(Prayers of Intercession)

(Evening)
Forgive me, Enlightening One, if, throughout this day, in any way I have hurt rather than helped, clouded rather than brightened, made poorer rather than richer, any life that intersected with mine.
(Prayers of Intercession)

Illuminating One, you are the light of the world. May I learn from my mistakes so that tomorrow my life will more fully reflect your will and ways.

(Morning)
God, be now my light throughout the light of this day! Amen.

(Evening)
God, grant me rest, I pray, in the knowledge that I am in the loving care of you who neither slumbers nor sleeps. Amen.

TUESDAY, JANUARY 7
(Read Psalm 72:1–7, 10–14)

(Morning)
Just and righteous God, as the psalmist prayed that the leaders of his day might rule in a fashion acceptable to you, so I offer my prayers this day for the leaders of the earth's nations.

(Evening)
Just and righteous God, Great Deliverer, my prayers tonight are for all who are oppressed for any reason. May they somehow feel your presence and know that they are in your love and care, and may their oppression cease.

May your Spirit lead all who are in positions of authority to be sensitive to and address the needs of the poor, the homeless, the hungry, and any who are oppressed because of their race, creed, or sexual orientation. May they strive for peace on earth and good will to all. May they find an example for their sovereignty in the justice, righteousness, and deliverance that characterize your rule of the worlds you have created.

(Morning)
Great Ruler of the universe, may I somehow today, through personal example and perhaps through contact with an elected official, do something to help bring to fruition at least one of these ideals.
(Prayers of Intercession)

(Evening)
Thank you, gracious God, for the opportunity I had today to minister to someone who was in need or oppressed. (Reflect on your day). Grant me sleep that will refresh and strengthen me to continue to act in your behalf in the days to come.
(Prayers of Intercession)

You are a just and righteous God.

(Morning)
Now may I go forth in the spirit of your prophet Micah to do justice and to love kindness as I walk humbly with you. Amen.

(Evening)
Tomorrow may my eyes continue to see someone, my ears hear someone, and my heart lead me to respond to someone in need, just as did Jesus, in whose spirit I pray. Amen.

WEDNESDAY, JANUARY 8
(Read Ephesians 3:1–12)

(Morning)
Infinite God of grace, although my finite mind cannot completely comprehend you, because of Christ Jesus, I know I can come to you in prayer at the beginning of this new day. You have created in me a God-shaped vacuum that I now invite you to fill.

(Evening)
Infinite God of grace, as the shadows deepen and I anticipate a night of rest, I pause to ponder your Word once again.

Like Paul, I want to be a prisoner of the Christ so that I can commit myself to being as Christlike as I can. In this role, may I share with others the good news and the boundless riches of your child—not in arrogance or judgment—but as a beggar telling them where I have found bread. Thank you for the church that binds me to those who have made similar commitments. Although we, the many members of the body of Christ, differ in our skills and gifts, you desire that we celebrate our uniqueness and be your servants in a variety of ways.

(Morning)
You are the creator of all. Today enable me to catch a glimpse of your Spirit in everyone I meet. May I thus reflect the spirit of the one whose prisoner and servant I want to be, even Jesus, the Christ.
(Prayers of Intercession)

(Evening)
Gracious God, as the shadows deepen and I anticipate a night of rest, I pause to share my thoughts and feelings. I must confess, "For I do not do the good I want, but the evil I do not want is what I do." Forgive me, Pardoning Parent.
(Prayers of Intercession)

Make me attentive to the good in others, not to their faults; and to what I have in common with them, not to our differences.

(Morning)
Guide me, great Jehovah, as I seek to serve, not for my glory, but for yours. Amen.

(Evening)
As I commit my family, my friends, and myself into your loving care this night, give us a refreshing sleep so that we may awaken strengthened for the activities of tomorrow. I pray in the spirit of the living Christ. Amen.

THURSDAY, JANUARY 9
(Read Matthew 2:1–12)

(Morning)
God of my Savior, today, may I be like the Magi; wise enough to seek to find and know Jesus, the Christ; wise enough to pay him homage by letting the Babe of Bethlehem become the man of Nazareth and my Savior; wise enough to dedicate to God's service my gifts of time, treasure, and talent.

(Evening)
God of my Savior, thank you, for offering me throughout this day, as you offered the Magi, direction, purpose, and a goal for which to strive.

God of Jesus and my God, I commit myself to "finding" the Christ. Thus, I will do my best to emulate your Child: to love as Jesus loved, to serve as Jesus served, and to be one of your expressions in the world in what I say and do. Just as Jesus grew in faith and knowledge of you, I will strive to do the same by turning daily to your Word, which is "a lamp to my feet and a light to my path."

(Morning)
Thank you, O God, for those people of old who have helped me find the Christ in the stories they wrote about him and through his teachings which they preserved.
(Prayers of Intercession)

(Evening)
Forgive me, parent of Christ Jesus and my parent, for the times today when I failed to "follow the star" and instead followed Herod, who sought to betray Jesus—the one who became the light of the world.
(Prayers of Intercession)

I seek the Christ.

(Morning)
Eternal Guide, I greet this day with the prayer that my life will cast light and not shadows on all whom I meet! Amen.

(Evening)
Guiding Light, grant me a good night's rest in the assurance that I can be wiser tomorrow. And I will try to be! Amen.

FRIDAY, JANUARY 10
(Read Genesis 1:1–5 and Psalm 29)

(Morning)
Creator and creating God, thank you for ancient, timeless stories reminding me of who you are and whose I am. As I open my eyes to the light of this new day, my heart sings with the one who wrote, "How Great Thou Art." You are great, O God, for you called the worlds into being.

(Evening)
Creator and creating God, thank you for ancient, timeless stories reminding me of who you are and whose I am. Thank you for the signs of your presence.

I live amid countless evidences of your creating power: sun, moon, stars, mountains, rivers, trees, shrubs, flowers, animals, and birds. I hear you in the thunder, see you in the lightning, and feel you in the wind. But I sense that the greatest evidence of your creativity is in my own life and in the lives of my family, friends, and neighbors. We all have been created in your image. I have been created to be like you—with the capacities to love, care, reason, relate, create, and choose. Thank you, Great One, for the breath of life and for the resources of the world in which I live. Grant me the strength to care for and use them wisely.

(Morning)
May I begin this day mindful of all of your natural and personal expressions that will surround me.
(Prayers of Intercession)

(Evening)
Ever-present God, whose Spirit has surrounded and embraced me throughout this day, grant me a night of peaceful rest. Forgive me if I failed to glorify you in what I said or did in my waking hours.
(Prayers of Intercession)

Thank you for the gift of this day as well as for the gift of this new year.

(Morning)
I commit myself to being a faithful steward of your many gifts that fill my life. Amen.

(Evening)
May I greet tomorrow's dawn with new resolve to be the person you created me to be—one who mirrors your image and who emulates Jesus. Amen.

SATURDAY, JANUARY 11
(Read Acts 19:1–7 and sing the first verse of the hymn "Holy Spirit, Truth Divine")

(Morning)
Holy Spirit of God, may I, throughout this day, be aware of and receptive to your presence within and around me.

(Evening)
Holy Spirit of God, you have been with me this day. Therefore I was able to face whatever came my way.

I praise you, O God, for all that I have learned about you this week from your holy Word. I was reminded that the various facets of the world in which I live speak to me of your creative power. You are the one who called the worlds into being and created me in your image. The scriptures also proclaim that I see you revealed in the life of Jesus whose birth I celebrated not long ago—the one who taught and showed me how to live. Now the apostle Paul has focused my attention on your Holy Spirit which is present within and around me at all times.

(Morning)
Spirit of the living God, fall upon me. Thus, may your Holy Spirit guide and sustain me throughout this day, resulting in my living as you want me to live.
(Prayers of Intercession)

(Evening)
For the comfort and power of your Spirit that has been with me this day, thank you, O God!
(Prayers of Intercession)

Holy Spirit, you are truth divine.

(Morning)
Thank you, Eternal Contemporary, for the assurance that during this day I will never walk alone! Amen.

(Evening)
May sleep now descend on me as I relax my mind and body, knowing that I am always in your love and care. Amen.

SUNDAY, JANUARY 12
(Read Mark 1:4–11)

(Morning)
Forgiving and renewing God, into whose Spirit I have been baptized, reading the story of Jesus' baptism challenges me to revisit my own baptism. *(Either)* Although I was too young to remember, I have heard of the vows taken by my loved ones on my behalf. *(Or)* I recall the day when I took my baptismal vows.

(Evening)
Forgiving and renewing God, into whose Spirit I have been baptized, reading the story of Jesus' baptism challenges me to revisit my own. I can rest tonight confident that I am yours.

Just as centuries ago Jesus was baptized by John and proclaimed to be your Child, through my baptism, the uniqueness, value, and worth of my life as your child were affirmed! My life was dedicated to you as I have come to know you through the Christ. And it was promised that I would grow in my faith as a part of the church, the body of Christ. Where I have been faithful to these vows, may I continue to be. Where I have failed to live up to them, forgive me.

(Morning)
Imperfect as I am, bathe me in your love, clothe me with your presence, and feed me the bread of life that comes only from you.
(Prayers of Intercession)

(Evening)
May I learn from my failures. May I turn away from that which is displeasing to you. And tomorrow may I be more the person you want me to be—more like Jesus, your Child, my Savior.
(Prayers of Intercession)

Holy Spirit of God, descend on me.

(Morning)
Descend on me, Holy Spirit, so that my life today will give you reason to say, "With you I am well pleased." Amen.

(Evening)
May sleep now descend on me like a descending dove. May my body, mind, and soul be refreshed, so that your Spirit will be evident tomorrow in what I say and do, just as it was in Jesus, the Christ, in whose name I pray. Amen.

MONDAY, JANUARY 13
(Read 1 Samuel 3:1–10 [11–20])

(Morning)
Gracious God, another day is here. Help me to be faithful to the tasks you are calling me to do.

(Evening)
Gracious God, this was a day full of challenges. As I reflect upon the day, help me to count my blessings. Help me tomorrow to be a blessing to someone in need.

Revealing Word of Life, I praise you for calling me by name, again and again. Thank you for insisting on my attention. God, you called Samuel in the days of his youth when your Word had not yet been revealed to him. You were always there as he went about his duties in the temple. It is scary and comforting to know that you are calling me. I am scared because I do not know what you will ask of me. Yet I am comforted because I know that you will provide my needs and make a way. God, keep calling my name until you have my undivided attention. Reveal to me that special task you have reserved just for me. Grant me the courage to respond as Samuel did: "Here I am, for you called me."

(Morning)
God, I pray for myself and others who need your protection today. In our ignorance, we boldly seize the day. Do not leave us alone as we go, but keep us in your care.
(Prayers of Intercession)

(Evening)
Today I encountered some who are disconnected from your love and grace. Grant unto them your peace and the courage to acknowledge your presence.
(Prayers of Intercession)

Here I am, for you called me.

(Morning)
Caring God, as I prepare for this day, keep me mindful of your presence. Let me not be distracted by petty things, but rather help me to focus on your goodness. Amen.

(Evening)
Caring God, the day has come, and now it ends. Brood and hover over me in the night. Then, with the dawn, bring forth the courage and wisdom I need to be your faithful and obedient servant. In the name of Jesus. Amen.

TUESDAY, JANUARY 14
(Read 1 Samuel 3:1–10 [11–20])

(Morning)
Eternal God of power and mercy, in the quietness of this hour, prepare me to face the uncertainty of this day with fortitude and grace.

(Evening)
Eternal God of power and mercy, this day was a good one because I felt your presence. I pray for those who have no peace.

God of mystery and patience, I praise you for being a God who hears and listens. Too often, dear God, my days are busy. I fill each day with too many things to do and I disrupt the quiet with noise. I refuse to slow down. The quiet and stillness are terrifying. Yet, O God, you challenge me to be still and know that you are God. In the stillness of the night, before the dawning of the day, you called Samuel. Breathe upon my anxiety and fear; transform them into confidence and courage. Open my ears to hear your still, small voice beckoning me closer to you.

(Morning)
God, I am tempted to fill this time with noise and activity. Help me to center and focus on you.
(Prayers of Intercession)

(Evening)
Thank you, God, for this personal and private retreat from the hustle and bustle of life. As I prepare for sleep, I rest in the comfort of your care.
(Prayers of Intercession)

Open my ears to hear your still, small voice.

(Morning)
God of calmness, thank you for these moments of peacefulness. When the day becomes busy, help me to remember how it feels to be quiet and still in your presence. Amen.

(Evening)
God of rest, as I sleep tonight, let me retire in the assurance of your love. May I awake on the morrow with only this prayer: "Sovereign, speak! For your servant hears." Amen.

WEDNESDAY, JANUARY 15
(Read Psalm 139:1–6, 13–18)

(Morning)
Gentle God of strength, thank you for awakening me so gently with your touch of love and mercy. I am ready to face the day.

(Evening)
Gentle God of strength, thank you for another day's journey. Because it is well with my soul, I rejoice and pray for those who struggle both during the day and during the night. Be for them what you have been for me: a steady presence of strength.

All-knowing God, I praise you because you love me in spite of my thoughts and deeds. Merciful God, I confess that I am not worthy of your love. Sometimes, I am unmoved by the misery of others. I am impatient with those who struggle. I am blind to the pain of the oppressed. I am tempted to be selfish and greedy. I am cynical when I should be caring; apathetic when I should be involved; passive when I should be bold. These and other frailties I lay before you. God of grace, I come before you seeking your transforming grace and never-ending mercy. Refashion me in your image and likeness.

(Morning)
Eternal and loving God, create in me a clean heart and contrite spirit. Leave me not to my own devices and whims, but fill me with your grace.
(Prayers of Intercession)

(Evening)
God, I place for your examination all that I did today. Take my failures, shortcomings, and weaknesses and transform them into opportunities to glorify you. I pray in Jesus' name.
(Prayers of Intercession)

"Even there your hand shall lead me, and your right hand shall hold me fast."

(Morning)
Creator God, I know not what this day holds for me—joy or tragedy, prosperity or poverty. I stand in the light of your love, knowing that whatever happens, you are still with me. Amen.

(Evening)
Thank you for the grace and mercy that sustained me today. Life is difficult, yet you brought me through again. I am grateful. Amen.

THURSDAY, JANUARY 16
(Read 1 Corinthians 6:12–20)

(Morning)
Creator of all that is good and true, I arise and give thanks for this day.
I seek to love you, my neighbor, and all of creation with my whole heart,
soul, mind, and body.

(Evening)
Creator of all that is good and true, take my life, all that is in it and in me,
and make it a thing of joy and beauty.

Maker of all there is, I praise your wisdom in making real for us the beauty and majesty of creation. In the days of the apostle Paul, some thought the physical body was not worthy of consideration. For them, the only important thing was the soul and spirit. Yet, O Wise One, you created us from the dust and breathed into our bodies the breath of life. Your Word became flesh, dwelt among us, died, and was raised up for us. Through your mighty Word and deeds, you elevate human beings to a place of dignity and worth. Your Spirit lives in us, and we are yours. Help us to live as your temples on earth.

(Morning)
Loving God, help me distinguish between that which is good *to* me and that which is good *for* me. Grant me the courage to choose wisely.
(Prayers of Intercession)

(Evening)
O God, my rock and refuge, strengthen me with your Holy Spirit. Grant me the wisdom to love and care for all of creation, which you pronounced good.
(Prayers of Intercession)

"For you were bought with a price; therefore glorify God in your body."

(Morning)
It is easy to judge my neighbor for not being like me. I thank you for Christ Jesus who looked beyond the superficial and bade us to love one another. For Jesus' sake. Amen.

(Evening)
As sleep brings rest and renewal, O God, let your Spirit instruct my dreams, thoughts, and actions so that I may awake with new zeal and fresh energy for the journey. Thank you for not giving up on me. In the name of Jesus Christ I pray. Amen.

FRIDAY, JANUARY 17
(Read John 1:43–51)

(Morning)
All-knowing and ever-present God, who knows what this day will bring? Help me to live this day as if it were my last. Be with me, and let my will be your will.

(Evening)
All-knowing and ever-present God, there is a restlessness within me that I cannot explain or understand. Use this energy for your glory. In Jesus' name.

Rock of Ages, you are made known to us in Jesus of Nazareth. Empower me to share the good news. Word of Life, I am not always comfortable sharing my faith. I feel awkward and unsure when I try to tell others what Christ has done for me. Give me the confidence to tell others what I have experienced. Give me the boldness to echo the words of Philip: "I have found him about whom Moses in the law and also the prophets wrote, Jesus son of Joseph from Nazareth." As this day unfolds, loosen my tongue and let me speak of what I know. If I am questioned about my faith, let me not cringe in shame or fear, but rather let me invite others to "come and see."

(Morning)
I envy the ease with which the disciples responded to Jesus' invitation to join him. Remind me of where I have been and where I am now. Remind me to speak up. The rest I leave in your hands.
(Prayers of Intercession)

(Evening)
God of creation, I pray for those who do not know Christ Jesus. I pray for their salvation even as I rest in the blessed assurance of my own.
(Prayers of Intercession)

"Do you believe because I told you that I saw you under the fig tree?"

(Morning)
O God, through the ages, you have revealed yourself to women and men who have declared your goodness. Today, it is possible for me to tell others what you have done for me through Christ Jesus. I pray for boldness in telling my story. Amen.

(Evening)
Eternal and loving God, as night blankets this day, I confess my failure to be a faithful disciple. Forgive me and grant me the courage to stand up for Jesus in the days ahead. Amen.

SATURDAY, JANUARY 18
(Read John 1:43–51)

(Morning)
Most loving God, thank you for the rest of last night and for the gift of a new day. Grant me the wisdom and energy to please and serve you.

(Evening)
Most loving God, protect me through the quiet hours of this night. May I rest in the knowledge that in a changing and chaotic world, you are steadfast and immovable.

God of peace, I praise you for being a God who calls and commissions. Make me an instrument of your peace in the world. Jesus saw Nathaniel sitting under the fig tree before Philip interrupted his meditation. The fig tree, a symbol of peace, is shady and leafy. Many have sat under its branches to rest and meditate. God, grant me the shade of a fig tree wherever I am, and show me how I can bring peace to the part of the world I inhabit. Help me to smile when I would rather curse; to whisper when I would rather scream; to comfort when I would rather strike out; to love when I would rather hate. In a broken, hurting, warring, and hungering world, use me as your instrument of healing, love, hope, and peace.

(Morning)
You promised to give power to the faint and strength to the powerless. I pray for myself and others who wait for you to renew our strength. Hear my prayer, O God.
(Prayers of Intercession)

(Evening)
O God, as I lay my weary head down this night, grant me a peaceful sleep, safe within the circle of your love and mercy.
(Prayers of Intercession)

"You will see greater things than these."

(Morning)
The trees are barren and stark. Sometimes I feel empty and barren. Fill me with the power of your Holy Spirit so that I may boldly live this day. Amen.

(Evening)
Somewhere tonight, both near and distant, mothers and fathers fear for their lives and the lives of their children. Be with them and let them know that they are safe in your care. In the name of the Bringer of Peace, I pray. Amen.

SUNDAY, JANUARY 19
(Read John 1:43–51 and Joel 2:28–29)

(Morning)
Good Provider, as a new morning dawns, so I, too, am made new. Be present in my life today. Give me the will to think and do what is right. Guide my steps and order my ways according to your good pleasure.

(Evening)
Good Provider, thank you for a day filled with miracles of love, life, companionship, and nourishment. Envelop me tonight in your grace and mercy.

Giver of every good and perfect gift, I praise you for making all things new. You declared, O Ancient of Days, that in the fullness of time, you would pour out your Spirit upon all flesh. According to your Word, men and women, young and old, slave and free, would dream dreams, see visions, and prophesy. You sent Jesus to show us a more excellent way—a way of peace, justice, harmony, and love. God of creation, do a new thing and begin with me. Kindle within me your vision for creation. Ignite in me a fire to do your will. Stir up within me the desire to serve your people. Put me where you can use me.

(Morning)
Sovereign, here I am! Send me into your creation to bring healing, health, and wholeness wherever I can.
(Prayers of Intercession)

(Evening)
God of serenity, allow me a night of rest and peacefulness, knowing that tomorrow is another opportunity to serve and glorify you.
(Prayers of Intercession)

I praise you for all things new.

(Morning)
O God, this is the beginning of a new day and a new week. The possibilities are endless. Make me worthy of the challenges that lie ahead. In Jesus' name, Amen.

(Evening)
Eternal God, I confess that I was not perfect today. Thank you for being a God who does not ask perfection of us. Help me to think about how I may do my best tomorrow. I pray for your revelation and the courage to say yes to your will. In Jesus' name. Amen.

MONDAY, JANUARY 20
(Read Jonah and Psalm 62)

(Morning)
God of light, your presence is a gift in my life. This day I give thanks for the people who are lights in my life.

(Evening)
God of light, as the day draws to a close and the stars of the evening sky light up the sky, I rest in the light of your faithful presence.

Creator God, the revelation of the gift of your Child, Jesus Christ, still brings light into a world that seems desperately bleak and in need of saving grace. Just as you spoke to Jonah, to the Psalm writers, and to people of everyday life, let your Word, your hopes, and your visions come to light today, speaking through my words and my actions. These are the places in my life, my congregation, my community, and the world where your light is needed this day . . .

(Morning)
I remember especially your children who face times of gloom and despair, and I pray for them . . .
(Prayers of Intercession)

(Evening)
As my body and mind begin to unwind from the events of this day, I remember the people and the tasks that I faced this day . . .
(Prayers of Intercession)

In the name of the One whose revelation in Jesus Christ is always a constant yet consistently a new affirmation.

(Morning)
Move me to action this day that I may see and respond to the places and the people in need of your light and your presence. Amen.

(Evening)
Now as I close my eyes in rest, I sleep in the light of your presence in my life. Amen.

TUESDAY, JANUARY 21
(Read Psalm 62:1–12)

(Morning)
God who tends my soul, I wake, arise, and offer these moments of silence as my soul waits for you.

(Evening)
God who tends my soul, at last the noise of the day is over and the quiet of the evening comforts my body and my soul.

You are the God of epiphanal moments when light breaks through to reveal your power and love. With the psalmist, I affirm that you are my hope, you are my salvation, you are my fortress, you are the one in whom rests my deliverance and my hope, you are my mighty rock. For it is in you, O God, where I find my refuge. My soul is at peace and rests knowing that my trust is in you.

(Morning)
God, you patiently wait and hear the joys and concerns of my soul which I give to you this day.
(Prayers of Intercession)

(Evening)
I offer these moments of silence to you as I listen and patiently tend my soul which you know most intimately and love most deeply.
(Prayers of Intercession)

This I pray in the name of the one in whom I hope and live this day and every day.

(Morning)
Restore and renew me this day as I move through the tasks and demands that I will face. Amen.

(Evening)
Restore my energy through these hours of rest so I may face the challenges and opportunities of another new day. Amen.

WEDNESDAY, JANUARY 22
(Read Psalm 62:1–12)

(Morning)
God of the silent moments, I know that I am precious in your sight and the reality of this affirmation amazes me.

(Evening)
God of the silent moments, in the silence of my soul this day I heard . . .

If my soul indeed can wait in silence, then I must listen and attentively wait for that which you, O God, have to say. In your power and your steadfast love I find my refuge. In contrast to your constant love and creative power, I am a puff of air, lighter than breath. I put my trust in you; in confidence I know that all is well with my soul, for you hold it in your hand. I am secure in the arms of your faithful love.

(Morning)
I pray this morning for those for whom I am concerned—family and friends who are in my heart and my prayers this day.
(Prayers of Intercession)

(Evening)
I give thanks for the ways you have helped me know hope this day and for the fortress you have provided in my walk of faith.
(Prayers of Intercession)

This I pray in the name of God whose steadfast love will never let me go.

(Morning)
May the faith that surrounds me hold my family and friends securely and be present with them today and always.

(Evening)
I relax and let my body, mind, and soul experience the peace of your love.
Amen.

THURSDAY, JANUARY 23
(Read Jonah 3:1–5, 10)

(Morning)
Sometimes O God, like Jonah, I need to be awakened to the Word you would have me live this day.

(Evening)
Sometimes O God, I feel a need for peaceful sleep, even before night comes. Grant me rest this night.

God, you come to us in ways I cannot expect or prepare for. Into the midst of the reality of my comfortable world, you break through with a power and a purpose that disrupt the order of my life. Like Jonah, it sometimes takes a second touch on the shoulder, a gentle nudge, to wake me up to the new ordering of life to which you are calling me.

(Morning)
I admit that I am not always ready to respond to your call, nor do I always feel strong or prepared! Today, help me to respond and provide the strength I need.
(Prayers of Intercession)

(Evening)
Your Spirit's walk with me each day sustains my journey and brings me safely to the day's end. I thank you for this protection.
(Prayers of Intercession)

This I pray in the name of God who loves me, the Redeemer who saves me, and the Spirit who gives me life.

(Morning)
With the assurance of your faithful purposes, I lean into this day which is yours. Amen.

(Evening)
As I prepare for refreshing sleep, may your Spirit which nourishes and sustains me refresh my soul and my body for another day of faithful living. Amen.

FRIDAY, JANUARY 24
(Read Jonah 3:1–5, 10)

(Morning)
God of steadfast love, you call me this day to turn from evil and so I confess to you my sins . . .

(Evening)
God of steadfast love, you know my sins and yet your forgiveness is sure. Your love is abounding.

Like the people of Nineveh, I too can live into new ways of being, living and responding to you, O God. In turning from that which is evil in relationships, in vocation, and in the public realm, I am assured that you, the God who calls forth such changes, are also the God who is "gracious and merciful, slow to anger, and abounding in steadfast love."

(Morning)
I move into this day with the assurance and confidence of your presence with me.
(Prayers of Intercession)

(Evening)
As my eyes close on this day, open them tomorrow to the spaces and possibilities for my faithful living.
(Prayers of Intercession)

This I pray in the name of Jesus, the Christ.

(Morning)
I give thanks for this day and for your grace which is freely and compassionately bestowed on all the faithful, I pray. Amen.

(Evening)
I give thanks for this night which is freely and compassionately bestowed on all the faithful. I pray that I will awaken to a new day. Amen.

SATURDAY, JANUARY 25
(Read Mark 1:14–20)

(Morning)
Ever-fulfilling God, you call us at unexpected times into new places. You gently yet firmly insist that my faith take shape and form. For this day and for your nurturing, I thank you.

(Evening)
Ever-fulfilling God, I have walked with you this day. I have seen you in these faces and in these places . . .

Dear God, time is often precious and waiting. Lifetimes include moments of living into that which is fulfilling. Lifetimes also include transitions and changes that demand all of my survival skills. The gospel that Jesus preached still needs to be heard and responded to today. The time is fulfilled; your realm, O God, is at hand. It is time to repent and believe in your gospel. And like the disciples, I leave the known and predictable and step out on my journey of faith, assured of the questions and struggling for the answers that only time and faith will reveal.

(Morning)
This day, show me the places and reveal to me the people who need your love, your care, your justice, and your shalom.
(Prayers of Intercession)

(Evening)
These are the questions that trouble me . . . I can live with the questions knowing that you are with me this night.
(Prayers of Intercession)

This I pray in the name of Christ Jesus.

(Morning)
Sustain me, O God, as the nets of your love connect me to your children. Amen.

(Evening)
Fulfilling God, I can live with the questions knowing that you are with me. Amen.

SUNDAY, JANUARY 26
(Reread the readings for this week in the Season of Epiphany)

(Morning)
God of light, you are our epiphany. Reveal to me this day your purposes and intentions for my life.

(Evening)
God of light, in the depth of night, I look to the sky.

O radiant Christ, Incarnate Word, Eternal Love revealed in time; come, make your home within our hearts, that we may dwell in light sublime. Our bartered, busy lives burn dim, too tired to care, too numb to feel. Come shine upon our shadowed world: Your radiance bathes with power to heal. Your glory shone at Jordan's stream, the font where we were born anew. Attune your church to know you near; illumine all we say and do. O Light of Nations, fill the earth; our faith and hope and love renew. Come, lead the peoples to your peace, as stars once led the way to you (Ruth Duck).

(Morning)
Ever-present God, show me the paths of peace I need to walk this day.
(Prayers of Intercession)

(Evening)
Creator God, a shining star reminds me of your healing and restoring power.
(Prayers of Intercession)

This I pray in the name of God, whose radiance and glory bring hope and vision to this world.

(Morning)
Keep my life from being so busy that I don't have time to say thank you. Amen.

(Evening)
May the vividness of your evening creation, O God, remind me of the re-creation of your earth and all its people to which I am called this day. Amen.

MONDAY, JANUARY 27
(Read Deuteronomy 18:15–20)

(Morning)
Holy and awesome God, at the beginning of a new day, let wonder stir me and awaken me. I would be alert to your life-giving presence.

(Evening)
Holy and awesome God, this day, your gift to me, is nearly done. I thank you that your Word is a living Word.

Revealing God, I praise you that you have not left me alone. You have provided and appointed me with messengers, prophets, teachers and apostles of your surprising new creation. Holy One, as your people, Israel, came into the new and the promised land, you provided prophets who would be alert, attentive, and faithful to your Word. I know, O God, that I really cannot live by bread alone; that the bread of this world, even in ample supply leaves me famished for your Word and presence upon which I truly depend. Grant me the courage to listen for your Word, to watch for your presence. Grant me also, loving God, the gift of discernment. Help me to discern your voice among the many voices that call to me and upon me.

(Morning)
As I look to this new day, I hold before you those who are in special need of your encouraging Word.
(Prayers of Intercession)

(Evening)
I praise you for this day, and as I ponder its experiences, I seek what you would have me learn. I pray for sisters and brothers in need of your Word.
(Prayers of Intercession)

With a heart open to your way, I pray the prayer Jesus taught.
(Pray the Prayer of Our Savior.)

(Morning)
Send me now into this new day, alert and attentive, listening for your living-giving Word, open to your presence in all things. Amen.

(Evening)
I give myself to you, confident that I rest in the shelter of your wings. Amen.

TUESDAY, JANUARY 28
(Read Deuteronomy 18:15–20)

(Morning)
Calling God, even as the dawn calls forth a new day, you have called and claimed me, loving and holy God.

(Evening)
Calling God, I offer this day, with its incomplete words and deeds, to you in whom completion is found.

I praise you, O Holy One, for the persons and events, the stories and the experiences, by which you have called me to know and to serve you. Gracious God, sometimes your Word is like fire in my bones. You have called me to speak your Word, to bear witness to your truth. I confess, that it is not easy to be a messenger, a prophet, a witness, an apostle of your way. Often I am unsure of your Word and your will. I would rather leave this task to another. I lose heart. I fail to speak the Word you have entrusted to me. I am afraid of what it might cost me. Forgive the ways I have shut your Word up within me. Help me to tell your truth in love, and to trust your power to use me for the healing of your world.

(Morning)
For your prophets and martyrs today, for all who fearlessly speak your Word, and for the church throughout the world, I pray.
(Prayers of Intercession)

(Evening)
You who have called the worlds into being, you know the tiniest sparrow, hear my prayers for the needs of others, and for my own needs.
(Prayers of Intercession)

With a heart open to your way, I pray the prayer that Jesus taught.
(Pray the Prayer of Our Savior.)

(Morning)
Called to love and serve you, I go to this new day confident of your presence. Amen.

(Evening)
Now, hearing your promise, "Do not be afraid," grant me rest and peace. Amen.

WEDNESDAY, JANUARY 29
(Read 1 Corinthians 8:1–13)

(Morning)
Patient and Gracious God, I am grateful for the relationships in which you have placed me, and ask for your guidance to strengthen them.

(Evening)
Patient and Gracious God, I praise you, Holy One, for you exist in relationship; Creator, Redeemer, and Sustainer.

O God, whose new creation, summons and creates a new community, help me to hear in the story of your people in Corinth, possibilities of grace and growth for every congregation. O God, you are at work in the lives of congregations and communities. Sometimes in our congregations we too imagine that we are "in the know," that we are brighter, freer, more knowledgeable, or more spiritual than others. O God, whose ways are not our ways, I see that my knowledge counts for little unless it is guided and directed by love. Help me to place my knowledge and gifts in the service of a love that builds up others, that builds up the community as a witness to your gracious way and patient truth.

(Morning)
You have placed me in a fabric of human community. I pray for the needs of others and for my own needs in this day.
(Prayers of Intercession)

(Evening)
Grant me patience with others, even as you have been patient with me. I pray for those who have been patient with me, and for those who need my patience.
(Prayers of Intercession)

With a heart open to your way, I pray the prayer which Jesus taught.
(Pray the Prayer of Our Savior.)

(Morning)
Open my eyes to the opportunities of this day to build up others and to strengthen the weak. Amen.

(Evening)
Assured of your constant care for all your creation, I ask that you would grant me restful sleep. Amen.

THURSDAY, JANUARY 30
(Read 1 Corinthians 8:1–13)

(Morning)
O God in whom all things exist, the light of your love opens my eyes to the connection of all that is, and I thank you.

(Evening)
O God in whom all things exist, I open myself in prayer to your restoring compassion for me and for all.

Compassionate God, I praise you for your vision of a new community, and seek that possibility as I listen to the story of your people and church at Corinth. Perhaps, O God, our individualism is but an illusion, a chimera, a confusion. Perhaps you have not called us one by one, but community by community. Perhaps at the judgment we shall not stand before you alone or one by one, but community by community, congregation by congregation, people by people that you may see what kind of community we have been together, that you may see who we have left out. Compassionate God, grant me grace to see the connections, to reweave the fabric where it has been frayed, and to discover that in thinking of others, it is myself I have thought of as well.

(Morning)
In prayer for the needs of others, as well as my own, I would restore and strengthen our connections.
(Prayers of Intercession)

(Evening)
As I remember in prayer before you my sisters and brothers, heal, I pray, your broken body.
(Prayers of Intercession)

With a heart open to your way, I pray the prayer Jesus taught.
(Pray the Prayer of Our Savior.)

(Morning)
As I go to love and serve you, I am not alone. I am surrounded by all the faithful. Amen.

(Evening)
You know me, O God. In this is my rest and my safety. Amen.

FRIDAY, JANUARY 31
(Read Mark 1:21–27)

(Morning)
Liberating God, break me open, and make me new this day.

(Evening)
Liberating God, by your gracious powers, I am sustained, granted healing and wholeness.

I marvel at you for your astonishing power as I listen to the story of Jesus encountering demonic powers in the sanctuary. Holy One, you come to engage the powers of evil. You come to challenge everything that distorts, diminishes, and disfigures your intention for humankind. Evil knows you. It senses your presence, your power, your threat. You find it in its sacred sanctuaries. Forgive me that I have made peace where you engage in struggle. Forgive me that too often I have dismissed the astonishing, the miraculous, the transforming possibility. Let the report of your disturbing power to change, challenge and heal spread in our lives, congregations and world.

(Morning)
Your power to make all things new is nearer than I imagine. Bring newness and hope to those engaged in the struggle with evil.
(Prayers of Intercession)

(Evening)
I pray now for those whose lives are distorted by pain, evil or oppression.
(Prayers of Intercession)

With a heart open to your way, I pray the prayer Jesus taught.
(Pray the Prayer of Our Savior.)

(Morning)
Today, grant me the grace to trust your promises and to live into them. Amen.

(Evening)
Your power is beyond my grasp, yet within reach of my trust. In trust, would I rest now. Amen.

SATURDAY, FEBRUARY 1
(Read Mark 1:21–27)

(Morning)
Passionate God, Astonishing One, speak with authority, that I may know that this day counts.

(Evening)
Passionate God, let me now ponder with wonder and awe, your presence in the day that is ending.

Jesus the teacher, teach me. Teach me of your life-giving power and your claim as author of my life. We learn little—strangely—from Mark's story of what Jesus actually taught. We do learn that his teaching had power—life-changing, demon-disturbing, awe-inspiring, people-healing power. Amazing! Help me to know anew the power of the Gospel, of the Word, of the church. Deliver me from all discounting, domesticating, dismissing of this amazing power that has, in some measure, been entrusted to me. Free me from fear. Set me free to share, to trust, to teach, and to live with the power of the Good News.

(Morning)
I look to this new day with its possibilities for healing for others and for myself.
(Prayers of Intercession)

(Evening)
Tonight I hold in prayer those who have given up hope, and for those who hide from hope.
(Prayers of Intercession)

With a heart open to your way, I pray the prayer Jesus taught.
(Pray the Prayer of Our Savior.)

(Morning)
I surrender myself to you, O God, to love and serve you as fully as I am able this day. Amen.

(Evening)
Quiet my anxieties that even as I sleep I may be receptive to your love and truth. Amen.

SUNDAY, FEBRUARY 2
(Read Psalm 111)

(Morning)
Holy and Awesome God, with this new day I remember your mercies throughout this week, and your abiding care.

(Evening)
Holy and Awesome God, a day of recalling your constant care now ends. Let me rest in the knowledge that you do care for me.

Faithful God, guided by the psalmist, today I tell of your goodness, your faithfulness, your trustworthiness. Some days and seasons, holy one, you seem hidden and far off; and it is courage to say so. Not today. Today, my whole being sings. Today I praise you because of your great works. Praise is also an act of courage. Today, Gracious One, I praise you in the midst of the congregation, offering my own testimony to all who would hear of your enduring love. May I so lose myself in your love, that I may be found more authentically in your service.

(Morning)
In the confidence of your care, I pray for the needs of the world, and of the church.
(Prayers of Intercession)

(Evening)
I thank you for the people of the congregation, and I ask your care for them.
(Prayers of Intercession)

With a heart open to your way, I pray the prayer Jesus taught.
(Pray the Prayer of Our Savior.)

(Morning)	(Evening)
I want to know joy today. Help me to seek the one needful thing, your presence. Amen.	Your praise, O God, endures forever; sung by night stars, by the breath of wild creatures, and by me. Amen.

MONDAY, FEBRUARY 3
(Read 2 Kings 2:1–8)

(Morning)
Radiant Giver of all life's joys and peace, I wake with thanks for your gift of companions who share my life and make it rich.

(Evening)
Radiant Giver of all life's joys and peace, I seek the gift of rest this night and recall with joy all those you send into my life.

Marvelous God, the friendship and loyalty of Elijah and Elisha open new horizons for all my relationships with others. You were in the heart of Elisha when he journeyed with Elijah through Bethel, Jericho, and Jordan. You poured a spirit of unflinching loyalty from Elijah into Elisha's very soul. Elisha did not fail Elijah or you. Forgive me, O God. I do not love others with all the strength you shower upon me daily. Search me, know me, and lead me in new paths of friendship and love with those around me.

(Morning)
Be with me in the midst of this day so that my love for others may grow stronger.
(Prayers of Intercession)

(Evening)
I pray for all whose lives have touched mine today. May I be worthy of their love.
(Prayers of Intercession)

Confident of your love and presence I pray.
(Pray the Prayer of Our Savior.)

(Morning)
Send me into the world today, renewed, strengthened, eager to be faithful to all my companions in the world. Amen.

(Evening)
I rest in your love, O God, strengthened by your presence and by comrades you send to me. Amen.

TUESDAY, FEBRUARY 4
(Read 2 Kings 2:9–12)

(Morning)
Gracious God, our hope and help, I greet this day longing to believe that you respond faithfully to my prayers.

(Evening)
Gracious God, our hope and help, my day closes with good news: I have learned your answers to prayer are varied and wondrous.

Eternal God, answer to every mystery of life, I search your response to Elisha for assurance that you answer prayers. Most merciful God, when Elisha requested a double share of Elijah's spirit, you answered that earnest hope; Elisha received Elijah's prophetic mantle. In every generation, you promise abundant life for all who trust you. Once again, grant me signs of your transforming Spirit in my life. As I pray, remind me again that your encouraging, strengthening, and empowering love is the full, final, and sufficient answer to every prayer.

(Morning)
Be with me throughout this day, gracious God, that my heart may be open to your Spirit, alive in me.
(Prayers of Intercession)

(Evening)
Loving God, help me always to remember your varied answers to all my prayers, spoken and unspoken.
(Prayers of Intercession)

Now, as our Savior taught the disciples, I pray.
(Pray the Prayer of Our Savior.)

(Morning)
Send me forth this day to serve my world and you, confident of strength that only your Spirit provides. Amen.

(Evening)
Trusting in you, I turn to sleep, and to rest for tomorrow's need. In the name of Jesus. Amen.

WEDNESDAY, FEBRUARY 5
(Read Psalm 50:1–3)

(Morning)
Almighty and ever-righteous God, in the quiet of the morning you speak to me as you have spoken to your followers in every age.

(Evening)
Almighty and ever-righteous God, I close this day with new strength.
I have listened for your call; I have heard you speak to me.

I offer you my praise because each day, from the rising of the sun to its setting, your presence among your children is evident. In days of old, the psalmist said, you summoned your people continually; you were not silent among them. You came to them in the beauty of the morning, and in a devouring fire. In an awesome tempest, everyone knew you were God! Forgive me, O God; I am not always mindful of your incredible majesty and marvelous power.

You created the earth and all that is in it; your love continues to sustain the world, and so I praise your glorious and mighty name.

(Morning)
Almighty and ever-righteous God, in the quiet of the morning you speak to me as you have spoken to your followers in every age.
(Prayers of Intercession)

(Evening)
Almighty and ever-righteous God, I close this day with new strength. I have listened for your call; I have heard you speak to me.
(Prayers of Intercession)

Now, as our Savior taught the disciples, I pray.
(Pray the Prayer of Our Savior.)

(Morning)
Throughout this day help me to know that even in all your glory you speak to me, calling me to faithfulness and abiding trust in your constant goodness. Amen.

(Evening)
May I be renewed tonight by both the mercy of sleep and the knowledge of your Spirit alive in me! Amen.

THURSDAY, FEBRUARY 6
(Read Psalm 50:3–6)

(Morning)
Righteous God, Judge of all humankind, as morning gilds the skies, I arise from sleep reminded that you are the final judge of all things good or ill.

(Evening)
Righteous God, judge of all humankind, the long day closes and night descends. I have new courage because of your presence and judgments about me.

Majestic God, you are righteous; your judgments are forever dependable and just. In that conviction there is comfort and power for me.

The psalmist reminds me that you call your people to gather regularly and be judged for their words and deeds. I lay bare before you today every secret of my heart; you know them as nobody else can. I confess my weaknesses and failures: I have not persistently followed the pathways you marked; I have not done the things I could have done; I have left undone the things I should have done. Because I have heard about your love in every age, I seek your judgment, confident of your mercy toward all children of your covenant. Prove me, O God, and try me; test my heart and mind.

(Morning)
Righteous God, Judge of all humankind, as morning gilds the skies, I arise from sleep reminded that you are the final judge of all things good or ill.
(Prayers of Intercession)

(Evening)
Righteous God, judge of all humankind, the long day closes and night descends. I have new courage because of your presence and judgments about me.
(Prayers of Intercession)

Now as Jesus taught, I pray.
(Pray the Prayer of Our Savior.)

(Morning)
May the knowledge that you are holy and merciful empower me to be faithful to your call. Amen.

(Evening)
I give thanks that you are my judge, and I bare my soul to your justice, mercy, and love. Amen.

FRIDAY, FEBRUARY 7
(Read 2 Corinthians 4:3–6)

(Morning)
Sovereign God, light of all who know you, what splendid joy is this: I begin my day bathed with the life and hope you send with every dawn.

(Evening)
Sovereign God, light of all who know you, I end my day as it began, imbued with your gift of light and life and hope.

God of the loving heart, I thank you for sending your beloved Child to earth with amazing news about your magnificent love. Because Jesus lived, seductive pleasures and alluring gods of this world can never blind me. You shine gloriously in my heart, the brightest light of all the world. I know life's richest blessings endure in your realm alone. Light of the World, enlighten and illumine my clouded heart, till everything within me is exalted by your divine Spirit, till I am a new creation bounding from Christ's love and yours.

(Morning)
Gracious God, as the day wends its way, help me to make your light the only light of my life.
(Prayers of Intercession)

(Evening)
As I close my eyes for sleep, kindle the torch of your love in me once more, that I may be renewed and refreshed.
(Prayers of Intercession)

Now, as Jesus taught, I pray.
(Pray the Prayer of Our Savior.)

(Morning)
With the light of your love shining in me, O God, may I be ever faithful to you. Amen.

(Evening)
May your peace and love and light strengthen my hopes and deeds tomorrow. Amen.

SATURDAY, FEBRUARY 8
(Read Mark 9:2–6)

(Morning)
Mighty and mysterious God, as morning dawns, today my heart awakens, "May Jesus Christ be praised!"

(Evening)
Mighty and mysterious God, as shadows of the evening appear, I sing joyously again: "May Jesus Christ be praised!"

All laud and honor be to you, gracious God, for setting Jesus of Nazareth apart, transforming, glorifying, and empowering him forever. One day, on a high mountaintop, you transfigured Jesus and anointed him with your own Spirit. Peter, James, and John witnessed this high mystery; later they shared this news with all the world. What a splendid Word: You sent Jesus among us to live, die, and rise again, and to offer new life to all who believe.

(Morning)
Redeeming God, during this day fix my mind on the wonder of this glorious gift: Jesus Christ, your revelation of divine love.
(Prayers of Intercession)

(Evening)
Ere shades of sleep overtake me, fasten forever in my heart the shining moment in Galilee when you set Jesus apart.
(Prayers of Intercession)

Blessed are you, O God, and blessed is Christ Jesus your Beloved, to whom be all glory, laud, and honor. World without end.

(Morning)
Help me, dear God, to be worthy of the great love and sacrifice of Jesus, who died that I might live. Amen.

(Evening)
Come, holy Jesus, and lead me in God's paths of love, justice, and peace—this night and all my days. Amen.

SUNDAY, FEBRUARY 9 (TRANSFIGURATION)
(Read Mark 9:7–9)

(Morning)
God of wonders far beyond human comprehension, I give you thanks this day for your gift of Christ Jesus, to whom I listen for every secret of abundant life.

(Evening)
God of wonders far beyond human comprehension, another day you have given me ends. I am grateful for the presence of your beloved One.

God of all compassion, in gracious mercy you sent your beloved Child into the world to bring amazing news. As I listen to the Transfigured One, I begin to perceive your inexhaustible and boundless love. The promises of Jesus are wondrous and astounding. I learn about life—rich, just, peaceful and eternal—and my heart is overjoyed. But, forgive me, O God. I do not always act as though I have heard the words of Jesus. Too often my thoughts and deeds are unworthy of love so amazing, so divine.

(Morning)
Energize me today, O God, to listen more responsively to your beloved Child.
(Prayers of Intercession)

(Evening)
Even as I close my eyes to sleep, help me to listen again for Jesus' words of life.
(Prayers of Intercession)

Hear me now as I pray the words Jesus taught to the disciples.
(Pray the Prayer of Our Savior.)

(Morning)
May my ears and my heart be open anew today to the words and wisdom of your Beloved. Amen.

(Evening)
I pray, O God, with a humble and contrite heart, that all my thoughts and deeds may be worthy of your love. Amen.

MONDAY, FEBRUARY 10
(Read Genesis 9:8–17)

(Morning)
God, who established your covenant for your people, it is your light that awakens me. May it truly brighten this day.

(Evening)
God, who established your covenant for your people, your sign of light and of love has kept me together for yet another day. For that I give thanks.

Noah with his family was the only one left who pleased you, O God. You saw fit to punish the rest and to save Noah. The very thought frightens me. And yet as daylight returns after the night, so does your rainbow. The sunlight that makes it shine allows all of us to dare to enjoy the light. It allows us to cast behind us any fear of the unknown and of that which we cannot see or comprehend. God, the covenant you offered us is the only kind of love that truly liberates any of us from the fears of destruction. We cannot avoid the fears; they seem to be in the midst of life. But we can experience the sign and symbol of the rainbow even more freely, for they are your gift for the day and the light in our lives.

(Morning)
May your covenant light guide me through this day.
(Prayers of Intercession)

(Evening)
Another night is coming, free me from all fears. Cradle me under your arch of grace and power.
(Prayers of Intercession)

And now pray the prayer that Jesus taught his disciples.
(Pray the Prayer of Our Savior.)

(Morning)
May your rainbow dispel the shadows of my fears. Let me rejoice in your love. Amen.

(Evening)
Another night is coming, free me of anxiety and restlessness. Cradle me under your arch of grace and power. Amen.

TUESDAY, FEBRUARY 11
(Read Joel 2:1–2, 12–17)

(Morning)
God of power and grace, let me know that your day is near and that you always call me to know where you are.

(Evening)
God of power and grace, I give thanks for your presence with me, letting me know that you kept me close.

God of grace, sometimes we live with great fears. We see skies that are gray with foreboding clouds, which we know, at worst, can create the flood that Noah experienced. Our relationships and situations can feel as if there is nothing but fear and trembling to encounter. Wars are real, whether they be within a family, in a workplace, or far away, viewed on the television screen, where horrible images can cause nightmares. "Yet even now," says Christ Jesus, "return to me with all your heart." In spite of the worst, your power is so great that it can reach into a life filled with fear and anxiety. For you are "slow to anger and abounding in steadfast love." Your love is indeed the power to dispel the gloom that sometimes overwhelms us, making us powerless. With your love, O God, we are not left powerless. As you love us, so your power does not hide from us.

(Morning)
Let me face this day, O God of power and grace, secure in your love.
(Prayers of Intercession)

(Evening)
Now be with me as the night draws near.
(Prayers of Intercession)

And now with confidence, I pray.
(Pray the Prayer of Our Savior.)

(Morning)	(Evening)
Let me face this day secure that your love holds me and feeds me. Amen.	Sanctify this night that I may rest in your grace and power. Amen.

WEDNESDAY, FEBRUARY 12 (ASH WEDNESDAY)
(Read Psalm 51:1–17)

(Morning)
God, do not despise me, but open my lips to praise you. I awaken knowing I have transgressed against you and your people. I pray, O God, have mercy; blot out also my iniquities.

(Evening)
God, do not despise me, but open my lips to praise you. The day has not been easy; humility is not easy to practice. But give me forgiveness and rest.

It is hard to accept that we are sinners, because we live in a culture that often strives to be the "best and purest" in the world. Every day we are told we are the greatest, that we are the saviors of this world, that the world needs the benevolence of our superpower. Yet by your mercy, we know we are not you. That burden is not ours. What you require of us is not power but honesty; honesty with ourselves and among ourselves. Knowing one's place with you entails daring, being freed to look into one's own soul, and discovering that you both judge and accept the heart as one discovers it broken.

(Morning)
God, as I move today among your people, teach me to understand my transgressions.
(Prayers of Intercession)

(Evening)
Hear my praise tonight as I discover you at my side, in spite of myself.
(Prayers of Intercession)

And now with confidence as your child, I pray.
(Pray the Prayer of Our Savior.)

(Morning)
God as I move today, give me the courage to know my place with you and to be humble before you. Amen.

(Evening)
God, you are teaching me today and everyday who I am and who you are. I rejoice in your presence and look forward to my rest, knowing your acceptance even of me. Amen.

THURSDAY, FEBRUARY 13
(Read Isaiah 58:1–12)

(Morning)
God, who cares for the whole community, I am confused this morning because I understand what oppresses me and I see that I, too, oppress others. Give me strength to accept your guidance.

(Evening)
God, who cares for the whole community, this day has been long, its lessons difficult. I give thanks for your guidance and for the glimpses of your justice among us.

To some of us, God, you seem demanding. To others, you offer freedom from homelessness, poverty, nakedness, and hunger. I am well fed and cared for, live in a home that meets my needs; but that is not what you demand from me. Serving myself is not your goal for the believer. Nor is fasting or the practice of righteousness on my terms. God, your justice and guidance are not separate departments of a human government. Hypocrisy is not acceptable to you. But breaking the yoke of oppression (our own and others'), living free, walking free with strong bodies, rejoicing in the wellspring of your pleasure—that is to glorify you.

(Morning)
God, I need your guidance even today. Answer my call for help.
(Prayers of Intercession)

(Evening)
As I prepare to rest, hear my prayer for those who need you.
(Prayers of Intercession)

And now, I humbly pray.
(Pray the Prayer of Our Savior.)

(Morning)	(Evening)
God, I need your guidance. Free me from my own prisons, use me today as your servant to loose the bonds of oppression. Amen.	As I prepare to rest, may your guidance help me see and feel. Restore among your people peaceful communities to live in. Amen.

FRIDAY, FEBRUARY 14
(Read Psalm 25:1–10)

(Morning)
God of truth and mercy, I am fearful this morning that this day may bring shame to me.

(Evening)
God of truth and mercy, the day has been a hard one, filled with challenges and confrontations. I pray that you in your mercy will forgive my impatience and shortcomings.

To trust in you, O God, sometimes seem to bring about difficulties. We need words and actions that are demanding and require all of our integrity. It can be difficult to face colleagues who seemingly disregard that you are the God of salvation for all of us and that, therefore, we are sisters and brothers. At such times, I can only trust and hope in your mercy that the ridicule to which I am exposed will not be worse than I can bear. And that I will continue to understand that your mercy is for all of us, on all sides of the issues that divide us. Your mercy will indeed show the way toward steadfast love and faithfulness in spite of the tensions that abound.

(Morning)
I am fearful this morning that the place where I work will be full of tension and worry and that your name will be forgotten.
(Prayers of Intercession)

(Evening)
This day has been a hard one, filled with challenges. I pray that you, in your mercy, will forgive my impatience.
(Prayers of Intercession)

And now I pray the prayer that Jesus taught his disciples.
(Pray the Prayer of Our Savior.)

(Morning)
Give me the strength to know that I face the difficulties of this day knowing you in your mercy. Forgive me and all who turn to you. Amen.

(Evening)
I give thanks for your mercy and your truth, which allow me to know that it is your uprightness that leads all along your path of faithfulness. Amen.

SATURDAY, FEBRUARY 15
(Read 2 Corinthians 5:20–6:13)

(Morning)
God of all righteousness and grace, each new day means a new chance in life. Help me today to accept the grace you have offered as you gave the life of your Child, Christ Jesus, for your people.

(Evening)
God of all righteousness and grace, as I prepare to rest, please let me do so in the trust that your righteousness will be enough for me, too.

Gracious God, maybe no other person has prayed as much for others as the apostle Paul. No other person has suffered so much hardship to communicate your gracious offer of salvation to the people for whom he cared. Some days I feel like Paul, praying and begging you to have those around me accept and live your words of grace and salvation. Some days I honestly wonder whether I even remember what you say to me, what you do for me, every day and every hour of my life. Other days, I feel as if I am being punished, almost to the limit of my capacity, for merely trying to hang on to the faith you have given me. Others then open their hearts to me, and thereby again open my eyes to see and to rejoice in the salvation you have offered in Jesus Christ.

(Morning)
Make this a day, O God of grace, a day where I may be able to bear whatever hardship may come my way.
(Prayers of Intercession)

(Evening)
I pray for those with whom I spoke today and tried to tell about your love. May they hear your Word and rejoice.
(Prayers of Intercession)

And now I pray the prayer that Jesus taught his disciples.
(Pray the Prayer of Our Savior.)

(Morning)
Make this a day in which I can freely share my faith in you. Amen.

(Evening)
I give thanks for those who spoke your Word to me and reminded me that today was indeed an acceptable time and a day of salvation. Amen.

SUNDAY, FEBRUARY 16
(Read Matthew 6:1–6, 16–21)

(Morning)
God, who hears and sees and notices all that we do, this is the special day in which the community gathers to worship. We pray together, sing together, and give alms for your church and its mission. May we come together with you, O God.

(Evening)
God, who hears and sees and notices all that we do, a new week has begun, and I turn again to you to give me enough rest to be strong for the challenges ahead.

Creator God, we are called to follow your way, your path of righteousness, and then we are told not to share it publicly! Yes, Sunday is a day to celebrate your willingness to be present among us and to respond to your presence with prayer and almsgiving. But our private life of prayer and of sharing the richness that you provide is not to be anything other than a reflection of you. Sunday is a gift in which to rejoice, a day to celebrate your generosity to us, a bounty that far outshines all else. This is a day to rejoice for just being a child among all of your children.

(Morning)
God, make this a day in which I never forget that you are with me.
(Prayers of Intercession)

(Evening)
God, teach me to pray as you wish, let me learn that all you have given me is still yours, for I am yours.
(Prayers of Intercession)

I now pray.
(Pray the Prayer of Our Savior.)

(Morning)
God, make this a day in which I can remember you so clearly that I forget myself. Amen.

(Evening)
Let me rest so that tomorrow I may rejoice in the gift of a new week full of days to glorify you. Amen.

MONDAY, FEBRUARY 17
(Read Genesis 17:1–2, Psalm 22:23, Psalm 46, and 2 Samuel 6:12–15)

(Morning)
O God who searches me out, I begin the day knowing you have renewed our relationship. Each day we start afresh together.

(Evening)
O God who searches me out, I stumbled many times today. Yet you upheld me. I can sleep in peace knowing that you are God.

Like Abraham, I have little to offer. Yet you sought me out to follow you. Like Sarah, I was filled with regret and emptiness. Yet you lifted me up and bestowed your promise on me. You enter into an agreement with me, O God. But how can this be? You are righteous and dependable. I am not. You are strong. I am not. You do not need me for anything, and it is I who need you. Yet you stand eye to eye with me. If I walk before you, you tell me I will be blameless. I am a nobody whom you have made into a somebody. You have raised me into partnership with you. I walk each day before you, as David danced before the ark!

(Morning)
What a morning to walk before you, O God, in the world! May I be blameless today in the sight of all.
(Prayers of Intercession)

(Evening)
My steps faltered this day. My dance too soon turned into drudgery. My spirit of confidence faltered. I am tired.
(Prayers of Intercession)

O God, the house of my soul is narrow; enlarge it, that you may enter in (St. Augustine).

(Morning)
Grant me confidence and steadfastness to live my part of our covenant. Let me feel your presence and strength beside me today. Amen.

(Evening)
You have sustained me this day, O God. I have been preserved. I rest praying that my life has made a difference. Amen.

TUESDAY, FEBRUARY 18
(Read Genesis 17:1–7 and John 15:1–11)

(Morning)
Abundant and fruitful God, this day I pray that I will make a difference in the world. I pray that my life may bear fruit.

(Evening)
Abundant and fruitful God, my high expectations were not met. Yet things did happen. Your presence in me mattered.

To live in covenant relationship with you is to accept the invitation to bring blessings into the world. In covenant we are called to bear fruit. Abraham and Sarah were called to create a posterity, generations who would be fruitful. O God, our lives are obsessed with creating "product," not bearing fruit. What we produce is so often dead on arrival. We are not branches connected in a living way with Christ Jesus, the vine. We allow ourselves to be controlled by impersonal systems that produce "goods and services" that people are told they want and need. But we are called to be fruitful. I pray that my life may be a bearer of blessing, not an instrument of dehumanization. I pray that I may say no to anything that does not give life.

(Morning)
I pray for centeredness in my day. I pray that I may not lose touch with the source of living water.
(Prayers of Intercession)

(Evening)
The pressures bore down on me today. I struggled. I am afraid I compromised too much. I "went along" too often.
(Prayers of Intercession)

Help me to spread your fragrance everywhere I go (John Henry Newman).

(Morning)
All the earth and heavens proclaim life, O God. The sounds of nature and the buzz of human activity welcome me to the world. Amen.

(Evening)
I find peace in my exhaustion. My bed will heal my frayed edges. I look back on my day with relief and fondness. Amen.

WEDNESDAY, FEBRUARY 19
(Read Genesis 17:15–17, Romans 4:18–22, and Jeremiah 1:4–10)

(Morning)
Trustworthy God, I awake and feel overwhelmed even before my day has begun. How can you sustain me in the face of what I will encounter?

(Evening)
Trustworthy God, I am filled with thanksgiving. Impossible things happened. I was sustained. What I stand for was not defeated. You were indeed with me, O God!

I trust in you, O God, to keep the promise, even in the face of all the evidence that it is impossible. How can a man of one hundred years and a woman of ninety years have a child? How can the wonderful promise you made to them depend on such an impossibility? How can I do what you have called me to do when I know how little I have to offer? It is all I can do to make it through the day and meet my basic responsibilities. How, therefore, can I be a healer and reconciler? How can I bring beauty, peace, and justice even to my own household, let alone the world? What you ask is impossible, O God; it is laughable. Yet I must do it—I must trust. Your trust in me allows me to trust myself.

(Morning)
I know what I am up against. I count the costs, yet I go forward knowing that you are with me.
(Prayers of Intercession)

(Evening)
I was not alone this day. I found friendship and support that I was not expecting. As you walked with me, O God, so did others, and I am thankful.
(Prayers of Intercession)

Sovereign God, grant us grace to desire you with our whole heart (St. Anselm).

(Morning)
May I find peace in the midst of struggle, beauty in the midst of ugliness, hope in the midst of what seems hopeless. Amen.

(Evening)
Sustained by your promise, I can better trust and more courageously hope. Amen.

THURSDAY, FEBRUARY 20
(Read Psalm 22:24–26 and Ecclesiastes 4:1–3)

(Morning)
Compassionate God, I know I am not alone this day. I rise eager to be with others.

(Evening)
Compassionate God, I noticed more today. I saw and heard a wider range of human experience.

Everywhere I see reminders of human suffering. I am overwhelmed by the amount of pain in the world. I am so aware of the pain of those around me. A homeless man asks for a handout. I am uneasy. A woman with a shopping cart talks to herself and glares at me. What am I to do? I am surrounded by affliction: poverty, racism, intolerance, and hatred. Not just where I work or live, but in my whole world. People cry out in their pain. I wish I could not hear them, but I do. Yet in covenant, you hear me. In my own pain and shame and abandonment, when I cry out, you are there for me. You promise healing. We all share affliction and pain. To understand this creates compassion in me. In compassion I can act. Your face does not hide from my affliction. Nor can I hide my face from others.

(Morning)
I will notice those I so often ignore. I will open my heart to suffering.
(Prayers of Intercession)

(Evening)
I carry with me memories of the pain I experienced today.
(Prayers of Intercession)

Christ has no body now on earth but yours (St. Teresa of Avila).

(Morning)
I pray that I may experience a sense of connection with those who seem different from me. Amen.

(Evening)
May I feel greater courage to cry out to God, for others and for myself. Amen.

FRIDAY, FEBRUARY 21
(Read Psalm 22:27–31 and Hebrews 12:1–2)

(Morning)
God of the ages, I wake with dreams fresh in my thoughts.
They are reminders of eternity.

(Evening)
God of the ages, today I was aware of the universality of human experience.
We all share so much.

I am aware today that I am surrounded by a great cloud of witnesses, a communion of the saints; those who have gone before and are yet to come. Before me came my father and mother, great- and great-great-grandparents. Yet they are not present. They stand behind me to encourage me. Though returned to dust, they are alive. After me comes my posterity; the people of God, the saints to come. Future generations will be told of you, O God. In every generation, voices like mine will proclaim your wonderful deeds. Your people have a foothold in eternity. My journey is their journey. The covenant journey of Abraham and Sarah is my journey, too. I live in their promise. Their story is my story.

(Morning)
May the communion of the saints strengthen and sustain me today.
(Prayers of Intercession)

(Evening)
My life touched many today. I was upheld by invisible hands.
(Prayers of Intercession)

God, of your goodness give me yourself; for you are sufficient for me (Julian of Norwich).

(Morning)
In each encounter I have, I will know that I am not alone. Amen.

(Evening)
My past, present, and future are in your hands, O God. I sleep in peace. Amen.

SATURDAY, FEBRUARY 22
(Read Mark 8:31–38 and Isaiah 53:7–9)

(Morning)
O God who knows suffering, I begin my day eager to confront the sources of pain and injustice in my world.

(Evening)
O God who knows suffering, today I was reminded of how hard it is to confront systems of oppression and cruelty.

Living in covenant makes astonishing and sobering demands upon me. I have been promised life in abundance. But I am also asked to give up something. I am being asked to let go and carry the cross of Christ. What must I sacrifice to be a bearer of blessing and reconciliation? my comfort? my security? my cherished notions of what is important? my ideas about what I need to be happy? Jesus spoke plainly to his disciples. He said he would undergo suffering, rejection, and death, and that he would rise. His disciples did not want to hear this. Nor do I. There is too much of this world that I love, too much of which I do not want to let go. To say that I will gain my life by losing it makes no sense to me. Must this covenant include this demand?

(Morning)
Today I will be aware of my attachment to this world. I will be conscious of wants that have become needs.
(Prayers of Intercession)

(Evening)
Today I was aware of the clutter that fills my life. I saw how distracted I was by "things."
(Prayers of Intercession)

Take, O God, all my liberty, my memory, my understanding, and my whole will.... Give me only your love and your grace. With this I am rich enough, and I have no more to ask (Ignatius Loyola).

(Morning)
Today I will count the costs of discipleship. Amen.

(Evening)
Issues became clearer to me. Today I experienced a taste of the love and courage of Jesus' sacrifice. Amen.

SUNDAY, FEBRUARY 23
(Read Romans 4:19–25, Matthew 13:31–32, and Mark 9:20–27)

(Morning)
O God who nourishes my growth, this morning I awake and long to fully trust you. Let me grow strong in my faith.

(Evening)
O God who nourishes my growth, today I let go and trusted more. And you were there for me.

Let faith replace the distrust and fear within me. Let me grow in faith as I give glory to you God. I yearn to have the faith of Abraham and Sarah. Let the little mustard seed of faith find a place in me. I believe that you can sustain me to help my unbelief. You have promised me this: If I trust you, if I give glory to you, I will grow strong in faith. I understand this. If I but give you glory, O God, if I walk before you blameless, my faith will deepen and be strengthened. My covenant with you, O God, is a covenant of faith. I believe in you who raised Jesus from the dead. So also shall I be raised.

(Morning)
In simple and direct ways, I will trust you more fully, letting go of myself.
(Prayers of Intercession)

(Evening)
Your presence carried me through this day, O God, with gentle surprises.
(Prayers of Intercession)

Christ be with me, Christ within me (St. Patrick).

(Morning)
Today I will say and do things that give glory to you, O God. Amen.

(Evening)
Has my faith grown? I don't know. Yet I can trust that the seed of faith grows secretly and mysteriously. Amen.

MONDAY, FEBRUARY 24
(Read Exodus 20:1–17)

(Morning)
God of righteousness, bring me out of the house of bondage today.
Release me from the guilt I carry at the word "commandment";
bring me into its grace. Sabbath me.

(Evening)
God of righteousness, I give you thanks for the capacity to live well, to be morally aware, and to do what I should. I didn't do it all, O God. But for what I did,
I give you thanks.

O God, let me not spout the commandments as though they make perfect sense to us. All we know is that they are on the right track—they show us the scent of sin. I don't know much about Sabbath, just that certain things should not be done on that day. And I know that stealing, killing, and adultery are obviously wrong. But coveting? Isn't that what our entire economy is based on? Are commandments real only when I can obey them? Or are they real even when they are hard and challenge the costly way of life that I practice? Let me know, God. Give me time to think today.

(Morning)
Let me not kill or covet. Keep me from dishonoring those I love. Make your words real in the way I live. Amen.
(Prayers of Intercession)

(Evening)
Let the day go now. Let what I did not shame me any further. Let what I did be good and useful to you.
(Prayers of Intercession)

Pray as Christ has taught.
(Pray the Prayer of Our Savior.)

(Morning)
Sabbath me, O God. Let there be a space in this day that is separate from the others. Let me plan it now. Amen.

(Evening)
Today was my life. You gave it to me, O God. I didn't always see it, but I kept on looking. In the shalt nots and the shalts, I find you. In my keeping on after I have failed, I find you. Keep me tonight so that I may keep you. In Jesus' name. Amen.

TUESDAY, FEBRUARY 25
(Read Psalm 19)

(Morning)
Creator God, let me be a bridegroom today, rushing out of my tent into the light.

(Evening)
Creator God, I have rejoiced as one strong to run a race, and now I am home. My going forth and my coming in, O God, you have blessed. Nothing has been hidden from the heat of this day. Thank you.

Sometimes you move into my life so surreptitiously that I don't even know you are coming. I remember the time you found me in the stained-glass workshop. It was early morning. The stained-glass repairers were already there, making colors, patching broken glass, and letting beauty find its way to light. You brought tears to my eyes. I repair stained glass for a living, too. I repair broken churches. You let me know the depth of my grief that day. You let me acknowledge how much beauty and color is already gone. Help me bring it back. Help the stained-glass repairers bring it back. Help the street workers bring it back. Help the youth group leaders bring it back. Let us help you bring it back.

(Morning)
Let me be strong and sure in the race. Let me know where I am going and let me remain intent on getting there.
(Prayers of Intercession)

(Evening)
Prepare me for a tomorrow as gracious as today.
(Prayers of Intercession)

I now pray.
(Pray the Prayer of Our Savior.)

(Morning)
Let my joy be clear to all who look. Let me be transparent, full of color, capable of light. Let me know how good this day is, how it is my life. Amen.

(Evening)
God of youth and strength, you are also God of age and weakness. Prepare me to know your many sides in my own life. In Jesus' name, Amen.

WEDNESDAY, FEBRUARY 26
(Read 1 Corinthians 18–25)

(Morning)
Surprising God, give me the courage for your foolishness today. Surprise me.
Be gentle with me. Erase the hard outline of the want ad I put out for you.

(Evening)
Surprising God, now I am weary of testing your foolishness in the world,
but I feel safer now than I can remember. Perfection no longer terrorizes me.
I begin to see, just barely, why you insisted on foolishness.

O God, you know how I imagined you: one who looks good, smart, clean shaven. I imagined you to look like the kind of person my church wants as members: Mom, Dad, two kids. Yet you give us teenage mothers and recovering addicts! Foolish you are. Keep me from complaining about your choices to be who you are. Help me understand them.

(Morning)
Let me see you in a nook, or in a cranny, or in a moment. Let me know that my
own foolishness is not nearly as bad as my own purported wisdom.
(Prayers of Intercession)

(Evening)
Now that I see more of your foolish way, I can imagine it more deeply. It is not my
usual way. I am going to need a lot of help to stay with you on this path. Send me
that help.
(Prayers of Intercession)

I humbly pray.
(Pray the Prayer of Our Savior.)

(Morning)
Wean me from my need to be smart, to
dress smart, to talk smart, to act smart.
Show me the way, today. Amen.

(Evening)
Let sleep's own wisdom come now, and
let it bring me peace. Amen.

THURSDAY, FEBRUARY 27
(Read 1 Corinthians 1:25)

(Morning)
O God, bring us strength to trust our way into a new world. Things are moving so fast; my head spins. Slow me down so that I may be ready for the new time.

(Evening)
O God, thank you for all the things I didn't get to today.
Thank you for my limitations.

Can we still say that you are strong, even if you don't have a 486 or a CD-ROM? You say your strength is weakness and that it is stronger than the sleek threads of cyberspace. How? Perhaps it is your wisdom not to compete, to act but not to force. Your strength looks to us like weakness. It is not.

(Morning)
Let me not be so afraid of my weakness, just as you did not fear yours.
(Prayers of Intercession)

(Evening)
Thank you for the hope I have in tomorrow, not that I may be stronger but that I may be more settled in my real self.
(Prayers of Intercession)

I humbly pray.
(Pray the Prayer of Our Savior.)

(Morning)
Let my weakness become my strength, once I know its shadow name. In the name of Jesus who didn't fear the cross. Amen.

(Evening)
Tonight I want to undress slowly, wash slowly, remember slowly, and count my blessings slowly. I want to treasure my weakness, not my strength. I want to trust your weakness, O God, and to know it as strength. Show me the way. Amen.

FRIDAY, FEBRUARY 28
(Read John 2:13–22)

(Morning)
God of grace, God in Jesus and Jesus in God, why do you always do things differently? How can we understand the time you live in, much less our own? Let me live with my tension with you this day; my tension is real with your ways and my ways.

(Evening)
God of grace, I rest in your difference. Make me yours.

Let me seek to know you, O God, in your difference from what I had thought you would be. You remember that your servant Flannery O'Connor sought the "action of grace in territory occupied by the devil." Let me do so as well. And if I can't find your grace, let me know others who can. Bless, O God, the teenager I saw yesterday, wearing a T-shirt that read "Deal with It." Bless the person walking down the street with the button "The Meek Are Getting Ready." Please meek, please God, hurry. The time is getting short.

(Morning)
You move quickly, O God, when you want to. Let me be ready. Amen.
(Prayers of Intercession)

(Evening)
I rest in your completeness, O God. Make it mine.
(Prayers of Intercession)

I now pray the prayer that Jesus taught.
(Pray the Prayer of Our Savior.)

(Morning)
You love our temples less than we do. Let me love my temple but love you even more. Amen.

(Evening)
I rest in your speed, O God. Let your time be mine. Amen.

SATURDAY, MARCH 1
(Read John 2:13–22)

(Morning)
O God, I love the Sabbath, and I hate the Sabbath. I love church, and I hate church. I love weekends, and I hate weekends. Do something with me.

(Evening)
O God, how much zeal do I need? Sometimes I am so dry, so dusty, so remote from even myself. And then you come. Your organ prelude brings me back. I burn. Bring me to worship this weekend. Bring me to zeal. Let it flame me.

Help me understand sanctuary, O God. Everyone, including my daughter, says that we can worship God in a meadow—we don't need church. And surely church has devoured its children on more than one occasion, even in the time of the Gospel of John. Jesus loved the temple so much he threw out "people selling cattle, sheep, and doves, and the moneychangers seated at the table." He acted for you. Let my love of the sanctuary be yours. Let meadow and morning worship both call your name. And, when I worship, let me hear it. Let me be moved this Sabbath so that I return to my week with new respect for sanctuary.

(Morning)
Sabbath me, today and tomorrow. Separate me from my usual routine.
Use me in a different way.
(Prayers of Intercession)

(Evening)
Let me worship this weekend. Get the pastor's sermon out of the way. Let me listen deeply enough to hear the beat of the world's heart in my own sanctuary.
(Prayers of Intercession)

Refresh me as I pray.
(Pray the Prayer of Our Savior.)

(Morning)
Refresh me, O God, let me be free of my own zeal. Amen.

(Evening)
Sit me down in the sanctuary and don't let me move until you are ready for me to move. In the name of tomorrow. Amen.

SUNDAY, MARCH 2
(Read John 2:13–22)

(Morning)
God, let me remember the temple of my body and the temple of our body today. Let me find its meaning in words and deeds.

(Evening)
God, to be risen from our bodies is to be so free. Thank you for holding out the promise of the resurrection and for letting me taste it today.

Show me the connection between my body and the temple. Show me how real the connection is between the way one embodies the Word and how another embodies the Word. When next I go to a committee meeting, let me remember what I learned about the temple, about Jesus, and about his risen body. Let me act out of that knowledge. Let the praise of the Sabbath sanctuary be so incorporated in me that I can't forget it and that I speak it on Monday and Tuesday too.

(Morning)
Let me not be a prisoner in my body but a guest.
(Prayers of Intercession)

(Evening)
Thank you for the time today to be, and to know that I both am and am not my body. Incarnate your Word in me and let me know your Child and the magnitude of the way he became Word, in flesh, and dwelt among us, even now.
(Prayers of Intercession)

I now pray.
(Pray the Prayer of Our Savior.)

(Morning)
Let me embody your Child. Make me like Jesus, and let my body be like his.
Amen.

(Evening)
Not everything was easy today, O God, but I did my best, and I offer it to you.
Amen.

MONDAY, MARCH 3
(Read Numbers 21:4–9)

(Morning)
Gracious God, thank you for providing visions of life for humanity.
May I never lose hope in you.

(Evening)
Gracious God, there are times when I feel that I am in life's wilderness
with no possibility for nurture.

You heard the cries of the Hebrews as they were held against their will in Egypt, O liberating God. You entered their lives by selecting Moses to lead them into freedom's avenues. Help us to know that you still hear the cries of hurting people in the world, and that you have risen up scores of women and men to work for freedom and justice. May we never lose hope in your ability to transform the world. May your Spirit equip us for the ministry of liberation, knowing that you will always be with us.

(Morning)
I am excited by your visions, help me to faithfully work for their fruition,
even if it seems that I am accomplishing little. May I never lose hope in you.
(Prayers of Intercession)

(Evening)
I thank you for letting me know that you have not abandoned me.
In you I can trust.
(Prayers of Intercession)

Gracious God, you equip women and men to be leaders.

(Morning)
Thank you for the leadership skills that you have given me, O God. Enable me to be alert to the Holy Spirit's direction, and the needs of those around me so that I may be faithful to your vision for humanity. Amen.

(Evening)
God of wisdom, it is easy for us to give up on you when life seems to fall apart. Help us to remember your good works; may they propel us into a future characterized by hope. Amen.

TUESDAY MARCH 4
(Read Psalm 107:1–3, 17–22)

(Morning)
Liberating, loving God, I praise you today for I have been redeemed and transformed by your steadfast love.

(Evening)
Liberating, loving God, today I learned how hard it is to love as you love. I rest tonight trusting you to free me from today's fears and failures as you strengthen me to serve you tomorrow.

Loving God, when I recall the events of my life, I realize that not all of my memories are happy ones. There were times when I experienced pain, not only at the hands of others but sometimes from my own actions. Yet during each period of sorrow, O God, you listened to my voice as I called out to you for help. You, liberating God, healed me from all wounds, self-inflicted and from outside sources. I will always offer you thanksgiving and sing songs of joy to tell others of your goodness.

(Morning)
You alone know of my life's journey; you chose to love me and called me to be an agent of your grace on this new day. I accept your call with gratitude.
(Prayers of Intercession)

(Evening)
I praise you, O God my great redeemer, for each episode of your grace that I experienced today.
(Prayers of Intercession)

O liberating, loving God, you are the redeemer of my soul and body.

(Morning)
Today I pray that your joy, O God, may radiate from the depths of my being, reminding me of your love for me and for all who walk this earth. Amen.

(Evening)
Before I close my eyes tonight, forgive me for the times when my actions did not spread your love to those around me. Give me rest and then send me out again. Amen.

WEDNESDAY, MARCH 5
(Read John 3:14–21)

(Morning)
O Kind Creator, help me pay attention to those around me today, that I may see the gifts present in each life.

(Evening)
O Kind Creator, often it seems so much easier to find fault and condemn others than it is to lift them up.

Frequently, O God, life presents us with many difficult circumstances, and I confess that at times it is hard to maintain an attitude of hope. As a result, confusion and condemnation have become ways of life for too many of us. Yet how refreshing it is to know that you sent your Child, Jesus, into the world, not to add to humankind's madness, but to redeem us. Redemption has ushered in a new way of life for me, and I will share my resources with those around me, that they may know that you give hope!

(Morning)
Help me today to engage myself in activities that nurture my sisters and brothers as you have nurtured me.
(Prayers of Intercession)

(Evening)
Forgive me when I too quickly judge others while conveniently forgetting how your love has overcome my faults.
(Prayers of Intercession)

You are a loving God whose grace redeems us and gives us hope.

(Morning)
Send me out on this new day, O God, that I may participate in all that is good, uplifting, and redeeming. May this day be characterized by joy. Amen.

(Evening)
Tonight I will rest my body in the full assurance that I need not be saddled with the weight of condemnation, for through Jesus Christ, I have the comfort of knowing that salvation has entered my life. Amen.

THURSDAY, MARCH 6
(Read Numbers 21:4–9)

(Morning)
Caring God, whose love and compassion meet every human need, I thank you for providing food and water that sustain me and your Spirit that guides me.

(Evening)
Caring God, I am amazed at how much we waste! Forgive me for the times I waste the gifts you have given to me. Help me to be a faithful steward.

How astounding it is, gracious God, that so many people conclude that you are disinterested in humanity because they cannot seem to find evidence of your love. Yet each day we throw away enough food and waste enough water to nourish scores of people. Instead of turning away from you, may we turn toward your righteousness and accept your vision of a world where no one hungers or thirsts. May we spread your love—already given—through our sharing with those around us.

(Morning)
I will walk with confidence today, knowing that you have blessed me;
may I be a blessing to others.
(Prayers of Intercession)

(Evening)
As often as I saw people working to eliminate poverty, hunger, violence,
and injustice, I observed you at work.
(Prayers of Intercession)

Caring God, you nurture my body and soul.

(Morning)
O God, during this new day, may I be nourished with food and water and through insight provided by your Spirit. May my faith and trust in you grow stronger throughout this day. Amen.

Evening
All day I saw you at work in the world, O God, and I realize all the more just how wondrous your love really is.
Amen.

FRIDAY, MARCH 7
(Read Psalms 107:1–3, 17–22)

(Morning)
Dear God, how glad I am to be linked to persons of faith from every generation who have experienced redemption through your grace. As one who has been redeemed, may my life testify to your goodness. I do not want to be silent!

(Evening)
Dear God, as I rest from the activities of this day, I confess that often I would rather keep silent than make known my faith in you.

How amazing it is to look around and realize the great diversity among humanity. God, I am altogether excited to know that people from the East, West, North, and South speak of your steadfast love and your vision for humanity. Help us to discern your presence among all of humankind as we embrace our diversity and work for unity.

(Morning)
Great God, I take delight in the vastness of your creation and your love for us all. May I not be afraid to form partnerships with segments of humanity whose ethnicities and cultures are different from my own.
(Prayers of Intercession)

(Evening)
Sometimes I am not willing to love those who refuse to love me. Enable me to remember how your love transformed my life and to know that your love for humanity will not fail.
(Prayers of Intercession)

In our broken and hurting world, I will not be silent about the transforming love of God.

(Morning)
May I listen to the stories of others and share my own, all for the common good. Amen.

(Evening)
Yes, God, I know that many parts of the human family are broken. Yet I know that when we, your redeemed people, take actions rooted in your steadfast love, dividing walls will fall and justice will prevail. May it be so. Amen.

SATURDAY, MARCH 8
(Read Ephesians 2:1–10)

(Morning)
O God, who was present with my ancestors, I thank you for your loving presence today. I am a recipient of your past and present acts of love. May my steps help future generations know of your goodness.

(Evening)
O God, thank you for enabling me to do good works in your name today. I know that I cannot earn your love through works; yet because of my gratitude to you, I accept your call to service, both now and always.

I confess to you, forgiving God, that I live in a world of people who are impressed by financial wealth. Frequently, I, too, am overly concerned with affluence. Yet today I am reminded of the great wealth that you possess. Indeed, you are rich in grace and mercy. Help me to realize my richness in your grace and my affluence in your mercy, so whenever I become indifferent to my neighbors, I will remember that all I am or ever will be is by your grace and mercy.

(Morning)
I am glad to be alive today, O God. May my life be a testimony to my gratitude to you and the vibrant hope I have in your love.
(Prayers of Intercession)

(Evening)
Transforming God, I praise you for the ways in which your love has revolutionized my life.
(Prayers of Intercession)

O God, the hope of our ancestors, your grace and mercy are known to all generations.

(Morning)
I am a recipient of your loving acts of the past and the present. May the steps I take today help future generations to know your goodness. Amen.

(Evening)
When I was dead in my sins, your grace made me alive in Christ. I rest tonight knowing that my life is anchored in your grace. Amen.

SUNDAY, MARCH 9
(Read John 3:14–21)

(Morning)
O God, I thank you for the light of Jesus the Christ that is in my life!

(Evening)
O God, thank you for the nurturing fellowship in which I participated today. Enable me to rest now, that I may be prepared to lift up Jesus this week through acts of love and kindness.

It is clear to me, loving God, that when you look at humanity, you see us not only as we really are, but for who we really can become through you. Your love for humankind is so intense that you sent Jesus into the world, not to condemn us but to save us, to teach us how to love one another as you love us. The more I consider your enthusiastic love and how it has transformed my life, the more committed I feel to go beyond the realms of the normal and the traditional in order to express love in the avenues where it is needed the most.

(Morning)
As I worship you today, may the joy of my salvation radiate to all around me.
(Prayers of Intercession)

(Evening)
Dear God, thank you for taking the risk of loving humanity.
(Prayers of Intercession)

In you, O God, we find strength to love without fear.

(Morning)
This is a new day, O living God. May your love empower me to break all old allegiances to indifference and fear in order to take part in your agenda of hope for this day. Amen.

(Evening)
Forgive me for my reluctance to risk my name and status to love as you love. Enable me to rest tonight and awaken tomorrow knowing that you still love me and will never give up on me.
Amen.

MONDAY, MARCH 10
(Read Jeremiah 31:31–34)

(Morning)
O God who sends springtime, the day begins with a hint of a rebirth in the good earth. I pray for patience to await the renewal.

(Evening)
O God who sends springtime, the day ends in the quiet. I long for the renewing power of rest.

I confess, renewing God, that sometimes I try to force change and renewal in my corner of your creation without acknowledging your power and presence. You spoke to my brother, Jeremiah, and told him of a new covenant written not upon stone but upon the hearts of your people. Renewing God, we seem, in our time, so cut off from your realm and your covenant. Some of your servants long for the day, the time, the season of renewal. Grant to us the wisdom and the courage to trust in your timeless power. Renewing God, we struggle to understand and to do your will in a fragmented and fractured world. We pray that you will touch our lives, our families, our churches, and our communities. Renew and refresh us with your Spirit.

(Morning)
As I begin this day, make me ever mindful that it is a precious gift.
(Prayers of Intercession)

(Evening)
As I reflect upon the gifts of this day, I pray for wisdom to learn and grow from what I have seen, heard, and done.
(Prayers of Intercession)

I offer labor of my hands and heart as I pray.
(Pray the Prayer of Our Savior.)

(Morning)
If it is your will, O God, make me an instrument of your renewal. Amen.

(Evening)
May my efforts and my prayers be acceptable in your sight, O God. Amen.

TUESDAY, MARCH 11
(Read Psalm 51:1–5)

(Morning)
O God who knows my pain, as the day begins I ask for strength not to get bogged down with guilt. I pray for balance in my life.

(Evening)
O God who knows my pain, you know of the times when I fall short of sin. Forgive me and help me to forgive myself.

Powerful and gentle God, there are surely times when I am aware of the pain and discord I create, sometimes with the best of intentions and sometimes not. Powerful God, the psalmist reminds us that we are all guilty of a narrowness which focuses upon our own needs to the exclusion of others. Gentle God, while we know that you forgive your children, we confess that sometimes we find it difficult to forgive ourselves and others. Powerful God, we seek to balance the wonderful knowledge of your power to forgive with the painful reality of sin. Gentle God, as the rains of late winter wash away the snow and slush, we ask you to wash away our guilt and forgive our sins.

(Morning)
With some hesitation, I come to this new day. Grant me the courage and the wisdom to forgive.
(Prayers of Intercession)

(Evening)
As I reflect upon the day now ending, I confess that I tend to see opportunities missed. Help me to forgive.
(Prayers of Intercession)

With humility I come to you, O powerful and gentle God, to pray.
(Pray the Prayer of Our Savior.)

(Morning)
God grant me confidence and humility in roughly equal portions to face this new day.

(Evening)
As I come to the time of rest, grant to me, O God, tranquillity.

WEDNESDAY, MARCH 12
(Read Psalm 51:6–12)

(Morning)
O God of energy and eagerness, it's a glorious day which you have made. But some days are more glorious than others.

(Evening)
O God of energy and eagerness, the day is all but over and I pray that I have brought brightness and light to your world.

O God of energy and eagerness, I confess that there are days when it is hard for me to be either energetic or eager. Cleanse my heart and break through my cynicism. God of energy, as the sun warms each day, warm my willingness to serve. God of eagerness, let me hear joy and gladness; too often I seem to hear only the voices of gloom and sadness. God of energy, there are days when I'm so tired. Breathe life and warmth into my cold soul. God of eagerness, help me to see that service in your name should be an empowering joy. God of energy, put in me a new and right spirit, a spirit that allows others to see me articulating a vision of hope and fullness. God of eagerness, I seek a willing spirit. Guide me to a new day.

(Morning)
The rising sun signals the power and light which are your good creation.
(Prayers of Intercession)

(Evening)
The setting sun signals the time to rest and reflect. We ponder the hope that the creation will see light tomorrow.
(Prayers of Intercession)

With the energy and eagerness of a child, I boldly pray.
(Pray the Prayer of Our Savior.)

(Morning)	(Evening)
Grant me this fresh day a hint, a suggestion, of the opportunities presented to me. Grant to me also a willing spirit. Amen.	I rest the rest not of smug satisfaction, but the rest of a servant of God who will try to nurture and support others. Amen.

THURSDAY, MARCH 13
(Read Psalm 119:9–16)

(Morning)
O God of learning and wisdom, may this new day bring to me new insights and fresh perspectives.

(Evening)
O God of learning and wisdom, I pray that the learnings of this day may bring wisdom to my life.

God of learning and wisdom, you have created us in your image. God of learning, help me to see that learning is a lifelong task. God of wisdom, help me not to take too seriously the degrees and certificates, a gift that is owned by many who have not been given the advantage of education. God of learning, bring me to an awareness that the gift of this day will present a plethora of opportunities to learn. God of wisdom, grant that I may grow to humility as I strive to acquire wisdom. God of learning, help me to be a patient teacher. God of wisdom, as I share myself and my story, give me ears to listen to the stories of those who share my world.

(Morning)
As I prepare to face the day, I pray that I will be able to listen and grow.
(Prayers of Intercession)

(Evening)
Well, God, you know that I could have done a better job of listening today. Help me to be patient.
(Prayers of Intercession)

As I struggle to understand what it means to be created in your image, I pray.
(Pray the Prayer of Our Savior.)

(Morning)
Send me forth into the light with your statutes in my heart. Amen.

(Evening)
I rest in the assurance of your powerful presence in my life. Amen.

FRIDAY, MARCH 14
(Read Hebrews 5:5–10)

(Morning)
O God, to whom I submit, I confess that submission is not something I'm comfortable with.

(Evening)
O God, to whom I submit, although I'd rather be in charge, I come to know that you must know me.

O God to whom I submit, I confess that I struggle with issues of authority. I want to decide. I want to control. And yet, ultimately, I give my life to you. Our reading this day reminds us that Jesus struggled to learn, to obey, and to submit. On some days, it feels right to take over things and people; help me to provide caring, strong, and gentle leadership. O God to whom I submit, the world would seem to be a better place with more order and compassion; help me to avoid the temptation of coming to believe that I have all the right answers and all the right questions. As Jesus came to accept his difficult and painful mission, help me to undertake my ministry in humility, with courage, and with the sure and certain knowledge that you are my God and my hope.

(Morning)
I rise with the hope that I will treat all with respect and dignity.
(Prayers of Intercession)

(Evening)
Your ordinances and your way, O God, have supported and guided me.
(Prayers of Intercession)

**As I submit to your teachings and your commandments,
I pray with appreciation.**
(Pray the Prayer of Our Savior.)

(Morning)
May the brightness of this morning give me hope and a gentle countenance.

(Evening)
The day is all but gone. I pray that all with whom I've dealt have seen a glimpse of you, O God, in my work.

SATURDAY, MARCH 15
(Read John 12:20–26)

(Morning)
O God of glory and honor, I see glory in the beginning of this new and fresh day.

(Evening)
O God of glory and honor, I find honor in having served in the ministries of Christ's church.

O God, Christ Jesus makes it abundantly clear that while glory and honor are much a part of a life of faith, suffering and service also are required. O God of glory, I stand humbled by the majesty and beauty of the springtime about to unfold. O God of honor, I strive to discover and maintain a balance between leadership and servanthood. O God of glory, there are surely times when service in your name brings unwarranted appreciation. O God of honor, sometimes when I honor your way I find myself in lonely places. O God of glory, I celebrate and raise my voice in song and prayer. O God of honor, I ponder, as did Mary, my sister in faith, the mysteries and wonder of you.

(Morning)
I pray that I will bring a small measure of glory to this day.
(Prayers of Intercession)

(Evening)
The struggles of the day nearly gone remind us of the honor which is service in God's name.
(Prayers of Intercession)

With honor and a glimpse of your glory found in the good creation, I pray.
(Pray the Prayer of Our Savior.)

(Morning)
May this day bring glory to your holy and powerful name, O God. Amen.

(Evening)
I seek to follow and to be a servant of Jesus Christ. Amen.

SUNDAY, MARCH 16
(Read John 12:27–33)

(Morning)
O God who comforts and God who unsettles, I slip from the warm comfort of my bed to face the uncertainties of a new day.

(Evening)
O God who comforts and God who unsettles, may the labors of this day bring comfort to those who are troubled.

O God who comforts and unsettles, the words of Jesus certainly must have seemed confusing to his friends and followers. O God of comfort, I see pain and suffering. Empower me to bring a little relief. O God who unsettles, I see so much self-satisfied smugness. Empower me to bring a little unease. O God of comfort, Jesus was aware of the pain ahead in his life, yet he sought to enlighten and bring the comfort of understanding. O God who unsettles, the friends and followers of Jesus struggled to understand the unsettling meaning of his words. O God of comfort, grant peace to all who know loss, grief, and suffering. O God who unsettles, unsettle and disturb those who create discord, distress, and pain. O God of comfort, grant us your presence always.

(Morning)
"Help me to comfort the afflicted" (a pastor).
(Prayers of Intercession)

(Evening)
"Help me to afflict the comfortable" (a prophet).
(Prayers of Intercession)

As I seek a delicate balance of pastor and prophet, I pray.
(Pray the Prayer of Our Savior.)

(Morning)
Grant to your servants courage and conviction of a sturdy faith. Amen.

(Evening)
Grant to your servants humility and the powerful capacity to comfort. Amen.

MONDAY, MARCH 17
(Read Philippians 2:5–8 and Mark 14:35–36)
(Sing "My Soul Gives Glory to My God")

(Morning)
God of obedience and humility, let me be of the same mind as you, whom I seek to love without measure.

(Evening)
God of obedience and humility, Eternal One, may I listen fearlessly for your voice.

O God, taking the form of a slave, your child Christ Jesus humbled himself and became obedient. I need to heed those words carefully so as not to apply them recklessly to my life. Humility is not a denial of one's human dignity. Slavery and servitude are not virtues if there are no other options. Obedience in such circumstances is a means of survival, nothing more. Instead, let us look to the example of Jesus, who "was in the form of God." Forgiving God, Jesus "emptied himself, taking the form of a slave." He was fully himself, and from that position of abundance, chose to give of himself. To follow Christ Jesus, we must decide to give our lives in service and to realize that involuntary servanthood is not discipleship.

(Morning)
Deliver me, Faithful Creator, from the impulse to sacrifice myself before
I have a self to sacrifice.
(Prayers of Intercession)

(Evening)
Giver of Life, you have created me and renewed me. Formed in your image,
I will find my fullest joy in giving of my life.
(Prayers of Intercession)

"My soul gives glory to my God, my heart pours out its praise."

(Morning)
Not my will, not my limited view, not my personal preoccupations, but yours. O give me strength, Author of Life, to pray it and to mean it. Amen.

(Evening)
Make me brave, Creator, to trust that in giving myself away I become more clearly who I am. Amen.

TUESDAY, MARCH 18
(Read Psalms 31:9–11 and Isaiah 50:4–9a)
(Sing "Great Is Your Faithfulness")

(Morning)
Enlightening God, morning by morning you awaken my ear to listen. Let me hear your Word, O Strength of My Life. Open my ears to the divine grammar of abundant life for all people.

(Evening)
Enlightening God, borne on the breath of Jesus of Nazareth, who acted your thoughts and spoke your heart, come live in me.

"God helps me," Isaiah says. "God helps me and is near me, so I am not ashamed." God helps me also. What is it, God, I wonder. What is it that Isaiah was doing that made him so unpopular that he had to give his back to those who struck him and his cheeks to those who pulled out his beard? Why was he subjected to insults and spitting? What he was doing was taking your message beyond Israel. This enraged his fellow Israelites. "What do you think you're doing, Isaiah? Why are you taking our sacred beliefs and giving them to people who don't appreciate them?" Caring God, let me not pour our religion down a hole but learn respect for your will.

(Morning)
Give me the tongue of a teacher, that I may sustain the weary with a word of hope, a word of liberation.
(Prayers of Intercession)

(Evening)
May I regard your Word more highly than human favor.
(Prayers of Intercession)

Your faithfulness is great, O God Creator!

(Morning)
May I be undaunted when you summon me to speak words of challenge. Amen.

(Evening)
Piercing the night stillness like the wail of a siren, your Word rouses me, even at the end of day. Grant me rest tonight, Great Spirit, that I may awaken tomorrow with open ears. Amen.

WEDNESDAY, MARCH 19
(Read Psalms 31:12 and Mark 14:3–14:10)
(Sing "When Morning Gilds the Skies")

(Morning)
God of remembrance, you have overrun creation with wild colors and lavished upon me life beyond measure. "Thank you" is inadequate in the face of your irrepressible generosity.

(Evening)
God of remembrance, bursting the constraints of decorum, the woman poured out precious oil. May I likewise be bold in love's expression.

Creator God, memories are fleeting when we cannot make sense of a situation. "Truly I tell you, wherever the good news is proclaimed in the whole world, what she has done will be told in remembrance of her." Yet, O God, it has not been told. The story of Judas who betrayed Jesus unto death is remembered and retold. The story of the woman who anointed Jesus in anticipation of new life is virtually forgotten. Let us remember this anonymous woman who might have anointed a body for burial, or with true prophetic recognition, anointed a monarch for coronation. Because of her, your Child, Jesus, went to his death and to his glory anointed.

(Morning)
Help me, ancient of days, to remember sacred history. Guide your church so that we may remember, and thus re-member, the body of Christ.
(Prayers of Intercession)

(Evening)
Keep me, O Heart of the Universe, from doling out my love, my dreams, my time, in harsh and measured servings.
(Prayers of Intercession)

My heart awakens to pray.

(Morning)
For what good service will I be remembered, star-abiding one? Grant me the perseverance to do the needful. Amen.

(Evening)
For what good service will I be remembered, star-abiding one? Grant me the imagination to see through all the layers of truth, from history into promise. Amen.

THURSDAY, MARCH 20
(Read Psalms 31:13–15 and Mark 14:1–2, 53–65, 15:1–32)
(Sing "Abide with Me" or "Stand by Me")

(Morning)
God of all times and beyond time, my times are in your hand.

(Evening)
God of all times, my trust is in you. You are my God.

Merciful God, terror all around! This was a dangerous time for Jesus. The whispers and the stealth, the plotting and the covert operations, are all arrayed against the agent for life. Within the territory of death. The fluidity of love confronts the rigidity of law. The body politic cannot withstand this outbreak of compassion, this contagion of health. Antibodies form and carry him away, lest the infectious infection spread.

(Morning)
Though I hear the whisperings of those who bear me nothing but ill will, disgrace will never immobilize me so long as you are near, O Steadfast One.
(Prayers of Intercession)

(Evening)
Where is my vindication, O Comforter? When troubles beset me, when friends betray me, stand with me, I pray. Then shall I repel all shame.
(Prayers of Intercession)

"Abide with me; fast falls the eventide; the shadows deepen, God with me abide."

(Morning)
When my finest offerings tarnish, when my attempts at justice and compassion fail, when my friends abandon me, O Hope of the Desolate, let me find the valor to keep on. Amen.

(Evening)
When I am insulted, when my work is discredited, when people detest me and wish me dead, may I not forget that scorn and treachery can be as undeserved as grace. Amen.

FRIDAY, MARCH 21
(Read Mark 14:10–52, 66–72)
(Sing "When Jesus Wept" or "Si Fui Motivo de Dolor")

(Morning)
Companion God, keep awake! Keep me watchful today, that I may not forsake my commitment to follow in the path where Christ Jesus leads me.

(Evening)
Companion God, we know not the day nor the hour when our resolve will weaken, our vision blur with weariness. Even as my body seeks restoring rest, let my spirit keep watch with you and in you.

"You will all become deserters." "Surely not I." We know the odds, the unevenness, of pitting our pitiful strength against the enormity of the slow crawl of indifference, of the ribald energy of evil. Yet surely we would not desert you when we saw you in the flesh. when we heard you teaching in the temple? day after day? when we ate with you, and drank with you, and traveled together in one company?

(Morning)
Christ is present in all those I meet today. There is no denying it.
(Prayers of Intercession)

(Evening)
We all become deserters. There is no denying it. Surely it is I.
(Prayers of Intercession)

"When Jesus wept, the falling tears in mercy flowed beyond all bound."

(Morning)
You are present in the poor and the suffering, in all who are outcasts and in all who seek to turn the colossal tides of greed and rancor. Let me know that I am present there also. Amen.

(Evening)
You betray yourself. You reveal yourself in the tears of those who mourn, in the hunger of the poor, in the joy of the righteous, in the work of the peacemakers. Let me not flee from you. Let me not desert you. Amen.

SATURDAY, MARCH 22
(Read Psalm 31:15–16 and Mark 15:33–36)
(Sing "There Is a Balm in Gilead" or "Sometimes I Feel like a Motherless Child")

(Morning)
Ever-present God, Bright Daystar, shine upon me. Save me in your steadfast love.

(Evening)
Ever-present God, do not forsake me or forget me in my distress. Disperse the mists that hide you from me.

The gray mists and lowering skies settle over me, dampen me, tamp me down. Where, O Morningstar, are you? Where am I going? Is this the path? My eyes cannot cut through cloud. My ears are taut with the strain of listening into echoing silence. Where is the dart of lightning that will slash through the dim curtain of my doubts? I wander, O Holy One. I am God-forsaken yet magnetized and drawn to you: metal to your lodestone. What attraction, always present! Yet it does not drag me with its pulsing current. I crave a steely steadiness and it eludes me. Draw near; draw me near; that I may take comfort in your closeness.

(Morning)
Blessed One cloaked in silence, in silence during the day, comfort me.
(Prayers of Intercession)

(Evening)
Blessed One cloaked in silence, in silence during the night, comfort me.
(Prayers of Intercession)

"There is a balm in Gilead, to make the wounded whole."

(Morning)
Whose heart would be so staunch as to choose the reasonable thing in the face of misery? Not mine, I pray, not mine. Amen.

(Evening)
You did not keep yourself aloof from my pain. Save me from comfort for myself purchased at the price of detachment from the pain of others. Amen.

SUNDAY, MARCH 23 (PALM/PASSION SUNDAY)
(Read Philippians 2:9–11 and Mark 15:37–47)
(Sing "What Wondrous Love Is This" or "How Firm a Foundation")

(Morning)
O Author of Life, this day, like all others, will bring its portion of misery as well as happiness. Let my steps be light as I walk into the unknown today, encouraged by you who have gone before me.

(Evening)
O Author of Life, I put my trust in you. You are my God. You never abandon me.

Most Holy One, you wanted so desperately to know humanity as we are—in the brilliant and glittering dancing of our souls and in the dank and musty heaviness of our spirits—that you, through Jesus, took on betrayal, humiliation, pain, fear, rejection, abandonment, and unjust execution. With generous passion, you taught us that even our most terrible moments can be redeemed. We are not alone. You know us. You have shared our common lot. When Jesus gave a loud cry and breathed his last, his cry was a shout of victory. All has been redeemed!

(Morning)
Truly, Christ Jesus is the offspring of the Most High. Let me recognize Christ in all who suffer. Let me proclaim the presence of the Holy Spirit in all who bring deliverance from the forces of death.
(Prayers of Intercession)

(Evening)
Fount of new life, I ask for vision, that I may not mistake beginnings for endings nor promises for curses. Let my spirit see with the eyes of faith and not be blinded by fear.
(Prayers of Intercession)

"What wondrous love is this, O my soul!"

(Morning)
Thanks be to you, my Redeemer. You have broken the bread of compassion, sipped the wine of bitterness, and spread the table of hope that I may have new life. Amen.

(Evening)
Redeemer and Sustainer, Hope of the Weary, Source of Delight, remind me that you know me and cherish me. Amen.

MONDAY, MARCH 24
(Read Isaiah 42:1–9 and John 12:1–11)
(Reflection from Psalm 36:5–11)

(Morning)
Steadfast and faithful God, how precious is your steadfast love! In the light of a new day, I give thanks and pray for awareness of your love in all I do and say.

(Evening)
Steadfast and faithful God, we have feasted today on the abundance you have provided. You provided for us drink from the river of your delight. You are present with me now.

Your righteousness is like the mighty mountains, your judgment like the great day. Your salvation comes to the upright of heart. In Jesus Christ you demonstrated to us the power of life over death, the triumph of hope over despair. You rejoiced over Mary's generosity and devotion, and wept over Judas' insincerity. The poor found in Jesus a champion and defender, and prisoners received a new kind of freedom. Guide me, holy God, through the treachery of Holy Week. Keep me from deserting and betraying the Savior. Help me to honor and fulfill your covenant with me.

(Morning)
Equip me today to speak and act in ways that bring forth justice and show your mercy.
(Prayers of Intercession)

(Evening)
Grant courage to let go of former things, that the renewal you offer may be fully realized as I sleep and when I awake.
(Prayers of Intercession)

Rejoicing in your steadfast love, I pray.
(Pray the Prayer of Our Savior.)

(Morning)	(Evening)
May I be upright of heart, O God, as I receive your light in the hours ahead. Let me be light to others I meet. Amen.	Your love is in the obscurity that surrounds me. In confidence, I rest in your abiding faithfulness. Amen.

TUESDAY, MARCH 25
(Read Isaiah 49:1–7, 1 Corinthians 1:18–31, and John 12:20–26)
(Reflections from Psalm 71:1–14)

(Morning)
O God, my rock and refuge, I want to listen to your Word as the day begins and to pay attention to your message every waking minute.

(Evening)
O God, my rock and refuge, today I have labored and spent my strength. It has been my aid to serve you. May the work I have done be pleasing to you.

You are my hope and my trust. You have supported me from my birth through all my years on earth. Your care for me is eternal. O God, I wish to see Christ Jesus. Like the inquiring Greeks, I want to know you in the flesh. It is my aim to follow, to rise, and to serve. Let the compassion of Jesus be seen in me. Bless me so my life may be a blessing to others. May I, like Philip and Andrew, bring others to Jesus. Forgive my unwillingness to embrace the cross and the many times I have stumbled over its message. Release me from the arrogance of my limited vision and periods of half-hearted commitment.

(Morning)
Today I may encounter unjust criticism; help me to remember the scorn and disgrace that Jesus faced with calm assurance.
(Prayers of Intercession)

(Evening)
Help me to discern ways I have failed you today, that I may seek and find forgiveness and glorify your name.
(Prayers of Intercession)

Then let me pray with hope the prayer Jesus taught.
(Pray the Prayer of Our Savior.)

(Morning)
In your presence, O God, I find wisdom and courage for the day. Use my weakness to reveal your saving love. Amen.

(Evening)
As your glory has been with me all day long, your praise will fill my dreams. Renew my strength as I rest in your care. Amen.

WEDNESDAY, MARCH 26
(Read Isaiah 50:4–9a, Hebrews 12:1–3, and John 13:21–32)
(Reflection from Psalm 70)

(Morning)
Amazing God, Creator and Teacher of all who have ever lived, awaken all my senses that I may taste, hear, feel, and see evidence of your love all around me.

(Evening)
Amazing God, Creator and Teacher of all who have ever lived, I have seen the beauty of your creation and caught the fragrant scent of your presence.

Let all who seek you rejoice and be glad. You are our help and our deliverer. We will not lose heart amid all your witnesses. O God, you were with the disciples as they learned from Jesus; you were available to Peter as he stumbled through life. You were the God of Judas, even in his cruel treachery. We confess that we have often seemed adversaries to your way, rather than followers of Jesus. We have retreated in confusion when challenged to run the race, rather than look to the pioneer and perfecter of our faith. Forgive us, we pray, for our weariness in well-doing and our failure to stand with Christ in trying times. Keep us from adding to the hostility that sent Jesus to the cross.

(Morning)
O God, you are helping me even now. Your gifts are not delayed by my slow response.
(Prayers of Intercession)

(Evening)
Tonight, I lay aside all bitterness and regret and all that might separate me from you or from any of your children.
(Prayers of Intercession)

In awe and wonder, I pray the prayer Jesus taught.
(Pray the Prayer of Our Savior.)

(Morning)
Thank you for the glory that surrounds me as I face today's challenges. I am ready to hear, see, and feel your guidance and assurance. Amen.

(Evening)
O God, you are greater than my imagining. I lie down to rest with joy and gladness filling all my being. Amen.

THURSDAY, MARCH 27 (MAUNDY THURSDAY)
(Read Exodus 12:1–14, 1 Corinthians 11:23–26, and John 13:1–7, 31b–35)
(Reflections from Psalm 116:1–2, 12–19)

(Morning)
Loving and judging God, I recall on this day of remembrance that I am your servant, joined in covenant to all whom you love.

(Evening)
Loving and judging God, at the end of an intense and emotion-filled day, I turn in trust to you, confident that your love will sustain me through the night.

Take me again to the table where Jesus broke bread. Let me taste once more and be drawn into communion with Christ. I take from Jesus' hand the cup of the new covenant and am strengthened, even in the shadow of death. I feel warm water splashing over my feet and see an even greater warmth in the eyes of one who dries my feet and says I will understand someday. When I forget that I am your child, reclaimed by a costly sacrifice, forgive me, I pray, and cause me to remember. I will pay my vows to you in the community of faith. In the presence of your people, I will lift up the cup of salvation.

(Morning)
Brought to consciousness from the depths of sleep, I am ready to travel wherever you send me.
(Prayers of Intercession)

(Evening)
Bind me to you in faithfulness this night, that I may know to whom I belong when a new day dawns.
(Prayers of Intercession)

May your love lead me to pray with renewed commitment.
(Pray the Prayer of Our Savior.)

(Morning)
Let me return my best to you during the hours of this day. Spare me from disaster that I may continue to serve you. Amen.

(Evening)
Now grant rest to your disciple. I rest in your love, knowing that I can pass on that love tomorrow. Amen.

FRIDAY, MARCH 28 (GOOD FRIDAY)
(Read John 18 and 19)
(Reflections on Isaiah 52:13–53:12, Psalm 22, and Hebrews 10:16–25)

(Morning)
Ever-present God, your goodness is very real to me as the day begins. Help me to see the good, even through tiredness and pain.

(Evening)
Ever-present God, your goodness is very real to me as the day ends. Help me to see the good, even through tiredness and pain.

Surely Christ Jesus has borne our infirmities and carried our diseases. He was wounded for our transgressions, crushed for our iniquities. Through him, we are forgiven and healed. Walk with us to the quiet garden where we may watch and pray. Save us from the evil of pious pretensions and from angry retaliation against those who wrong us. Grant us courage to claim our Christian identity, even when we are questioned and ridiculed. Let us be guided by truth that is personal in Christ rather than by our own narrow constructions of truth. Empower us to view the world through the eyes of Christ, to see beyond present circumstances and limited vision. Draw us to the cross, lest we miss the meaning of this day.

(Morning)
Help me to trust, O God, even as I pray for all who feel alone and forsaken.
Hear my prayers for my brothers and sisters.
(Prayers of Intercession)

(Evening)
At Jesus' feet, I pray for all the families of the nations and especially for those who needs are known to me.
(Prayers of Intercession)

With these, for whom I have prayed, I pray also the prayer of Jesus.
(Pray the Prayer of Our Savior.)

(Morning)
May the poor, who found a friend in Jesus, also find a friend in me this day. Let me provoke others to love and do good deeds. Amen.

(Evening)
In quiet confidence, I accept the gift of sleep, praising you for the encouragement of undefeated love. Amen.

SATURDAY, MARCH 29 (HOLY SATURDAY)
(Read Job 14:1–14, 1 Peter 4:1–8, and Matthew 27:57–66)
(Reflections from Psalm 31:1–4, 15–16)

(Morning)
Patient, suffering God, I awaken in dread that death has triumphed and there is no release. Yet you are my refuge and strong fortress. Help me to face this day.

(Evening)
Patient, suffering God, you have waited with me through the agonies of uncertainty and the excesses of misspent hours. Let your face shine on me now.

Save me in your steadfast love, holy God, even as you dwelt with Job in his pain and rebellion. Let Peter teach me to discipline myself, according to your will. Even though we have heard the rest of the story, this is not an easy day for us. We are impatient: It is hard to wait at the tomb, knowing we have betrayed and denied one who demonstrated your constant love. When our lives are laid low, we have many questions; when we suffer, it is hard to find answers. Forgive me, patient God, for all the complaints that mute and destroy the melodies of love. Turn me from self-centered idolatries, lest I be unprepared for the surprises you may offer.

(Morning)
Lift my eyes beyond my own desires, that my prayers for others may be in tune with your purposes for them.
(Prayers of Intercession)

(Evening)
Take away my need to always be in control, that I may grow in your love that covers a multitude of sins and cares deeply for those I pray for now . . .
(Prayers of Intercession)

Remembering Jesus, I pray the prayer he gave us.
(Pray the Prayer of Our Savior.)

(Morning)
My times, this day and always, are in your hands, O God. Rescue me if I stray and let your face shine on me, I pray. Amen.

(Evening)
To you, O God, I offer an accounting of this day, confident that you forgive and restore. May I live again, when the new day comes. Amen.

SUNDAY, MARCH 30 (EASTER SUNDAY)
(Morning: read John 12:1–18; evening: read Luke 24:13–49)
(Reflections from Acts 10:34–43, Psalm 118:1–2, 14–24, and Colossians 3:1–4)

(Morning)
Impartial and inclusive God, how rich are your surprises and how bountiful your gifts! I awaken with great anticipation on this resurrection day.

(Evening)
Impartial and inclusive God, thank you for the joys of this day, for the exciting promises of new life and its realization in me.

In awe before you, amazing God, I bow in wonder that you accept me as your child, chosen and precious, offering me life in all its fullness. With Mary Magdalene, I approach the tomb, amid the shadows of grief, seeking to honor Jesus. Yet he is not in the tomb or on the cross; the risen Christ lives in the disciples. Christ lives in the community of faith, gathering to celebrate. Christ lives in me; and through my tears, I sense a presence. Along lonely pathways and at table with others, I know the Christ in broken bread and healing conversation. I am raised with Christ to newness of life! Let all the world rejoice in this day God has made!

(Morning)
With resurrection joy, I lift up to you, O God, the pain and the gladness of those traveling with me through this life.
(Prayers of Intercession)

(Evening)
As I continue to discover the presence of Christ in colleagues and friends, I pray for them and for many in need around the world.
(Prayers of Intercession)

Now, with echoes of resurrection stirring within me, I pray.
(Pray the Prayer of Our Savior.)

(Morning)
Open to me the gates of righteousness that I may enter and give thanks to you, wondrous God, rejoicing in the resurrection. Amen.

(Evening)
Walk with me, risen Christ, through the days ahead. I recommit myself to your way of love and accept the gift of your peace. Amen.

MONDAY, MARCH 31
(Read Psalm 133)

(Morning)
Creator God, you order the planets and set the sun at their center. So give order to my life this day that I may find fulfillment in your purpose.

(Evening)
Creator God, you scatter the stars in the sky as signs of life in deepest space. So give me light this night, and let me shine as one of your stars on earth.

How good it is when people live together in unity. You do not ask us to overlook differences, or always to overcome them. You ask us to look at what distinguishes and not to let that determine our divisions. You give, as a gift, persons who are not like me. God, help me to recognize differences within the human family. Then help me to accept that you created us all and love each of us equally.

(Morning)
I give thanks for the members of my household and for my extended family everywhere.
(Prayers of Intercession)

(Evening)
I celebrate the varieties of life among my family, my friends, my acquaintances.
(Prayers of Intercession)

Now, as our Savior Christ has taught us, I pray.
(Pray the Prayer of Our Savior.)

(Morning)
Guide me waking and guard me sleeping, that awake I may walk in your way and at sleep I may rest in peace.
Amen.

(Evening)
Guide me waking and guard me sleeping, that awake I may walk in your way and at sleep I may rest in peace.
Amen.

TUESDAY, APRIL 1
(Read Psalm 133)

(Morning)
Anointing God, thank you for songs of birds and signs of spring.
Give me heartfelt joy this day.

(Evening)
Anointing God, thank you for leaf buds on trees and flower petals
that fold at night. Grant me gentle rest this evening.

Oil, the precious compress of seeds, the extract of earth. It anoints our bodies and adorns our food. It greases our machines and lubricates our lives. Without oil, motion would cease, our skin peel away. It provides fuel and light and life. How precious this gift, O God, how luxurious to be bathed with scented beads, perfumed from head to toe, blessed in our whole being by your extravagant grace.

(Morning)
Anoint me this day, O God. Bless my body for your service.
(Prayers of Intercession)

(Evening)
Reveal to me the ways I have been blessed this day and the ways in which my life
has been a benediction to others.
(Prayers of Intercession)

Humbly I pray.
(Pray the Prayer of Our Savior.)

(Morning)
Guide me waking and guard me sleeping, that awake I may walk in your way and at sleep I may rest in peace.
Amen.

(Evening)
Guide me waking and guard me sleeping, that awake I may walk in your way and at sleep I may rest in peace.
Amen.

WEDNESDAY, APRIL 2
(Read Acts 4:32–35)

(Morning)
O Christ, you roused the sleeping and raised the dead.
Open my eyes to new life this day.

(Evening)
O Christ, you are the light of the world, the fire no shadows can overcome.
Stay with me, for it is evening.

From all according to their ability; to all according to their need. That was the apostles' manifesto, the ideal of the early church. There were no private possessions, only a public trust, born of your grace, O God, and the resurrection of your Christ.

(Morning)
Help me to act responsibly in the face of human need.
(Prayers of Intercession)

(Evening)
Help me to care for the earth, my planet home.
(Prayers of Intercession)

Now, as our Savior Christ has taught, I pray.
(Pray the Prayer of Our Savior.)

(Morning)
Guide me waking and guard me sleeping, that awake I may walk in your way and at sleep I may rest in peace.
Amen.

(Evening)
Guide me waking and guard me sleeping, that awake I may walk in your way and at sleep I may rest in peace.
Amen.

THURSDAY, APRIL 3
(Read John 20:19–31)

(Morning)
Spirit of the risen Holy One, you penetrate walls made by human hands.
So enter my heart this day.

(Evening)
Spirit of the risen Holy One, my house is closed against the night.
Yet enter in, abide with me.

Three times you came, O Christ, passing through walls, offering peace to your followers huddled in fear. And still you come, not only opening when we knock, but finding us when we cower in corners. You treat as nothing the barriers we build to protect ourselves. You beckon us out to overcome hostilities of past and present. Your perfect love casts out our fear, and your peace fills even our imperfect lives with the possibilities of new beginnings.

(Morning)
May I reflect on the signs of peace in the world and give God thanks for this gift.
(Prayers of Intercession)

(Evening)
May I be aware of the fear in the world and pray for God's peace to enter in.
(Prayers of Intercession)

Humbly I pray.
(Pray the Prayer of Our Savior.)

(Morning)
Guide me waking and guard me sleeping, that awake I may walk in your way and at sleep I may rest in peace.
Amen.

(Evening)
Guide me waking and guard me sleeping, that awake I may walk in your way and at sleep I may rest in peace.
Amen.

FRIDAY, APRIL 4
(John 20:19–31)

(Morning)
Faithful God, like Thomas who doubted, I doubt too.

(Evening)
Faithful God, I believe. Help my unbelief.

So many times I have thought, even prayed, that if only a certain thing were to happen, then I would believe. You taught us, Jesus, that if we ask we shall receive. You answered Thomas's prayer, appearing to him beyond all doubt. But then you offered the even greater hope of unanswered prayer, the assurance of faith that sight is not required for belief, but that believing makes sight possible.

(Morning)
Open my eyes that I may see glimpses of truth you have for me.
Open my eyes, illumine me, Spirit Divine.
(Prayers of Intercession)

(Evening)
Close my eyes that I may see glimpses of truth you have for me.
Give me faith's sight, illumine me, Spirit Divine.
(Prayers of Intercession)

Now, as our Savior Christ has taught, I pray.
(Pray the Prayer of Our Savior.)

(Morning)	(Evening)
Guide me waking and guard me sleeping, that awake I may walk in your way and at sleep I may rest in peace. Amen.	Guide me waking and guard me sleeping, that awake I may walk in your way and at sleep I may rest in peace. Amen.

SATURDAY, APRIL 5
(1 John 1:1–2:2)

(Morning)
Forgiving God, for all birds of air and beasts of ground; for all crawling creatures and ocean inhabitants, I praise you, Adonai.

(Evening)
Forgiving God, for all who lie restless at day's end and all who labor this night; for all who cry out for comfort and all who offer them care, I pray your presence, Emmanuel.

How tempting it is to say I do not sin, that others are at fault, but not I. The truth is, of course, that all of us have fallen short of the glory of God. What a relief to know that even though I sin, I do not sin alone, and that God is not only watching, but watching over me. God, you gave Christ to the world not only for my sins, but for the sins of all. Let me lead my life in great thanksgiving.

(Morning)
God, help me to admit my shortcomings this day. Let your forgiving Spirit dwell with me.
(Prayers of Intercession)

(Evening)
God, help me to let go of the ill I have done this day. Let your freeing Spirit lie with me.
(Prayers of Intercession)

Humbly I pray.
(Pray the Prayer of Our Savior.)

(Morning)
Guide me waking and guard me sleeping, that awake I may walk in your way and at sleep I may rest in peace. Amen.

(Evening)
Guide me waking and guard me sleeping, that awake I may walk in your way and at sleep I may rest in peace. Amen.

SUNDAY, APRIL 6
(John 20:19–31)

(Morning)
God, Creating Spirit, Source of life and being, I call upon you.
Let my soul magnify your name.

(Evening)
God, Creating Spirit, I praise you, divine power over all and in all.
Let me depart this day in peace.

In the beginning you were, O God, you, your Spirit and Word. In Christ you came again, and in the Spirit you continue still. All who open their hearts receive the gifts of your grace, the truth of Christ, the spirit of peace and power. It is peaceful because it is of you, O God; it is powerful in that we are given the ability to begrudge or forgive. The gift is yours; the choice is ours.

(Morning)
Let me forgive and know that you are God.
(Prayers of Intercession)

(Evening)
Let me receive and know that you are God.
(Prayers of Intercession)

Now, as our Savior Christ has taught, I pray.
(Pray the Prayer of Our Savior.)

(Morning)
Guide me waking and guard me sleeping, that awake I may walk in your way and at sleep I may rest in peace.
Amen.

(Evening)
Guide me waking and guard me sleeping, that awake I may walk in your way and at sleep I may rest in peace.
Amen.

MONDAY, APRIL 7
(Read Acts 3:12–19)

(Morning)
God, I know that you seek to continually surprise me. Help me to remember to look under every rock I pass, behind every tree I see, but especially in every face that I meet for signs of your grace.

(Evening)
God, forgive me for turning my face and closing my ears when you tried to surprise me today.

When I was in college, a streaking craze swept through campuses across the country. Streaking involved removing all of one's clothing and running through a public place. Even after twenty years, I remember distinctly the heightened sense of awareness that everyone on campus experienced—after all, you never knew when a totally nude person would come dashing past you! How different would each day be if I had the same sense of expectation of meeting you, God, anywhere and anytime? Peter was puzzled at the amazement of those who witnessed this healing—"What, you don't expect God to break into our lives with grace when it's needed?"

(Morning)
God of surprising grace, give me some hints as to where you will be waiting for me today.
(Prayers of Intercession)

(Evening)
God of unlimited grace, thank you for those moments today when I was open to your amazing grace and love.
(Prayers of Intercession)

God grant me the gift of awareness.

(Morning)
With faith I rise to meet a day full of your presence. Amen.

(Evening)
With faith I commit this day to your blessing. Amen.

TUESDAY, APRIL 8
(Read Psalm 4:1–4)

(Morning)
God, help me this day to sense your presence even in the wide spaces.

(Evening)
God, forgive me for interpreting silence as indifference.

Scripture provides a multitude of images of your concern for us. When I am experiencing distress, the images that first come to mind are generally those in which you are portrayed as close, comforting, or enfolding. But sometimes I experience your presence in difficult times as space. Sometimes when you grant me relief from the pressures that threaten to smother, crush, or engulf me, the oppressive closeness of these troubles is replaced with your space—space in which to mediate, be still, and know that you have indeed acted. Sometimes you provide a cloud by day and a pillar of fire by night to assure me that I am cared for. But sometimes I simply must remember where the cloud or the pillar was and trust in your constancy.

(Morning)
God, my refuge, help me to know this day that I am sheltered by you even when the refuge is so large that I do not feel its walls, floor, or ceiling.
(Prayers of Intercession)

(Evening)
God, my redeemer, thank you for those moments today when I trusted your faithfulness in the open spaces of my life.
(Prayers of Intercession)

God grant me the gift of trust.

(Morning)
With faith I rise to meet a day full of your presence. Amen.

(Evening)
With faith I commit this day to your blessing. Amen.

WEDNESDAY, APRIL 9
(Read Psalm 4:5–8)

(Morning)
God, help me this day to sense more deeply that in you I am safe.

(Evening)
God, forgive me for the fear that separates me from your love.

Safety is one of the most primal instincts that we experience. When we are threatened, our adrenaline level increases, leading to a whole host of physiological responses. God, you promise to provide us with safety. Why do I find that promise so hard to claim? Perhaps one reason is that my idea of safety doesn't necessary match yours. Often I desire safety from discomfort, safety from embarrassment, or safety from uncertainty. But God, your promise of safety is at a more fundamental level. Much of what I fear losing is in reality excess baggage that diverts my energy from the truly important parts of my life. I am asked to simply trust that you will preserve that part of my being that is essential and basic.

(Morning)
God, my security, help me to know this day that no part of me will ever be lost from your care.
(Prayers of Intercession)

(Evening)
God, in whom I trust, thank you for those moments today when I trusted your care for me in the midst of threatening situations.
(Prayers of Intercession)

God grant me the gift of safety.

(Morning)
With faith I rise to meet a day full of your presence. Amen.

(Evening)
With faith I commit this day to your blessing. Amen.

THURSDAY, APRIL 10
(Read 1 John 3:1–3)

(Morning)
O God, who loves me as mother and father, help me this day to live in the joy and security of being your child.

(Evening)
O God, forgive me for the times today when I have acted like an orphan.

"We are like your children." But John's emphasis is clear; we *are* your children. Frankly, it sometimes scares me to think about being your child. The intensity that comes with being part of a human family can be overwhelming; how much more so when you are part of the family! But I tolerate the turmoil of my family because I know that I need the intimacy and connectedness that I can only find there. Likewise, as I search my soul, I find needs there that can only be satisfied when I claim my role as your child.

(Morning)
God, source of all love, help me to claim this day, all of the joy, freedom, and responsibility that come with being your child.
(Prayers of Intercession)

(Evening)
God, whom I love, thank you for those moments today when I felt the closeness and care that can only come in your family.
(Prayers of Intercession)

God grant me the gift of being your child.

(Morning)
With faith I rise to meet a day full of your presence. Amen.

(Evening)
With faith I commit this day to your blessing. Amen.

FRIDAY, APRIL 11
(Read 1 John 3:4–7)

(Morning)
O God, who loves me without reservation, help me this day to live as one who has been granted your righteousness.

(Evening)
O God, forgive me for the times today when I lived in my own sense of righteousness.

God, sometimes John can be uncomfortably straightforward. It can't really be this simple, can it? "No one who abides in him sins"—no finely tuned theological definitions, no exploration of subtleties or nuances. But I know that I don't live a perfect life, a life without shortcomings or blemishes. Is abiding in your Child, Christ Jesus, then not possible for me? Perhaps I have been overly focused on sin and not focused enough on abiding. My job is not getting rid of sin—that job belongs to Christ. Rather, my role is simply to abide in Christ's presence and to live my life in the awareness of Christ's love for me.

(Morning)
God, source of forgiveness, help me to live this day not in the light of my own finitude, but in the light of your boundless grace.
(Prayers of Intercession)

(Evening)
God, my righteousness, thank you for those moments today when I sensed your forgiveness surrounding me like the air I breathe.
(Prayers of Intercession)

God grant me the gift of forgiveness.

(Morning)
With faith I rise to meet a day full of your presence. Amen.

(Evening)
With faith I commit this day to your blessing. Amen.

SATURDAY, APRIL 12
(Read Luke 24:36b–43)

(Morning)
O God, who created me as a human being, help me this day to walk in increased wonderment for the possibilities of being human.

(Evening)
O God, forgive me for the times today when I focused solely on the limitations of being human.

God, Jesus went to great lengths to convince the disciples that he had appeared to them in his full humanity and not as some disembodied spirit. Why was this such an important point? Jesus understood that his disciples, like all of us, had to live their lives as physical, human beings. We perhaps know instinctively that any resurrection that only involves our spirit or soul is not a resurrection of our whole being. Your son sought to reassure his disciples that he understood both the limitations and the possibilities of living in a body and that you would bless and claim all the aspects of their beings. God, you created us, body and spirit, and you will reclaim us, body and spirit.

(Morning)
God, source of life, help me this day to honor this creation, my whole self, that you see fit to include in your resurrection.
(Prayers of Intercession)

(Evening)
God, my righteousness, thank you for the gift of your affirmation of all that I am.
(Prayers of Intercession)

God grant me the gift of resurrection.

(Morning)
With faith I rise to meet a day full of your presence. Amen.

(Evening)
With faith I commit this day to your blessing. Amen.

SUNDAY, APRIL 13
(Read Luke 24:44–48)

(Morning)
O God, who satisfies all my longings, help me this day to have the courage to bring my desires and expectations into your presence.

(Evening)
O God, forgive me for the times today when I feared that I would find you inadequate to satisfy my longings.

Christ Jesus embodies the fulfillment of the great longings expressed in the Hebrew Scriptures. Your Child showed us a way of righteousness that enables us to live lives of justice and responsibility, as required by the law of Moses. He challenged the self-satisfaction of the power elites as he followed the example of earlier prophets. And he modeled an honesty before you, O God, that is mirrored in the wide range of emotions exhibited in the Psalms. The writers of the Old Testament speak for me and my longings in all of these ways and more. And so Jesus' call to me is to trust him to fulfill those yearnings of my heart.

(Morning)
God, who hears all of my desires, help me this day to live in the expectation that you are good enough and strong enough to meet my desires.
(Prayers of Intercession)

(Evening)
God, who satisfies the desires of my heart, I thank you and praise you for your all-sufficiency.
(Prayers of Intercession)

God grant me the gift of fulfillment.

(Morning)
With faith I rise to meet a day full of your presence. Amen.

(Evening)
With faith I commit this day to your blessing. Amen.

MONDAY, APRIL 14
(Read Acts 4:5–12)

(Morning)
In your tender care, O God, I have rested through the night. Remain close to me and to the church, that like your servants Peter and John, we might be encouraged by your Word.

(Evening)
In your tender care, O God, in your tenderness and love, you bring me now to the close of another day of my life. Let me rest at peace in your embrace through Jesus Christ.

Why is it that I often take my place among the rulers and choose a seat among the elders, resisting your Word, O God, with my stubborn disbelief? You have summoned me to the cost and joy of discipleship and fed me with the very bread of life. You meet me amidst the denials and crucifixions that are part of who I am. You assure me of salvation and renew my hope. How will I understand this except as a miracle, undeserved and beyond my imagination? Help me to be truly grateful and despite my confusion and lack of faith, my tentativeness and superstition, to seek to follow Jesus Christ.

(Morning)
You invite me to pray for others as well as for myself, for the church, and for the world you love. Hear now my prayer.
(Prayers of Intercession)

(Evening)
May your love accompany me through the hours of the night to come, O God, and may we rest in your everlasting arms forever.
(Prayers of Intercession)

In your tender care, I pray.
(Pray the Prayer of Our Savior.)

(Morning)
Grant me grace, O God, to begin and end this day in the name of Jesus and in the service of your Word. Amen.

(Evening)
May your love accompany all your children through the hours of the night to come, O God, and may we rest in your everlasting arms forever. Amen.

TUESDAY, APRIL 15
(Read Psalm 23)

(Morning)
Good and Faithful Shepherd, guide me and those I love, through the day to come, that we may place our lives joyfully in your hands and be nourished by the wonder of your love.

(Evening)
Good and Faithful Shepherd, into your hands I commend my body and soul, asking you to protect me through the night to come, so that I may awaken to the glory and wonder of the morning.

You are my shepherd, Jesus. You are the true shepherd of the sheep. Among the many who tempt me to follow, only you bring me into the green pastures of truth. Only you can lead me beside the still waters of grace. Only your Word can quiet the restlessness of my soul and inspire in me courage to travel along the paths of righteousness. Despite the dry, desert places of my unbelief and the searing heat of my remarkable pride, teach me again today how to confess you before the world, Good Shepherd of my life.

(Morning)
You invite me to pray for others as well as for myself, for the church, and for the world you love. Hear now my prayer.
(Prayers of Intercession)

(Evening)
Bless not only me and those I love this night with a peaceful sleep, but also be with your children who look to you as the source of life and true shalom.
(Prayers of Intercession)

Faithfully I pray.
(Pray the Prayer of Our Savior.)

(Morning)
Gracious God, you have placed the sun in the heavens to nourish the earth and the moon in its orbit to accompany us through the night. Feed my soul today and be my companion like a faithful shepherd. Amen.

(Evening)
Bless those I love this night with a peaceful sleep. Amen.

WEDNESDAY, APRIL 16
(Read Psalm 23)

(Morning)
I give you thanks, O gracious and merciful God, for the sleep of the past night and for the gift of this new day.

(Evening)
I give you thanks, Christ Jesus, asking you to forgive my words and deeds that have compromised my faith and wounded your love.

It is a comfort to know that you are present like a faithful shepherd, O God, even in the deepest valleys of my life. Where the shadows fall and I am tempted to lose my way; where night descends and I am unable to discern your truth; where the storms of my arrogance rage and I struggle not to compromise my soul, you promise to be present. It is astonishing, this grace of yours. Help me today to confess it gratefully and to live in its light, despite the soothing and delicious idolatries with which I am tempted to make friends.

(Morning)
You invite me to pray for others as well as for myself, for the church and the world you love. Hear now my prayer.
(Prayers of Intercession)

(Evening)
May your truth, O God, revealed to me through Jesus Christ, help me to rest my body and soul completely at peace tonight, in the certainties of your love.
(Prayers of Intercession)

Once again, I turn to you praying.
(Pray the Prayer of Our Savior.)

(Morning)
I know not, Christ Jesus, where you will meet me in the course of the day to come. Awaken me to the soft, gentle rain of that grace, that I might not miss the thunder of your Word. Amen

(Evening)
I know not, Christ Jesus, where you will meet me in the course of the day to come. Awaken me to the soft, gentle rain of that grace, that I might not miss the thunder of your Word. Amen

THURSDAY, APRIL 17
(Read 1 John 3:16–22)

(Morning)
O God, morning has broken again, a sign of your grace towards the world.
Grant that I, may proclaim that your Word is a lamp unto our feet and a light unto our path.

(Evening)
O God, I come to you this night, bent with the burden of my sin.
For I have neither loved you nor loved my neighbor as I should.

You summon us to speech, O God, and call us to the language of love. It is more than words you await from us, but truth and deeds. Yet we are not able by ourselves to accept our high calling, and so we ask you to send us your Holy Spirit, that we might abide in your commandments. Take all falsehood from us, and the arrogance that keeps us from loving one another. Give us faith to bear one another's burdens, to reach out to one another in genuine love, as you in Christ have reached out to us. Yes, come to us, O God, abide with us, Emmanuel.

(Morning)
You invite me to pray for others as well as for myself, for the church, and for the world you love. Hear now my prayer.
(Prayers of Intercession)

(Evening)
Grant to the world this night in all its fragile pieces, the gift of your peace.
(Prayers of Intercession)

I am summoned to pray.
(Pray the Prayer of Our Savior.)

(Morning)	(Evening)
Grant, O God, that your love abide in me and I in your love throughout the day to come. Amen.	This night, grant the church, in all its fragile pieces, the gift of your peace and the consolation of your love amidst all the tears that have been present on the earth today. Amen.

FRIDAY, APRIL 18
(Reading from 1 John 3:23–24)

(Morning)
Refreshing God, refresh my soul today, and the souls of all who look to you, so that our lives may bear witness that you remain in love with the world. Awaken our senses to the wonder of your forgiveness and the gift of human life.

(Evening)
Refreshing God, grant that I might sleep this night not in the restlessness of having to prove my worth, but in the assurance of your grace, which covers the multitude of my sins.

Send your Holy Spirit once more, O God, that we who claim the name of Christ Jesus might live the truth of our many confessions. Take away what is false, remove cheap spirituality, the empty word and the halfhearted, counterfeit deed. Stir among us a restlessness for your truth and a passion to serve you, basin and towel in our hands, glad to be summoned to love one another as you have commanded us, through Jesus Christ, your Child.

(Morning)
You invite me to pray for others as well as for myself, for the church and the world you love. Hear now my prayer.
(Prayers of Intercession)

(Evening)
My faith, O God, flickers like a candle before the wind's swift gusts. Breathe life into this fragile faith of mine when I awake in the morning.
(Prayers of Intercession)

Refreshed, I pray.
(Pray the Prayer of Our Savior.)

(Morning)
If this day I should be called to carry a cross, help me to do it willingly, patiently, and in the name of Christ Jesus. Amen.

(Evening)
My faith, O God is like the embers of a dying fire. Breathe life into this fragile faith of mine. Amen.

SATURDAY, APRIL 19
(Reading from John 10:11–15)

(Morning)
Gracious God, for the sweet silence of the night that is past and the refreshing dawn of this new day, I give you thanks.

(Evening)
Gracious God, you have brought me to the close of another day of my life. Like a mother in love with her restless child, hold me close to your breast through the night to come.

Save us again today, Good Shepherd, from all who seek to tear us away from your flock. Save us from the hired hands who speak piously but do not take your Word to heart. Save us from the ravaging wolves; the myths and lies that tear at your gospel, seeking to rip us away from our vocation as witnesses to your truth. Save us from cheap idolatries that tempt us with their seductions. Save us from our arrogant and insatiable urges to live above the world, indifferent to your call to us to kneel in the crevasses and valleys where so much of life is lived. Yes, save us again today, Good Shepherd, from all in us that pushes you off to another day, another time, another place.

(Morning)
You invite me to pray for others as well as for myself, for the church and the world you love. Hear now my prayer.
(Prayers of Intercession)

(Evening)
The light of day fades, evening surrounds me. Let me rest now, dear God, secure in you.
(Prayers of Intercession)

In sweet silence, I pray.
(Pray the Prayer of Our Savior.)

(Morning)
Take my hand, gracious God, for I tremble. Take my will, my heart, my soul, and conform them all to your purpose, through Jesus Christ our God. Amen.

(Evening)
The stars appear, evening surrounds me. Let me rest now, dear God, secure in you. Amen.

SUNDAY, APRIL 20
(Reading from John 10:16–18)

(Morning)
I offer you my thanks, Good Shepherd, for all who have awakened to the promise of this new day, for your love with which you help me face its joys and sorrows.

(Evening)
I offer you my thanks, and ask forgiveness for those things which today have belied my love for you. Grant me the grace I need to begin again.

Lift my vision, O God, from the petty concerns that peck away at my faith, to the broad, spacious landscape of your love, which stretches far beyond my imagination. Lift my soul above the confining precincts of my disbelieving heart to the wonder of your grace, with which you embrace the whole creation. Give birth in me and in the church to a faith that is generous, open, capable of wonder and amazement. Faith, that we may neither scold the world nor retreat from its demands, but enter it with the joy of knowing that the Shepherd's heart beats for all your scattered sheep.

(Morning)
You invite me to pray for others as well as for myself, for the church and the world you love. Hear now my prayer.
(Prayers of Intercession)

(Evening)
Hold me in your arms, Good Shepherd, close to your heart, and keep me through the deep night and into the morning, through Jesus Christ our God.
(Prayers of Intercession)

Without pretension, I pray.
(Pray the Prayer of Our Savior.)

(Morning)
Christ Jesus, as this new day begins, I thank you for the love revealed in your birth, your life, death, and resurrection. Help me to be calmed by this love.
Amen.

(Evening)
Hold all the creatures you have made in your embrace through the deep night and into the morning, through Jesus Christ our God. Amen.

MONDAY, APRIL 21
(Read Acts 8:26–31)

(Morning)
Loving and ever-present God, I am ever grateful for your presence in my life. Guide me throughout this day. Keep me open to your messengers and your message.

(Evening)
Loving and ever-present God, thank you for walking with me today. Now grant me rest, in the knowledge that you guide me even while I sleep.

I listen for you to speak to me through the story of Philip and the Ethiopian eunuch. God, so often I do not listen to your directions to go on the unfamiliar roads of life. Yet Philip's story tells me that it is only when I am bold enough to follow the road less traveled that I will find your special messenger to me. Open my ears, O God, so that I might hear your Word. Open my eyes, God, so that I might see the guide you send. Open my heart, Holy One, so that I might receive your guidance.

(Morning)
I pray for your guidance in my day and the day of these others . . .
(Prayers of Intercession)

(Evening)
Continue to be with me on my journey, God. Be with those others whose journeys are lonely and frightening and new.
(Prayers of Intercession)

So often I feel like the Ethiopian, reading your Word, but without a guide.

(Morning)
Lead me and guide me today
So that I cannot stray.
God, walk with me,
And lead me today. Amen.

(Evening)
In your holy name. Amen.

TUESDAY, APRIL 22
(Read Acts 8:30–35)

(Morning)
Transforming and patient God, you have changed my life in so many ways, sometimes it has frightened me. Sometimes it has energized me. Always it has awed me. Allow your unexpected guide into my life this day and every day.

(Evening)
Transforming and patient God, as this day draws nigh, I thank you for leading me in your path.

God, you sent the angel to guide Philip down that unpopular road. You sent Philip to guide the Ethiopian to new faith. You sent the Ethiopian to guide Philip to a new ministry. Help me get past my own expectations of your guide for me. My guide may be very different from me but may challenge me in untold ways. Help me trust that I will be blessed by your guidance.

(Morning)
I pray today for all those who have guided me in the past, and I pray for those who might guide me this day.
(Prayers of Intercession)

(Evening)
Help me recall those moments during this day when you guided me.
I pray that others may be open to your guides.
(Prayers of Intercession)

Guided by you, I pray now.
(Pray the Prayer of Our Savior.)

(Morning)
May I have the wisdom to know your guide and the openness to hear your guidance. Amen.

(Evening)
May I rest, assured of guidance and your love. Amen.

WEDNESDAY, APRIL 23
(Read Psalm 22:25–31 and Acts 8:36–41)

(Morning)
Holy and Wonderful One, I sing praises to you, knowing that you are there to guide me throughout this day.

(Evening)
Holy and wonderful One, to you, indeed, will all who sleep on the earth bow down.

God, like the Ethiopian, I strive to understand your holy Word. Like him, I seek to hear the good news about Christ Jesus in my life. Let me be energized, excited, and eager like that new convert. Be a powerful presence in my life, O God, so, that I might sing forth your praise.

(Morning)
As I begin this day, I pray for guidance about these things especially . . . and I pray that you will guide the leaders of all nations. I pray for guidance for these others also . . .
(Prayers of Intercession)

(Evening)
I pray especially this evening for my pastor and all those who seek to open the hearts and minds of your people.
(Prayers of Intercession)

Help me to recall my own baptism and to be refreshed and ready to start anew.

(Morning)
Spirit of the living God, fall afresh on me throughout this day which you created and create still. Amen.

(Evening)
I rest now, knowing that you, O God, rule over all creation. Amen.

THURSDAY, APRIL 24
(Read Psalm 22:25–31)

(Morning)
Deliverer of all humankind, I awake singing your praises. I awake full of the knowledge that all will worship you. I awake singing your praises.

(Evening)
Deliverer of all humankind, I will live for you.
O Sovereign God, I will live for you.

God, even when I feel most forsaken, most alone, deep down I know you do not hide from me. You hear my cries. You will feed the poor and heal the afflicted. You hear their cries. May we praise your holy name.

(Morning)
I pray especially for the poor and for those who are sick.
(Prayers of Intercession)

(Evening)
The earth is yours and the fullness thereof. Let all the nations praise you.
(Prayers of Intercession)

I will tell future generations about you and proclaim your deliverance even to those yet to come.

(Morning)
Help me, O God, to rededicate myself to you this day and every day. Amen.

(Evening)
I praise your name, O God, forever and ever. Amen.

FRIDAY, APRIL 25
(Read 1 John 4:7–16)

(Morning)
God who is love, I awake this morning reminded anew of your great love for me and for all your creation. I give you thanks, O God.

(Evening)
God who is love, I am able to rest because of your love for me. I am humbled and awed. I give you thanks.

Loving and perfect God, your love surrounds me, permeates me, overwhelms me. Your love commands me to love others as you have loved me. You showed your love for me by sending Christ Jesus to be sacrificed for me. I can show my love for you by sharing it with others.

(Morning)
I pray for the ability to love even those whom I do not know; those whom I do not like; and those who are most unlike me.
(Prayers of Intercession)

(Evening)
Be with me throughout the night, infuse me with your love.
(Prayers of Intercession)

I feel your love and the powerful presence of your Holy Spirit in my life. I give you thanks.

(Morning)
Help me share your love with others this day. Amen.

(Evening)
Make me an instrument of your love and peace. Amen.

SATURDAY, APRIL 26
(Read 1 John 4:16b–21)

(Morning)
God of abiding love, I marvel at your love. You are love divine.

(Evening)
God of abiding love, I give you thanks for your love.

Eternal Spirit, I recall the words "perfect love casts out fear." Allow that perfect love to fill me. Allow it to chase away all my fears—fears of others, fears of myself; fears that are rational and those that are not; fears that paralyze me and inhibit me from sharing your love. Allow that perfect love to fill me.

(Morning)
I pray that you will cast out these fears of mine and others.
(Prayers of Intercession)

(Evening)
I recall those fears that filled me this day. Let your perfect love cast them out.
(Prayers of Intercession)

Help me, O God, to love my brothers and sisters of this world, knowing that they, too, are your children and are loved by you.

(Morning)
Abide in me this day, God of love.
Abide in me. Amen.

(Evening)
Thank you for your abiding love and the gift of Christ Jesus. Amen.

SUNDAY, APRIL 27
(Read John 15:1–8)

(Morning)
Loving and guiding God, great is your love for me. Great is my love for you.

(Evening)
Loving and guiding God, I glorify your name. Abide in me as I rest this night.

You are the Creator, the Gardener of all life. Just as you were the vine grower for Jesus, so you are for me. Live in me. Flower in me. Let your Word infuse my being. Let your love be my guide. Live in me. Live in me.

(Morning)
As I begin this day, I pray that you will guide me, and shape me, and use me. I pray that you will remove from me those things that need to be removed and that you will allow others to flourish.
(Prayers of Intercession)

(Evening)
Thank you for touching my life today, for giving me the opportunities to grow which you gave me. Help me continue to be open.
(Prayers of Intercession)

Jesus taught, if we live in you and your Word lives in us, we have only to ask and you will answer our prayers. I pray now the prayer Jesus taught us to pray.
(Pray the Prayer of Our Savior.)

(Morning)
Emboldened by your love and your promise, I pray for my own needs and for the needs of others. Amen.

(Evening)
Let me be your disciple, God. Let me bear much fruit. Amen.

MONDAY, APRIL 28
(Read Psalm 98 and Acts 10:44–48)

(Morning)
Loving and creating God, in this new day I would be open and receptive to the joyful noise of spring and to the gifts of all whom I meet.

(Evening)
Loving and creating God, it is time for rest. I give thanks for this day now ended and ask your forgiveness for whatever deeds of love and mercy I have left undone.

I praise you, O God, for your inclusive love that reaches beyond the boundaries I draw with my opinions and prejudices. Help me to listen for your Word in the experience of Peter. You know how ready I am, O God, to be satisfied with my current knowledge and familiar friends. Even though I proclaim your love and the astounding movements of your Holy Spirit, you keep appearing in places where I was not looking. Forgive me for closing doors and for narrowing my vision. Help me to discover your presence in and among those I have called "outsiders." Be at work in me, and in all your people, that we may welcome one another with grace and peace.

(Morning)
As Peter so gladly proclaimed the peace of Christ at the center of his life, let my life also become proclamation. These are the needs I have and the needs I see this day . . .
(Prayers of Intercession)

(Evening)
Be with me now as I recall in prayer those whose lives have touched my own today, and those whose needs are great.
(Prayers of Intercession)

And now, with other faithful people I pray.
(Pray the Prayer of Our Savior.)

(Morning)
Send me forth now into the new day ready to extend a welcoming and caring hand to all I meet. In your name I go.
Amen.

(Evening)
Grant me a night of restoring rest as the earth turns again toward day. Let each breath I take as I sleep bring peace.
Amen.

TUESDAY, APRIL 29
(Read Psalm 98 and Acts 10:44–48)

(Morning)
Loving and creating God, help me to look for the movement of your Holy Spirit in the day ahead of me, that I might recognize the new things you are doing.

(Evening)
Loving and creating God, with thoughts of the day now ending I turn to you. Help me to examine this day with the mind of Christ, and then release it into your keeping.

I praise you, loving God, that you challenge me to love. Help me to understand the wisdom and actions of Peter as he responded to your call. You often argue through embodiment, O God. You, incarnate Christ, cause us to see others—and to see you in others—in ways we had not anticipated. Who are we to protest the ways of your Spirit? Who are we to withhold your gifts from others? Help me to share the witness of Peter: that we are more alike than unalike; that we who are baptized are claimed to be your witnesses to all; and that the Holy Spirit frees and unites us in love. Forgive me for my inhospitality and grant me opportunities to welcome others to faithful living. Give me an eagerness always to learn more of you and your love.

(Morning)
In anticipation of newness in this day, I pray for what I need and for the needs of others.
(Prayers of Intercession)

(Evening)
Be with me in these quiet moments, as my memories of today turn into prayers lifted to you.
(Prayers of Intercession)

With great hope, I pray.
(Pray the Prayer of Our Savior.)

(Morning)
Aware of your love and your glory, I go into this day to be your witness and ready to see that your people are alike. Amen.

(Evening)
Now let your peace flow into my being and grant me the renewal of rest and sleep. Let the night sounds of the earth keep me attuned to the wonder of creation. Amen.

WEDNESDAY, APRIL 30
(Read Psalm 98 and 1 John 5:1–6)

(Morning)
Loving and creating God, I greet the day knowing the fullness of your love. Help me to move through each moment, focused on loving you first of all.

(Evening)
Loving and creating God, if I have been loving in the day now past, I give praise to you, and I offer myself into your keeping this night.

For your gift of companionship and the guidance of your commandments, I praise you, O God. Lead me in the way of love, so that whatever I do flows out of my love for you. Whenever I speak and act for self-interest and gain, remind me that you are the loving parent who gave us your own Child to show the depth of your care for us. I cannot love others without loving you; nor can I love you without loving them as well. If your commandments seem burdensome, help me to comprehend their eternal wisdom. If I am seduced by other priorities, or dizzy with the whirlwind of my own affairs, lead me to a center in myself where I may know again the power and the discipline of your love.

(Morning)
Lead me through this day, aware of the joys and sorrows of those around me, praying always for your loving presence and guidance.
(Prayers of Intercession)

(Evening)
I lay aside today's work to seek a night of rest and renewal.
I pray for all your children, and especially for those who are dear to me and those who have special needs.
(Prayers of Intercession)

And now, with confidence in your love for us, I pray.
(Pray the Prayer of Our Savior.)

(Morning)
Let me be a blessing to those I meet today, sharing with them the love that you have so freely given. Amen.

(Evening)
Grant to me the peace of a restful night as I relinquish into your loving care the day now past. Amen.

THURSDAY, MAY 1
(Read Psalm 98 and 1 John 5:1–6)

(Morning)
Loving and creating God, I would arise in faith this day, full of the confidence your love brings and ready to offer both my faith and my love to serve your spirit of truth.

(Evening)
Loving and creating God, let the evening shadows surround me with the promise of rest and let me give into your keeping the day now past.

I praise you, O God, that you have given us victory over death and that you continue to conquer the world's evil through love. Help me to listen again to John, who reminds us that the world's salvation is in Christ. Too often, I believe that I must take care of the world, and that where humans fail to do good, there is no hope. Help me to remember the power of your victory and faith in all the trials and troubles that come to me. Help me to put aside the weapons to which I cling: walls of separation, a sharp tongue, a suspicious nature. Let faith grow in my heart, that I may join others who have conquered the world with faith and who have witnessed peace. Let me remember that I have come through the waters of baptism and may live in confidence and seek your truth without fear.

(Morning)
As I anticipate the work and the challenges of this day, I pray for what I need and for the needs of others.
(Prayers of Intercession)

(Evening)
This evening, help me to remember and let go of my daily tasks. Grant me rest and wholeness, peace and a clean heart, as I pray for myself and others.
(Prayers of Intercession)

And now, with faith in your conquering love, I pray.
(Pray the Prayer of Our Savior.)

(Morning)
Lead me through this day with courage and hope. Give me uncowering faith and clear vision so that I may reveal to all I meet the joy of loving you. Amen.

(Evening)
In peace I would rest now. In hope I would pray for a new day of faith. Let your loving arms enfold me as I sleep. Amen.

FRIDAY, MAY 2
(Read Psalm 98 and John 15:9–11)

(Morning)
Loving and creating God, with all that will happen in the day ahead of me,
I want most of all to abide in your love. Keep me mindful of what that means.

(Evening)
Loving and creating God, the day is over, and I come seeking your forgiveness
and peace. I want to abide always in your love and to remain in the joy
of your presence.

With a thankful heart, I praise you, O God. You continually call me to your realm of joyful obedience—a joy that is complete and whole. Yet I know, too, that there is cost involved, and that joy is made complete by obedience and by discipline. When I am tempted to take the easy way or the less strenuous journey, help me to understand what will be lost by my negligence or haste. When I think that love should be quick, costless, and without pain, help me to take the long view and to build the future carefully. Ease my sense of urgency with your gift of time and eternity, and help me release joy-preventing anxiety. Help me to follow Jesus' example and abide in the joy that you so graciously offer to me.

(Morning)
In the hours ahead of me, there are tasks to be done and people to meet.
I pray that your joy will go with me, and I pray for the needs I see.
(Prayers of Intercession)

(Evening)
Even as I release the cares of the day now ending, I pray that I may rest in the
peaceful hours of the night. Hear my evening prayers for those in need.
(Prayers of Intercession)

And now, with hope and joy I pray.
(Pray the Prayer of Our Savior.)

(Morning)	(Evening)
In this day, let me discover again the complete joy of obedience in keeping your commandments. Amen.	Now I rest in your enfolding love, grateful for today and hopeful for tomorrow. Amen.

SATURDAY, MAY 3
(Read Psalm 98 and John 15:12–17)

(Morning)
Loving and creating God, I awaken to this new day knowing that I am not alone in the world. You have given me others to love.

(Evening)
Loving and creating God, at the end of this day, I want to relinquish its sorrows and failures and cherish those whom I love.

I praise you, O God, that in Christ you have shown us a great love, and have gathered your people together as friends. You have given us life as a gift. I offer gifts to my friends by giving them well-meant tokens of my affection, but it's hard to imagine what it would mean to lay down my life for them. Yes, I know there are those who have done it. Most of all, Jesus did it, and his crucifixion still catches at my heart and stuns me with its power. He called us friends, and plainly declared, "This is my commandment, that you love one another!" Forgive me for my failure to live this commandment. With your patience and compassion, teach me again that we have one another and that with love we are truly made in your image.

(Morning)
As I think about the day ahead, keep me clearly focused on loving others.
I pray for my needs and for theirs.
(Prayers of Intercession)

(Evening)
Where I have failed to love in the day now past, forgive me, O God.
Open my mind and heart to learn more of love as I pray for myself and others.
(Prayers of Intercession)

And now, with confidence and hope I pray.
(Pray the Prayer of Our Savior.)

(Morning)
Send me into this day as an emissary of love, ready to live the commandment of Jesus and to rejoice in love shared. Amen.

(Evening)
Now I seek an evening calm and the respite of sleep. May your love grow in me, even through this night. Amen.

SUNDAY, MAY 4
(Read Psalm 98 and John 15:9–17)

(Morning)
Loving and creating God, I come to this new day as your chosen child,
knowing that to be chosen is to belong, and to belong is to serve you.

(Evening)
Loving and creating God, you gave me this day for worship and renewal.
I pray that I have used it well as an opportunity for loving others.

For the church and our life together in faith, I praise you, O God. You have given us to one another as a sign of your presence and have sent us into the world to bring good news and healing. Jesus calls disciples friends. In this friendship there are no secrets; everything is made known; there is profound belonging, which the world cannot take away; and there is the lasting love and reason enough to obey your command to love. Sometimes such profound love is hard to understand and to accept. Sustain me in my journey of faith and teach me to receive with grace the immeasurable acceptance and compassion with which you love me, so that I may, in turn, befriend others.

(Morning)
As I begin the day in hope, I pray for the leaders of the world and for those most affected by their decisions, and for the special needs I see.
(Prayers of Intercession)

(Evening)
For all this day has brought, I give thanks. For all my failings in it,
I ask forgiveness. Be with me as I reflect, and as I pray for myself
and all who are friends in Christ.
(Prayers of Intercession)

With faith and trust in your abiding love I pray.
(Pray the Prayer of Our Savior.)

(Morning)	(Evening)
As your beloved child, send me now. Help me to share my faith with others in what I say and do and in who I am. Amen.	Draw me to you, O God, and grant me peace. Through the tranquillity of this night, refresh me for a new day of loving. Amen.

MONDAY, MAY 5
(Read Ephesians 1:15–23)

(Morning)
O God, I awake with the possibility of tasks that require keen understanding and wisdom from you. Help me to become more sensitive to your Spirit.

(Evening)
O God, as I pause for this evening, help me to reflect upon the day's activities. May the praise of my lips become the last event of my activities. Thank you, God.

    I praise you for the spirit of your wisdom, for your words that bring healing to all who hear. Like Paul who prayed for his hearers to receive the spirit of wisdom and revelation, I wait upon you. God, you sent Paul to a church steeped in tradition. Your wisdom encountered him as he was furthering his own agenda. The wisdom of Jesus made Paul's wisdom look like foolishness. As Paul's eyes were opened, God open ours. Forgive me, and may your Holy Spirit flow like a river of all knowing. Help me to see all things through the lens of the Holy Spirit.

(Morning)
As I awaken into your presence, I pray that your holy presence will not be grieved through my busy lifestyle, may your wisdom reflect in quietness also.
(Prayers of Intercession)

(Evening)
God, I present my limitations to you. May the Holy Spirit bathe over my soul as I recline in your presence. Become the answer to my many questions.
(Prayers of Intercession)

And now with confidence as your beloved child, I pray.
(Pray the Prayer of Our Savior).

(Morning)
As your child, I ask for wisdom to heal the brokenhearted. May the presence of the resurrected Christ become near as I present to you a broken heart. In your all-knowing name I pray. Amen.

(Evening)
I rest in your name. May the sleep that you bring renew me. In your name I pray. Amen.

TUESDAY, MAY 6
(Read Luke 24:44–53)

(Morning)
God, I awaken refreshed, you have renewed me as you breathed life into me during the night. Help me to breathe out the freshness of your presence to others.

(Evening)
God, I thank you for your nearness. May I cherish the moments of your revelational knowledge in my heart, which yearns for more of you.

Thank you, God, for opening your Word to my parched heart. Your words have refreshed me as you flowed with your sweet presence. May your Word be incarnate in me. Christ, the Bread of Life, feed my hungry soul. God, as you appeared to the weary disciples and fed them from your hand, feed me from your manna above. Then will my understanding become more perfect. Like your disciples of old, I need your Holy Spirit. I await your promise. Come Holy Spirit, I need you.

(Morning)
I awaken refreshed. Thank you for being with me through the night.
Help me realize the gift of life more fully. As I feel my hands,
remind me of your scars for me. Amen.
(Prayers of Intercession)

(Evening)
O God, all of your creation gives so freely. Help me to see the gifts
you have given me more fully developed as I give them into your hands.
(Prayers of Intercession)

I humbly bow in your presence, as your beloved.
(Pray the Twenty-third Psalm.)

(Morning)
God, as you led the disciples to the Mount of Ascension, help me realize that you are not remote, but near. May your presence be near me each time I look up. Amen.

(Evening)
I worship you as I return to my Jerusalem. Thank you for the joy of your presence. You are all the comfort that I have needed. Amen.

WEDNESDAY, MAY 7
(Read Acts 1:1–11)

(Morning)
O God, I awaken with the reality of a busy day. Help me to wait upon you for direction this day, I pray.

(Evening)
O God, thank you for making this an eventful day, full of wonderful opportunities to trust you. I rest from my labor.

I praise you, God, for keeping your promises. You have never failed me, though I have failed you many times. Flow through me, Holy Spirit, flow through me. O God, as you empowered the apostles with your presence, empower me. I look at the weakness of each one of the disciples and I see myself clearly in each of them. Somehow you held them together until your Spirit filled all of their weakness with power. Help me to receive all you have for me, resurrected Christ.

(Morning)
Many mornings have been uneventful because I rushed out the door without your guidance for the day. O God, help me to gaze more perfectly at your image in me.
(Prayers of Intercession)

(Evening)
God, like the refreshing rain, you have refreshed me this day by your Holy Spirit. Will you refill me before I retire tonight? Come, Holy Spirit, I need you.
(Prayers of Intercession)

Christ Jesus, as your hungry child, fill me.
(Recite Matthew 5:6.)

(Morning)
As your empowered child, send me now. May your presence be sufficient for all tasks before me today. In your name. Amen.

(Evening)
Excitement is not the word! You thrill me beyond any words. May the power from the resurrected, ascended Christ keep me. Amen.

THURSDAY, MAY 8
(Read Psalm 93)

(Morning)
O God, not only is there an empty tomb, but there is power from an ascended Christ. May you reign supremely within my being this day.

(Evening)
O God, your power amazes me. The enemy of my soul is no match for your intercessory power. Thank you, God, for all of your unseen help today.

I praise you, resurrected and ascended Christ, for all of your words. They have become life to me, and strength when I was weary. Thank you for reigning in my heart. Jesus, you journeyed through this life with an aimless wandering people. Your disciples were weak, not realizing your plan for them. You arose from the grave, ascended, and the descent of your power transformed all of the disciples. Christ Jesus, will you do the same within my own life? Send me your presence, that I may glorify you, ascended Christ.

(Morning)
Sovereign, you have created both the day and night. This world seems peppered with sin. May the light of your presence shine like a ray of sunshine to all.
(Prayers of Intercession)

(Evening)
You have calmed the storms of my life today. I rest in your presence, I cease from all of my labor, renew me, Holy Spirit, I pray.
(Prayers of Intercession)

And now with gratitude, I pray.
(Recite Psalm 103:1.)

(Morning)
As your child, O God, who now realizes the need of your presence, fill me until I overflow, then will I spill over on others. Amen.

(Evening)
Now, God, I rest in your presence. May sleep be calm. In your name I pray. Amen.

FRIDAY, MAY 9
(Read Acts 1:15–17, 21–26)

(Morning)
O God, as I awaken this day, I am aware of the need for your presence.
Help me become more sensitive to your living presence.

(Evening)
O God, as I rest this night, I am aware of how you led my every step this day.
Thank you, God, for your leadership.

O Holy Spirit, Divine Paraclete, my very thoughts have been filled because of your grace. My heart is filled with thanksgiving for the beckoning call of your will. Like Peter, who stepped into leadership by your Spirit, may I, too, step into your presence. The witness of your resurrection was so important to the leadership of your church. May you, the resurrected, ascended Christ, empower our leadership. May your eternal presence transcend all time as we know it. Heal our wanderings, renew our brokenness. May your will become renewed in me. May the very thoughts of your resurrected, ascended power abide.

(Morning)
O God, may John's baptism be a reminder of your moving in my life.
Help me to recognize how much you desire others to experience your grace.
(Prayers of Intercession)

(Evening)
May your holy presence recall the brokenness I faced today. O God, you see the broken through eyes of renewal, renew all whom I have seen and thought of today.
(Prayers of Intercession)

With confidence in abiding in your will, I pray.
(Recite Psalm 19:14.)

(Morning)
As your chosen child, God, help me to walk humbly before you, and lead others in the righteous path of your leadership. In your name, I pray. Amen.

(Evening)
O God, I rest in your will. May the holy angels abide with me this night. In your name, I pray. Amen.

SATURDAY, MAY 10
(Read Psalm 1)
(Reading from 1 John 5:9–13)

(Morning)
Sovereign God, many are anxiously awaiting your voice. May I become the ambassador of heaven's voice today. In your name, I pray.

(Evening)
Sovereign God, I am exhausted, for your name has so much power and your power has changed so many lives today. Thank you, resurrected, ascended Christ.

I praise you, powerful Christ, for the witness you have birthed in me. May the Spirit, water, and blood renew me as I abide in you and in your holy name. Jesus, you came from heaven to a gloomy and dismal people who did not understand your intentions. We crucified you through our foolish pride. The very nails were held in my hands as I drove them deep into your flesh. But this did not stop you from loving me. The very ones who crucified you are now abiding in you. O God, help me to see clearly your presence in my life.

(Morning)
Dear Jesus, I thank you for this day that is filled with so many wonderful opportunities of grace. May I be the mouthpiece of your service.
(Prayers of Intercession)

(Evening)
God, my steps have been lightened this day because of your abiding presence. Thank you for carrying me.
(Prayers of Intercession)

And now with confidence as your child I pray.
(Pray the Prayer of Our Savior.)

(Morning)
O God, life eternal flows so freely from you. May this day be more relaxed in you than any day before. In your name, I pray. Amen.

(Evening)
O God, this has been a glorious week. Thank you for sharing this week with me. In your name, I pray. Amen.

SUNDAY, MAY 11
(Read John 17:6–19)

(Morning)
O God, as I remember the life that you gave me and the ability
of your Spirit working through me, I feel as though I have just begun the work
you have given me.

(Evening)
O God, you have prayed so many times for me. May I pray as effectively
for others whom I have met today.

I praise you, High Priest, for your effective intercession for me. Yet you are never far removed, but deep within. God, you have loved me with an everlasting love. The words of your mouth have changed my very life. Thank you for reaching beyond your generation into mine. Your words justify my existence and flow with life. I praise you for this very special time of knowing. May the desired effect of your words change others, as you have changed me. Help us all, as your children, to be more loving.

(Morning)
God, you have reconciled us unto yourself. With this thought in mind,
help me to go forth with your power.
(Prayers of Intercession)

(Evening)
May the very thought of your existence charge me with new energy.
Help me, Christ Jesus, to become more of a priest to my family.
(Prayers of Intercession)

And now as with new confidence I pray.
(Pray Isaiah 40:31.)

(Morning)
Each day has begun with the feeling of expectancy. Will you fill me with more anticipation today? I need your intercessory work flowing from me, Holy Spirit, and flowing through me.
Amen.

(Evening)
Christ Jesus, you ascended to heaven that heaven might descend upon us. Thank you as I relax in your peace. Descend upon me. In your name, I pray.
Amen.

MONDAY, MAY 12
(Read Ezekiel 37:1–10)

(Morning)
Promise-making God, my soul is parched and dry. I wait on your Spirit for life.

(Evening)
Promise-making God, your breath flowing through will bring me rest.

The question is not really Can these bones live? You, O God, the author of all life, know that by that divine grace and Spirit, they can. What is really at the heart of the matter is, How will these bones live? By their own spirit? Absolutely not! Living by their own will has left us deep in the valley, a heap of dry bones. But by the promise of your breath being blown into them, with sinew and flesh, there comes the promise of life, and the promise of knowledge. We will know who you are because your breath will flow through us like life-giving wind.

(Morning)
Encompass my soul as fresh air surrounds the morning.
(Prayers of Intercession)

(Evening)
For the renewal of spirit that enables peace and calm, thank you.
(Prayers of Intercession)

In anticipation of new life, I pray.
(Pray the Prayer of Our Savior.)

(Morning)
Come, Holy Spirit, as a rough and cleansing wind. Amen.

(Evening)
For every whisper of new life and hope this day, I am grateful. Amen.

TUESDAY, MAY 13
(Read Ezekiel 37:11–14)

(Morning)
God of grace, guide me through this journey.

(Evening)
God of grace, praise be to you for every act of reconciliation
I participated in today.

When we are obedient, God—when we prophesy, teach, heal, and stand with those who are dispossessed physically, emotionally, or spiritually—you enable us to be the vehicles of new life. With a word, we can bring reconciliation and restoration. Restoration and reconciliation bring new awareness, which brings new thankfulness for life, for home, for the gift of grace that you bring to us. There is life in us yet!

(Morning)
Let me move through this day as one who is reconnected with others.
(Prayers of Intercession)

(Evening)
Grant me rest in the name of the reconciler, Jesus Christ.
(Prayers of Intercession)

Pray now for someone who needs a broken relationship restored . . .

(Morning)
Bless me this day to know hope. Amen.

(Evening)
As I review this day, help me to know that I lived by your Spirit. Amen.

WEDNESDAY, MAY 14
(Read John 15:26–27)

(Morning)
Healing God, I need help to get through this day, and I wait on your visitation.

(Evening)
Healing God, what spirit will guide this night's sleep? Let it be yours.

In the ninth chapter of the Gospel of John, Jesus heals a young man who had been born blind. People who witnessed the event were scared or angry. The disciples were confused, and the religious leaders were incensed that Jesus had healed on the Sabbath. The young man's parents fled any responsibility, saying, "He is a grown man, he can speak for himself." The one who was healed spoke the truth, "I don't know what you all are arguing about. All I know is that I was blind, and now I can see." We say, "I do not know what to say." The Spirit says, "Just tell the truth about what you, O God, have done for us. We will not be alone."

(Morning)
For the energy that raised me from sleep, I am thankful.
(Prayers of Intercession)

(Evening)
I pray I was a sound witness today.
(Prayers of Intercession)

O God, thank you for these blessings in the last twenty-four hours . . .
(List ten blessings.)

(Morning)
Let my life be a witness for you today.
Amen.

(Evening)
Thank you for those who spoke your truth today. Amen.

THURSDAY, MAY 15
(Read John 16:4b–11)

(Morning)
Merciful God, I am anxious today. Quiet my spirit.

(Evening)
Merciful God, I believe. Help my unbelief.

When I was growing up, there was a television game show called "I've Got a Secret." Celebrity panelists had to guess the occupation or identity of the special guests. Though it was sometimes frustrating for the panel, it was always fun, and it was entertaining. The life of your Spirit, O God, is not a game show or parlor game. This is real life. There are some hard truths we must hear. Life is not always fair. Disappointment comes. Death is not prevented by age, kindness, or popularity. We can hear these things now because you, through Jesus Christ, have prepared us to hear and know the truth. Our helper is here.

(Morning)
Grant me wisdom and courage to believe that you are really present in my life.
(Prayers of Intercession)

(Evening)
Thank you, God, for not leaving us either helpless or hopeless.
(Prayers of Intercession)

I pray for enough humility to realize that I cannot go through life all by myself.

(Morning)
Gently, safely guide me through this day. Amen.

(Evening)
Holy Advocate, you were with me all day long. Thank you. Amen.

FRIDAY, MAY 16
(Read John 16: 12–16)

(Morning)
Spirit of the living God, the day is full of unknown possibilities.
Guide me through them.

(Evening)
Spirit of the living God, even as sleep comes, let my spirit listen to you.

These comings and goings are too much for me. Where are you? What are you saying? I am confused, and I need clear talk from you. Yet I will wait. I will bear this difficult moment with calmness, because you have promised that the Spirit will come. Christ Jesus, you keep your promises, so I know that the Advocate/Spirit will come. When it comes, you will be glorified and I will understand far better than I ever thought possible.

(Morning)
Open my heart, ears, eyes, and soul to take in your Word.
(Prayers of Intercession)

(Evening)
I close my eyes in trust.
(Prayers of Intercession)

Dear Jesus, I write the words of a song that keeps me going when I am down and confused . . . (Write down the words to a song.)

(Morning)
Remind me even in the times when I can't see you, that you are here with me. Amen.

(Evening)
Even as I dream this night, speak to me.
Amen.

SATURDAY, MAY 17
(Read Romans 8:22–27)

(Morning)
God of creation, this day is full of expectancy. You are about to do something.

(Evening)
God of creation, thank you for life, fullness, my family of faith, my home.

Several friends of mine have adopted children. One friend gave birth to a child after she and her husband had adopted two children. The presence of these little ones has brought joy and chaos into my friends' homes. They welcome the noise of inquisitive minds. They are raising good children because they are good parents who know that, through these children, their lives and their homes are fuller and livelier than they would have been otherwise. They live in hope for what you will do in their families, and they live with praise and gratitude for what you have already done. May all of us, your adoptees, O God, find home, hope, and happiness.

(Morning)
Holy Spirit, pray for me when I am too weak, scared, and small to pray for myself.
(Prayers of Intercession)

(Evening)
I greet this night in gratitude for all the places I feel welcome and at home.
(Prayers of Intercession)

O God, I resolve to talk to . . . , who remembers when I was born. (Speak with someone who remembers your birth.) I also reflect in gratitude on the birth of my loved one, . . .

(Morning)
Eagerly, I run into this day. Amen.

(Evening)
God, the day was worth the wait and hope. Amen.

SUNDAY, MAY 18
(Read Acts 2:1–21)

(Morning)
God of glory, break through. We are eager for you.

(Evening)
God of glory, teach me to listen so that I hear all of the voices that speak to me.

When the Spirit came, and the wind blew, and the fire rested, the glorious sight was witnessed by devout believers who were gathered in Jerusalem. They were perplexed by what they heard, because it was like nothing they had ever heard before. It was a moment of glory, because despite all of the ways in which the assembled observers differed, the Spirit gave them a sense of oneness to hear words of praise, each in his or her own language. May the Spirit of Pentecost, the Shekinah glory of you, be ours now and forever.

(Morning)
Help me as I go through this day to hear the many languages of the Spirit that will surround me.
(Prayers of Intercession)

(Evening)
Breathe in me, breath of God.
(Prayers of Intercession)

What would your world be like if it had your Spirit of Pentecost?

(Morning)
Spirit of God, abide in my soul. Amen.

(Evening)
Come, Holy Spirit. Alleluia. Amen.

MONDAY, MAY 19
(Read Psalm 29)

(Morning)
God, open me to your glory and your strength this morning.

(Evening)
God, I remember these intimations of your glory this day.

God, I know your voice thunders; I have heard you in great storms and seen you in sunsets. Even in terrible earthquakes you are not absent. You hold this planet in the palm of your hand; this precious, fragile island only existing because you hold it so tenderly moment by moment. Make it possible for me to hear your voice also when I walk on asphalt and sit in buildings where no fresh air enters, so that I may know that you are God.

(Morning)
Through the day, O God, speak more deeply than my thoughts,
that I may be refreshed and joyful to greet you today.
(Prayers of Intercession)

(Evening)
I remember these intimations of your glory this day . . .
(Prayers of Intercession)

Thank you for letting me hear your voice this day in creation.

(Morning)
Great God, show me your wonder of your voice through creation. Amen.

(Evening)
Through the night, O God, speak more deeply than my dreams, that I may wake refreshed and joyful to greet the day and you. Amen.

TUESDAY, MAY 20
(Read Isaiah 6:1–5)

(Morning)
Great God, let me see you with the eyes of my heart.

(Evening)
Great God, show me how you have been in my heart and life this day.

Let me see you this day, almighty God, in the throne of my heart; in the temple of the church, above the world's busyness and mine; in this world situation; in this year, month, day, and precise moment in which everything is happening. Above all, you are here, high and lifted up, and your presence fills everything.

(Morning)
Help me trust in your presence filling the world through the day.
(Prayers of Intercession)

(Evening)
God, may I be in your temple and you in the temple of my heart and life this night.
(Prayers of Intercession)

I have seen you this day, almighty God, and your presence filled everything.

(Morning)
God, may I be in your temple and you in the temple of my heart and life this day. Amen.

(Evening)
Help me trust in your presence filling the world through the night, even when I sleep. Amen.

WEDNESDAY, MAY 21
(Read Isaiah 6:5–8)

(Morning)
Creator God, bring me gently into the holiness of your presence.

(Evening)
Creator God, how did you cleanse me? And where did you send me today?

God, I have been here before—scalded by your touch, lips burned, heart torn by your holiness, exposing my shame, my guilt, my sin. I know I should be grateful, but it does hurt. Nevertheless, I do hear your voice from time to time, and by your grace, on this day healing and sending me. God, to whom shall I go now, and what shall I say?

(Morning)
Send me into renewal this day according to your Word.
(Prayers of Intercession)

(Evening)
God, I am open to your leading, wherever it takes me this night.
(Prayers of Intercession)

Even in the smallest things I have done as you have led me, and I am grateful.

(Morning)
God, I am open to your leading, wherever it takes me this day. Amen.

(Evening)
Send me into rest this night according to your Word. Amen.

THURSDAY, MAY 22
(Read John 3:1–8)

(Morning)
Show me, Christ Jesus, that I am born anew this morning and this day.

(Evening)
Show me, Christ Jesus, how have you born me anew this day.

I am already old, or I am young. It makes no difference. I am who I am. Patterns formed and life shaped in whatever confusion or clarity you have given me. And I have chosen. I am not about to enter into any womb again. Yet I long to—to have a second chance, a third chance, as many chances as it takes for your Spirit to rush through me and blow me about until I am born anew this day. Every day. In this moment, O Christ Jesus, bear me anew, from above.

(Morning)
I rise secure and serene in your arms.
(Prayers of Intercession)

(Evening)
Christ Jesus, I am born anew in you this night.
(Prayers of Intercession)

These old bones have been born anew.

(Morning)	(Evening)
Christ Jesus, I am born anew in you this day. Amen.	As a little child, I lay me down to sleep, secure and serene in your arms. Amen.

FRIDAY, MAY 23
(Read Romans 8:9–11)

(Morning)
Holy Wisdom, Holy Spirit, be in me this morning and this day.

(Evening)
Holy Wisdom, Holy Spirit, thank you. I remember you in me this day.

You say that you dwell in me, Holy Spirit. Wisdom, feminine grace, indwelling presence in me. Though my body is tired, my spirit flags, even when I am consumed with anger, anxiety—whatever. Your Spirit dwells in me, recalling me to myself. Remembering who I am. I can count on that. I can take that to the bank. I don't have to worry about that, because you are not fickle like I am. Thank you, holy, tender Spirit. I feel like crying for gratitude.

(Morning)
I rise, and at once I am awake. I move in you.
(Prayers of Intercession)

(Evening)
The Spirit of God dwells in me.
(Prayers of Intercession)

Though my body is tired, though my spirit flags, though I have lost it several times, Holy Spirit, I know you have been in me this day.

(Morning)
The Spirit of God dwells in me. Amen.

(Evening)
I lay down, and at once I fall asleep.
I rest in you. Amen.

SATURDAY, MAY 24
(Read Romans 8:12–17)

(Morning)
Christ Jesus, may I know I am your child and your heir.

(Evening)
Christ Jesus, show me how I have been your heir this day.

"Provided we suffer," God. I do not think what I go through can be counted here. There have been big losses and the time I felt I was dying. There have been smaller unhappinesses, frustrations, confusions, stresses, and modest attempts to serve you. There have been gains and losses on a daily basis. I don't feel like your heir as I suffer them. Please assure me, Christ Jesus, that there is meaning here as well, and opportunity to grow in love; that your Spirit bears witness with my spirit. Make me believe that I am joint heir with you, carving out your new realm of freedom in this little corner of your creation.

(Morning)
I claim my birthright in you today.
(Prayers of Intercession)

(Evening)
In everything that happens this night, I am your heir.
(Prayers of Intercession)

I know, Christ Jesus, how your Spirit has borne witness with my spirit. It has grown me in love this day. Make me fully free in you.

(Morning)
In everything that happens this day, I am your heir. Amen.

(Evening)
I claim my birthright in you this night. Amen.

SUNDAY, MAY 25
(Read John 3:9–17)

(Morning)
O Sabbath joy, I celebrate you this day.

(Evening)
O Sabbath joy, thank you for this time.

On this holy Sabbath, Christ Jesus, remind me of wonder. How can these things be? You have come to us, been born in us, abide in us. Your parent, God, so loved the created universe that it shines in glory. You so loved us that you give us life eternally, to shine in glory. I may condemn myself, but you do not. You only give me life, love, and the freedom to be yours forever. Thank you, Christ Jesus.

(Morning)
I awake rejoicing in you, Christ Jesus.
(Prayers of Intercession)

(Evening)
I glory in your love tonight.
(Prayers of Intercession)

Christ Jesus, you so loved the universe that you created it to shine in glory.

(Morning)
I glory in your love this day. Amen.

(Evening)
I go to sleep rejoicing in you, Christ Jesus, to wake to a new week in your love. Amen.

MONDAY, MAY 26
(Read 1 Samuel 3:1–10)
(Sing "Called as Partners in Christ's Service")

(Morning)
Gracious and holy God, during this day filled with many sounds,
I pray that I might be able to listen.

(Evening)
Gracious and holy God, at the end of this noisy day, I pray that I can still listen.

I am aware that I am like Samuel—living and sleeping in the "temple of God," but often failing to hear your divine Word. I pray, gracious God, that I might listen, that I might believe that your Word is not rare in these days, and that you, the Holy One, might even be speaking to me. I pray for patience and hope, that I might have the conviction that the "lamp of God has not gone out," and that I might have new courage to respond, "Here am I." And most important, I pray this day for ears to really hear.

(Morning)
Give me the capacity to wait upon you, God, and to put myself
into places where you are present.
(Prayers of Intercession)

(Evening)
Give me the capacity to know when I am called—to believe that
I am worthy and that I have the ability to respond.
(Prayers of Intercession)

"Speak, for your servant is listening."

(Morning)
As I move forward into this day of many noises, a day filled with the din of life, help me to listen—to listen in the midst of life. And when the Word comes, give me courage to keep on listening. Amen.

(Evening)
As this day draws to an end, I pray for the ability to lay down in my place now and to listen for your call. In the silence of this very night, make me newly aware that I am called to listen. Amen.

TUESDAY, MAY 27
(Read 1 Samuel 3:11–20)
(Sing "God Speak to Me, That I May Speak")

(Morning)
O God, who imparts knowledge and who calls us to be more than hearers of your Word, today I seek your blessing and support to share what I know.

(Evening)
O God, who imparts knowledge to many of us who would rather not know, I come to the end of this day newly aware that knowledge demands action.

Sometimes I learn of things that "make both ears of anyone who hears of it tingle." Sometimes I do not want to believe what I hear. Yet sometimes I am called to share what I know. I pray that I might be led like Samuel to know when you are speaking and not to resist new information. I pray that I will keep faith with my obligations to open the doors of your house each day that I live. I pray that I will be able to share my visions with others, even when I know that they do not want to hear what I have to say.

(Morning)
Give me strength to overcome my fears.
(Prayers of Intercession)

(Evening)
Give me courage not to hide the truth from those who ask.
(Prayers of Intercession)

Enable me to trust in you, confident that you will do what seems good to you—not what others want to hear and not what I wish I had heard.

(Morning)
As the activities of this day unfold, enable me to "grow up" as Samuel did, that none of my words fall to the ground. Amen.

(Evening)
As the activities of this day draw to a close, enable me to "grow up" as Samuel did, that none of the words I have said today fall to the ground. Amen.

WEDNESDAY, MAY 28
(Read Psalms 139:1–6, 13–18)
(Sing "Dear God, Embracing Humankind")

(Morning)
All-knowing God, it is good to start this day knowing that I am known.

(Evening)
All-knowing God, it is good to end this day knowing that I am known.

The knowledge that I was formed by you, that I am fearfully and wonderfully made, that I was known even before my creation, and that I will always exist in your love is "too wonderful for me." My being rejoices in thanksgiving. In this knowledge, I pray that throughout my life I might sit down and rise up to your glory. In this knowledge, I pray that the words on my tongue might always be guided by your love. In this knowledge, I pray that I might praise you and speak of your wonderful works.

(Morning)
Keep me from being overwhelmed by the weight of your thoughts!
For I know that I cannot count them.
(Prayers of Intercession)

(Evening)
Keep me confident in my knowledge that no matter where I go—even when I come to the end of an hour, a day, a decade, or a life—I am still with you.
(Prayers of Intercession)

In confidence, I pray.
(Pray the Prayer of Our Savior.)

(Morning)
Be with me, gracious God, in the tasks of the day ahead, that at the end of the day I will have even greater knowledge of you, even as I am known. Amen.

(Evening)
Thank you, gracious God, for your presence in the day just past. Strengthen my knowledge and renew my sense that you are with me through this night and in the days ahead. Amen.

THURSDAY, MAY 29
(Read Deuteronomy 12:5–15)
(Sing "God, You Have Set Us")

(Morning)
O God of holy places, make me aware this day that I do not choose the places of your love.

(Evening)
O God of holy places, make me aware this evening that I do not choose the places of your love.

Enable me to bring what I have to worship you—my offerings, my sacrifices, my tithes and donations, my votive gifts, my freewill offerings, and the first fruits of my work—that I might rejoice in all the undertakings wherein I have been blessed. Lead me to holy places, O God—places that you have chosen out of all the world to put your name. Guide me not to act as expected, according to my own desires, but bless me with your gifts, that I might live in safety as the ancient Hebrews did when they followed your promise and worshiped you in new places.

(Morning)
Keep me from offering my gifts in "any place I happen to see."
(Prayers of Intercession)

(Evening)
Inspire me to seek out only places chosen by you to offer my gifts.
(Prayers of Intercession)

Lead me to do what you command, according to the blessings that you have given me in these times.

(Morning)
Even as many people in this world do not know "where they are," I move out into this day seeking places chosen by you. I pray that I might find my place in your love. Amen.

(Evening)
Even as many people in this world go to bed this night not sure "where they are," I seek my rest knowing that there are places chosen by you. Lead me to that place, O God. Amen.

FRIDAY, MAY 30
(Read Psalms 81:1–10)
(Sing "Spirit of God, Descend upon My Heart")

(Morning)
God of words and of silence, be with me in the hours ahead, that I might sing songs and shout for joy with renewed awareness that you are with me.

(Evening)
God of words and of silence, at the end of this day I am thankful that I can sing songs and shout for joy in your presence.

For I know that you are the Holy One, who shares burdens, who rescues, who answers in "the secret place of thunder," and who tests our faith. I pray that I might remember your covenant with the ancient Hebrews, how they heard voices that they had not known. I pray that when I am in distress I will be able to call; and that when I call, you will not fail to rescue. I pray that your admonitions will not fall upon deaf ears; that I might listen to your voice, blow trumpets at new moons, full moons, and raise new songs.

(Morning)
Keep me focused, gracious God. Remind me of your command that "There shall be no strange gods among you."
(Prayers of Intercession)

(Evening)
Keep me from bowing down to false gods, to gods that come and go and that do not deserve adoration.
(Prayers of Intercession)

Fill me with the right words of praise and joy—and new courage to do your will in an unjust world.

(Morning)
During the coming day, holy God, fill my mouth with words that are needed and keep me silent when there is nothing to say. Amen.

(Evening)
At the end of this day, holy God, forgive my mouth that makes empty words and forgets to let you fill it. Make me humble in the face of your silence. Amen.

SATURDAY, MAY 31
(Read 2 Corinthians 4:5–12)
(Sing "Take My Life, God, Let It Be")

(Morning)
God of creation, enable me to place my confidence in you—the One who leads me through the shadows of each day.

(Evening)
God of creation, at the end of this day, I pray that you will restore my confidence in you—the One who has guided me through the shadows of this day.

I pray that new knowledge of your glory as known through Jesus Christ might rest upon me—that I come to know your extraordinary power and believe that salvation "does not come from us," but from you. Lead me to see your glory in the contrasts of life, so that when I am afflicted in every way, I am not crushed; so that when I am perplexed, I am not driven to despair; so that when I am struck down, I am not destroyed. Help me to understand the limits of my earthly life, so that the life of Jesus may also be made visible in me. And finally, in life, let me understand that I am always being given up to death. For even as death is at work in me, I am bold to affirm the wonder of my life in your love through Christ.

(Morning)
God, I celebrate the contrasts of life. Shine in my heart this day.
(Prayers of Intercession)

(Evening)
God, I celebrate the contrasts of life—births and deaths.
Shine in my heart this night.
(Prayers of Intercession)

In celebration, I pray.
(Pray the Prayer of Our Savior.)

(Morning)
Creator God, I celebrate the contrasts of life—successes and failures. Shine in my heart this day, so that I might do your will in the hours ahead. Amen.

(Evening)
Creator God, I celebrate the contrasts of life—beginnings and endings. Shine in my heart this night, that I might rise with another day to do your will. Amen.

SUNDAY, JUNE 1
(Read Mark 2:23–3:6)
(Sing "Joyful, Joyful, We Adore You")

(Morning)
God of the Sabbath, as I begin this day, I ask for new sensitivity to the importance of keeping Sabbath—of keeping some part of my week for you.

(Evening)
God of the Sabbath, as I conclude this day, I ask for new sensitivity to the importance of keeping Sabbath—of keeping some part of my week for you.

In the "grain fields" of my life, I wonder if anyone even notices what I am doing. Do the authorities question? Are my activities lawful or unlawful? I pray for new courage to challenge all my unexamined assumptions. Open me to more balanced understandings about the commitments of others. Give me priorities to know when rules need to be broken. And above all, strengthen my loyalty to Jesus Christ, who insists that the Sabbath is made for human well-being, not that humanity is made for the Sabbath. Yet even with new Sabbath freedom in Christ, I pray for strength to value Sabbath rhythms. If any would destroy my life, may it be because I have grounded my witness in the holy rhythms of your love.

(Morning)
I pray this day, therefore, that I might keep your commandment to remember the Sabbath day and keep it holy.
(Prayers of Intercession)

(Evening)
At the end of this day, therefore, I recall your commandment to remember the Sabbath day and honor its holiness.
(Prayers of Intercession)

Remembering the Sabbath, I pray.
(Pray the Prayer of Our Savior.)

(Morning)
As you rested on the seventh day, this day I too seek a renewed spirit of Sabbath in my life. Amen.

(Evening)
As you rested on the seventh day, at the end of this day I too seek a renewed spirit of Sabbath in my life. Amen.

MONDAY, JUNE 2
(Read 1 Samuel 8:4–11)

(Morning)
Dear God, help me to find a place to listen to your challenge to me and to help me carry out your will in this world.

(Evening)
Dear God, at the close of this day, I give you all the thanks for my journey. Grant me peace for the night.

God, because of your peace, your grace, and your mercy, I give you thanks this day. You have always been with me and with others who believe in you. And you have been a source of strength when evil would surround me and tempt me. Keep me still, God, in those times and in those places when I need patience and quietness. It is in those moments that I need to remember your Child, Christ Jesus, the one who died for me. Bless me now, O God, and for the rest of my days.

(Morning)
Dear God, you have given me your work to do as well as my own.
Help me this day.
(Prayers of Intercession)

(Evening)
God, I am constantly in praise of your goodness. Bless this night and all my days.
(Prayers of Intercession)

With confidence, I pray.
(Pray the Prayer of Our Savior.)

(Morning)
O God, help me to hold my life in balance and help me to give my best each and every day. Amen.

(Evening)
Gracious and loving God, grant me the faith that will not shrink, or waver, or complain, even in the face of adversity. Help me to grow stronger each day in your love. Amen.

TUESDAY, JUNE 3
(Read 1 Samuel 8:12–15, 16–20)

(Morning)
God of patience and faithfulness, I thank you for your patience with me and with others. When I awakened this morning, I felt your presence.

(Evening)
God of patience and faithfulness, as I close my eyes to this world,
I rest in your love and I am at peace.

Dear God, when I consider all the things that you have created for us and when I think about our sinfulness and greed in response to your gifts, I am ashamed and seek your forgiveness. I repent and ask that you accept my confession and let me try again to follow you and obey you. Please grant these petitions.

(Morning)
O God, there is beauty in our memories and hope in our time spent with you.
May the music of love linger with me all day.
(Prayers of Intercession)

(Evening)
May this night bring harmony and blessed joy.
May peace abide as I rest in your love.
(Prayers of Intercession)

With faith, I pray.
(Pray the Prayer of Our Savior.)

(Morning)
Dear God, may this day be the best day of my life and may I add to your glory and your love. Amen.

(Evening)
Thank you, God, for your continued blessings on my journey. Amen.

WEDNESDAY, JUNE 4
(Read Psalm 138)

(Morning)
Dear God, inspire my efforts to make this day a day of thanksgiving.

(Evening)
Dear God, thank you for the challenge and for your will in the world.

I praise you, O God, for entrusting me, as young as I am, with your plans for a better world. I love you enough to do the best I can in spite of my limitations and my weaknesses. I pray for strength, for guidance, and for wisdom to carry out your work until your realm comes on earth as it is in heaven.

(Morning)
I will praise you with my being; my mind, body, and spirit.
Today is the day of praise and thanksgiving.
(Prayers of Intercession)

(Evening)
Thank you, God, for being with me this day,
and I seek you now in these evening hours.
(Prayers of Intercession)

In thanksgiving, I pray.
(Pray the Prayer of Our Savior.)

(Morning)
I praise you, God, for this new day. I praise you, God, for last night's rest. I praise you, God, for my life. I praise you, God, for your grace. Amen.

(Evening)
I praise you, God, always and for everything. You are a good God, and your mercy is ever with me, both night and day. Praise God. Amen.

THURSDAY, JUNE 5
(Read Psalm 130)

(Morning)
O God, as I gather my thoughts and meditate on your Word, I give thanks to you and praise your holy name. Be of good cheer.

(Evening)
O God, thank you for this day, and for all the days of my life.

God, my hope is in you and in your mercies. You have brought me out of shadows and into the marvelous light of your love. You have been merciful to others. I thank you that you are generous and kind, full of grace and truth. I love you, God, and I pray that all the families of the earth will love you also. You are worthy to be loved by your creation and your creatures.

(Morning)
This is the day of caring. You have cared for me all the days of my life. It is time for me to reach out and care for others. Place me in the way of someone in need. Thank you, God.
(Prayers of Intercession)

(Evening)
I pray for those who need to accept you as the answer to their concerns and problems. Help me to be a positive witness in this land.
(Prayers of Intercession)

With patience, I pray.
(Pray the Prayer of Our Savior.)

(Morning)
Holy and upright God, direct my feet as I make my way to work and to a willing spirit of caring for others. Amen.

(Evening)
In the solitude of these evening hours, I need and want to thank you, God, for life, liberty, the pursuit of love, and the love of Christ Jesus for all people. Amen.

FRIDAY, JUNE 6
(Read Genesis 3:8–15)

(Morning)
Ever-present God, we try so hard to keep a mask on our faces and hide ourselves from you. Forgive us for being fearful.

(Evening)
Ever-present God, thank you for accepting our efforts to be real and to be open to others.

O God, do not let our love for you or for one another be like the morning dew. The dew goes away too soon when the sun comes up. Let our love be like an everlasting spring of mountain water, whose refreshment replenishes the ground, the thirst, and the spirit. Continue to be available to us, O God. I sincerely thank you for your constant presence.

(Morning)
O God, this day I pray for those whose lives are broken. Help them heal. For those who are sick in body or mind, bring health and healing.
(Prayers of Intercession)

(Evening)
Thank you for standing by throughout this day, O God. Watch over me and wake me to see another day.
(Prayers of Intercession)

With assurance, I pray.
(Pray the Prayer of Our Savior.)

(Morning)
As I reflect on your goodness each morning, I thank you, God, for my life from the beginning until now. I have experienced you and have received from you all the goodness I need or will need. For this I give you thanks. Amen.

(Evening)
I remember, O God, the prayers my mother taught me as a child. My father stood by, strong and still like a tree. As I grew older, my prayer life expanded. Thank you, God, for the memories.
Amen

SATURDAY, JUNE 7
(Read Mark 3:20–35)

(Morning)
Creator God, the soul that you have given me is pure! I thank you for creating and forming it. You have breathed your Spirit into me, and you are sustaining me day by day.

(Evening)
Creator God, I release all my fears and my sorrows to you. Take them and cast them aside, and let me rest in your love.

Dear God, I recognize and praise your name. This is your world, your earth, your creation, and we all belong to you. We are your family. Help us then to accept your will for our lives, and help me to love you and the rest of the family. I need special help to forgive those who abuse me. Your Child, Jesus, loved us and forgave us while he was on the cross. Thank you, God, for his love and for yours.

(Morning)
Heal us, O God, and we shall be healed. Help us and save us.
(Prayers of Intercession)

(Evening)
Thank you for another day. I praise and honor you, God.
(Prayers of Intercession)

In obedience, I pray.
(Pray the Prayer of Our Savior.)

(Morning)
O God, you are the one that I ask for strength to rise and to walk in faith in my loneliness. Thank you for the opportunity this day. Amen.

(Evening)
Dear God, I present myself to you before I rest this night and thank you for your kindness to me. I will sing my soul to you and give you all that is in my mind and my heart. Amen.

SUNDAY, JUNE 8
(Read 2 Corinthians 4:13–5:1)

(Morning)
God, it was grace that woke me up this morning, and I thank you for extending my life for one more day.

(Evening)
God, it has been a day full of thanksgiving and grace. Thank you for your love to me.

Gracious and eternal God, I want to open my heart to you and confess my sins, the one and the many. For any waste of my gifts, forgive me. For all the times I do not walk in your love, forgive me. For being hesitant in doing your will in the world, forgive me. And for not obeying you when I should have followed you, forgive me, O God. Accept my confession and my need for forgiveness.

(Morning)
O God, help me to live radiantly, joyously, amid the tensions of life.
(Prayers of Intercession)

(Evening)
As I rest in your grace, O God, make my sleep peaceful and pleasant.
(Prayers of Intercession)

I believe, therefore I pray.
(Pray the Prayer of Our Savior.)

(Morning)
Dear God, this is the day that you have given to me, and I am thankful. Help me to be sincere, to be trusting, and to be open to your Spirit. Amen.

(Evening)
Lift my heart, God, and lead me into your presence. I seek to find the power and the will to love you with all my heart, mind, and body. As I retire to rest, I pray for your continued presence. Amen.

MONDAY, JUNE 9
(Read Psalm 92:7–4)
(Reading from 1 Samuel 15:34–16:1)

(Morning)
God of all mercy, as I rise from sleep, remind me of your steadfast love
which will go with me all day.

(Evening)
God of all mercy, as I prepare myself for sleep, I thank you
for being with me today and all days.

I remember your good works through which I have received blessing. I listen for your presence, too, in the witness of Samuel. In the midst of grief and despair, you reached out to Samuel with promise. You promised him hope which would swallow up his grief. I, too, O God, am consumed at times with grief. I look about me and see only promises unfulfilled, work not accomplished, love not lived out. Then I am tempted to conclude that you are not with me; that you have abandoned me and your plans for me. Help me, as you helped Samuel to prepare myself for the journey of hope that will carry me beyond despair. Let me be filled with faithfulness. Let me step out in joy.

(Morning)
Let me start this day with the psalmist, by declaring that no matter what,
you and your love will never leave me.
(Prayers of Intercession)

(Evening)
As you hear me, let me remember three ways in which you blessed me today.
(Prayers of Intercession)

In the knowledge that you are listening to me now, hear me as I pray.
(Pray the Prayer of Our Savior.)

(Morning)
Send me forth in hope and joy,
knowing that no matter what this day
brings, you are with me. Amen.

(Evening)
Let me rest now in peace, having found
the answer to all my pain in your
ceaseless love. Amen.

TUESDAY, JUNE 10
(Read Psalm 20:1–2)
(Reading from 1 Samuel 16:2–5)

(Morning)
God of all mercy, I awake and wonder what this day will hold for me.

(Evening)
God of all mercy, hear me as I pray so that I may rest.

I remember all your good works through which I have received blessing. I listen for your presence, too, in the witness of Samuel. O God, you gave Samuel a mission that he believed impossible. So he asked for your help. You showed him the way. "Make a sacrifice in front of Jesse," you said, "and I will show you what you shall do." Help me to remember to seek your guidance at all times. When I am perplexed, when your call to witness seems too hard to bear, remind me that you will show me the way. Just as you led Samuel, lead me, today and every day. As I enter into peace with you, remind me to invite others to join us, as Samuel invited Jesse and his sons.

(Morning)
As I begin my day, I pray for your guidance.
(Prayers of Intercession)

(Evening)
As I prepare to rest, I recall the ways you showed me hope today.
(Prayers of Intercession)

In the knowledge that you are listening to me now, hear me as I pray.
(Pray the Prayer of Our Savior.)

(Morning)
I begin my day confident that you will show me the way. Help me to bring peace to those I encounter today. Amen.

(Evening)
Now I sleep, secure in your arms. May I sleep in your peace. Amen.

WEDNESDAY, JUNE 11
(Read Psalm 20:3–5)
(Reading from 1 Samuel 16:6–13)

(Morning)
God of all mercy, as I begin this new day, let all my plans be your plans,
let all my victories be yours.

(Evening)
God of all mercy, as I lay down to sleep, hear my prayers of thanks
for all you have done this day.

I remember all your good works through which I have received blessing. I listen for your presence, too, in the witness of Samuel. Mysterious God, you sent him to Jesse looking for a ruler. Samuel looked at the oldest, the strongest, the most responsible of Jesse's household, and he did not see the ruler for whom you had sent him. It seems your ways are surprising, for who should your ruler be but the little shepherd David! Teach me to look for your surprises in every place. Remind me that even Samuel had to search the entire household before he discovered the one you had promised. Let me not lose heart in my search for promise. Help me to delight in the seeking of your way and your will.

(Morning)
As I start this day, give me strength to minister in your name.
(Prayers of Intercession)

(Evening)
As I end this day, hear my prayers for all your children.
(Prayers of Intercession)

In the knowledge that you are listening to me now, hear me as I pray.
(Pray the Prayer of Our Savior.)

(Morning)
Help me to live this day expecting guidance and hope and promise. Help me to carry your peace into your world. Amen.

(Evening)
Tonight I release myself into your care. Let me dream dreams of unexpected joy. Amen.

THURSDAY, JUNE 12
(Read Psalm 20:6–9)
(Reading from Ezekiel 17:22–24)

(Morning)
God of all mercy, I greet this new day filled with a sense of your presence in and around me.

(Evening)
God of all mercy, with peace I greet the end of this day
Now, release me from the day's toil.

I remember all your good works through which I have received blessing. I listen for your presence, too, in the witness of Ezekiel. God of all possibilities, Ezekiel saw you creating the strongest tree from the most tender of shoots. Your nurture and care brought into being a tree that symbolized strength, security, and beauty—a true home for your creatures. Hear the longing in me for such a home. Help me to understand that only in you will I find the perfect refuge I seek. Just as you used the smallest twig to grow the tallest tree, use me, too. Let me grow in your Word. Let me stretch up toward the sky, trusting that all is in your hands.

(Morning)
As I start this day, give me strength to minister in your name.
(Prayers of Intercession)

(Evening)
As I end this day, hear my prayers for all your children.
(Prayers of Intercession)

In the knowledge that you are listening to me now, hear me as I pray.
(Pray the Prayer of Our Savior.)

(Morning)
Today, hold before me the vision of the mighty cedar tree. Let its shelter be my strength for this day. Amen.

(Evening)
Whether I was weak as a twig or strong as the cedar, I turn this day over to you. Tomorrow will be another day to grow in your love. Amen.

FRIDAY, JUNE 13
(Read Psalm 92:12–15 and 2 Corinthians 5:6–10)

(Morning)
God of all mercy, draw my first breath. I see myself planted in you.
Let me be a sign of your love.

(Evening)
God of all mercy, as I prepare myself to rest, today, I turn all my cares over to you.

I remember all your good works through which I have received blessing. I listen for your presence, too, in the witness of Paul, who taught that we "walk by faith, not by sight." It is hard to walk by faith, God of love. It is hard to be living testimonies to your love. It is easier to depend on our own eyes than to trust you to guide us. Grant me a sense of your trust in me. Help me to show all I meet what your love has done for this world. Grant me confidence in you and in your workings within me. Help me to look forward to serving you, so that on that glorious day when I meet you face to face, I will have many blessings to return to you!

(Morning)
As I start this day, give me strength to minister in your name.
(Prayers of Intercession)

(Evening)
As I end this day, hear my prayers for all your children.
(Prayers of Intercession)

In the knowledge that you are listening to me now, hear me as I pray.
(Pray the Prayer of Our Savior.)

(Morning)
Help me to flourish like the palm tree.
Let me be fruitful as I grow in you.
Amen.

(Evening)
I lay down to rest and give my cares over to you. Let me awake to greet the new day in your love. Amen.

SATURDAY, JUNE 14
(Read 2 Corinthians 5:14–17)

(Morning)
God of all mercy, as I draw my first breath, I envision my feet firmly planted in you. Today, help me to be a sign of your righteousness.

(Evening)
God of all mercy, as I prepare myself to rest, I turn all my cares over to you, confident that tomorrow will bring its own work.

I remember all your good works through which I have received blessing. I listen for your presence, too, in the witness of Paul. God of possibility, help me to understand myself and those around me in light of your love for all of us. Help me to live out of love. Let me see the new creation you have worked in me and are working in all your people. We are all people of your resurrection love—new creations no longer bound by sin or pain. No matter what has happened to me in the past, remind me that today I have started fresh again in your love.

(Morning)
As I start this day, give me strength to minister in your name.
(Prayers of Intercession)

(Evening)
As I end this day, hear my prayers for all your children.
(Prayers of Intercession)

In the knowledge that you are listening to me now, hear me as I pray.
(Pray the Prayer of Our Savior.)

(Morning)
Help me to see everyone I meet today in light of your love for them. Amen.

(Evening)
Hear my prayers for all those I met today. Let me rest now in your peace. Amen.

SUNDAY, JUNE 15
(Read Mark 4:26–34)

(Morning)
God of all mercy, I awake on this Sabbath day to rest and renewal.
I honor you by keeping this day holy.

(Evening)
God of all mercy, in you I have found peace today
Let me carry your peace with me into rest.

I remember all your good works through which I have received blessing. I listen for your presence, too, in the teaching of Jesus. O God, though I may be the tiniest part of all your creation, help me to grow in faith like the mustard seed. Cultivate me. Help me to grow in faith, love, and service for all your creation. Help me to see all the ways in which I am able to minister to your world. O God, as you have blessed me, let me bless all those you love.

(Morning)
As I start this day, I recommit myself to living in your joy!
(Prayers of Intercession)

(Evening)
Hear my prayers for all your world.
(Prayers of Intercession)

In the knowledge that you are listening to me now, hear me as I pray.
(Pray the Prayer of Our Savior.)

(Morning)
Help me to greet your world with love and joy. Amen.

(Evening)
As I lay down to rest, I look forward to serving you. Amen.

MONDAY, JUNE 16
(Reading from 1 Samuel 17:1a, 4–11, 19–23, 32–49)

(Morning)
God of holy valor, the day holds challenges of which I am not yet aware.
    Some may frighten me and sorely test my courage.

(Evening)
God of holy valor, in weariness I surrender the day you gave me,
    yielding to your judgment both its triumphs and failures.

But it is *your* day; and because I know your mercy in my flesh, I receive it with thanks and open myself to its lessons. David's is an amazing story, God. Though yet a lad, he embodied the courage that belongs to those who are grounded in your love. Least among his people, he led in trust of the divine promise, and offered his life as tribute to your trustworthiness. While cowardice groveled and arrogance jeered, he unsheathed your valor and snatched triumph from the jaws of death. I remember another, called Child of David, who took my flesh against fearful odds and conquered death itself.

(Morning)
Now bring David's courage alive in me, to teach that I can confront the giants
    of my own days.
(Prayers of Intercession)

(Evening)
Remind me, O God, that what I lacked today may come tomorrow,
    that I grow in courage as I grow in faith.
(Prayers of Intercession)

With David's confidence in you, I pray.
(Pray the Prayer of Our Savior.)

(Morning)
Go with me as I address this day in trust. May I return it to you unafraid. In the name of Christ. Amen.

(Evening)
Now I sleep secure that your mercy will guard my night as it guided my day. Amen.

TUESDAY, JUNE 17
(Read Psalm 9:9–12 or sing a familiar hymn)
(Reading from 1 Samuel 18:10–16)

(Morning)
Steadfast God, you alone are my rock, on whom my soul depends,
against whom no evil can prevail.

(Evening)
Steadfast God, you brought me safely through this day.
I yield again my thanks for sheltering love.

For your steadfast love that shields me, your constant nurture that keeps me, I sing your praise. How frightening it must have been for David, who, seeking to comfort his leader, received vicious enmity in return. How discouraging to face alone the enemy's champion and secure the victory, only to acquire a monarch's rage. What are we to do, merciful God, when the conduct of friends falsifies loyalty, and those we trust demean and torment us? Forgive me for my contribution to the forgery of friendship. Discipline your people when we steal trust from those who count on our constancy. Remind us that when we claim to be your people, others judge you by our actions.

(Morning)
As I begin this day, I pray to be more trusting and trustworthy;
more caring, and responsive to the caring of others.
(Prayers of Intercession)

(Evening)
At this day's close, bless those whose loyalty sustained me and give me grace
to forgive those who betrayed me.
(Prayers of Intercession)

And now, in the words of your most trusting Child, I pray.
(Pray the Prayer of Our Savior.)

(Morning)
Send me now to model your faithfulness, that others, seeing it patterned in me, may become bold to trust you. Amen.

(Evening)
Through this night, girdle me in your sheltering embrace, most trusted and trusting friend. Amen.

WEDNESDAY, JUNE 18
(Read Psalm 9:13–14 or sing a familiar hymn)
(Reading from 2 Corinthians 6:1–13)

(Morning)
God of our histories, you attend me as I prepare for the day,
declaring it an acceptable day.

(Evening)
God of our histories, from the trials of the day I come away
to remind myself who I serve and who serves me.

    I would not accept your gift in vain or hinder your promise. I hear your affirmation that you listen to us, and help us toward the day of redemption. So I praise you, God of my salvation, in all circumstances. Whether in trial or rejoicing—I will praise you! Thank you for saints whose long-stilled voices still chant, to my ears, your glory song. I laud their constancy in persecution and suffering and their insistence on praising you, even when life held only travail. Correct me when I whine about my troubles, refusing to embrace my pain and find in it the means to glorify you. Teach me to center myself in things eternal, to forget my pain, and get on with my life.

(Morning)
Restrain me this day to put no obstacle in another's way,
but to commend myself as a servant.
(Prayers of Intercession)

(Evening)
Show me where you helped me today, even when I did not see you,
and refresh my sense of infinite mercy.
(Prayers of Intercession)

Wherefore I pray.
(Pray the Prayer of Our Savior.)

(Morning)
Direct my day, you "who lift me up from the gates of death, so that I may recount all your praises!" Amen.

(Evening)
Thank you for my day, in all its variety, and grant me to serve you more fully tomorrow. Amen.

THURSDAY, JUNE 19
(Read Psalm 9:15–20 or sing a familiar hymn)
(Reading from Job 38:1–7)

(Morning)
Eternal God, in mystery and majesty you fill the morning of one
who is but mortal flesh and all unknowing.

(Evening)
Eternal God, your mystery and majesty have enveloped me this day
and helped me know my limits.

I would not presume to declare the boundaries of your majesty that exceed human comprehension, nor claim to know you at all, but that you call me beloved and bid me hear you. Speak to me now, mighty and mysterious One. I wait in holy dread for your Word and would be obedient to your will. For I cannot realize you except that you reveal yourself. I cannot know your purpose unless you make it known. I cannot obey unless your Spirit helps me. Wherefore I will be silent and wait upon your Word, until I am able with certainty to distinguish the purposes of God from the schemes of humanity.

(Morning)
Teach me today the meaning of silent reverence that affirms your mystery and
acknowledges my mortality.
(Prayers of Intercession)

(Evening)
As I sought to learn silent reverence at the day's beginning, I seek it still
at the day's closing.
(Prayers of Intercession)

While after your Child, born of Spirit and of flesh, I pray.
(Pray the Prayer of Our Savior.)

(Morning)
Let now your morning stars sing again together, Creator God, and my voice be in harmony with them all. Amen.

(Evening)
I close my eyes in peace, thankful for your majesty that will judge the nations by a righteous will. Amen.

FRIDAY, JUNE 20
(Read Psalm 133 or sing a familiar hymn)
(Reading from 1 Samuel 17:57–18:5)

(Morning)
God who is one God, the dawning day prompts me to weigh the difference between your intention and our actuality.

(Evening)
God who is one God, I have tried to see more clearly today the blessings of accord and the liabilities of discord.

Out of many, you have called us to be one; in you, and you alone, is our unity. We emphasize differences and foster division. The love of Jonathan for David accuses us of our stinginess of soul and models for us the depth potential of friendship. With sensuous joyfulness, the psalmist excites us to the sublime rewards that attend upon unity among God's people—the very gateway to divine blessing and life eternal. Forgive my reluctance to extend your embrace, O God, and endow me with such a spirit of unity that my whole being reflects your purpose, my every action a mark of healing.

(Morning)
Help me to make good my pledge this day to be a force for healing and unity.
(Prayers of Intercession)

(Evening)
Thank you, God, for what this day has taught me of the beauty of oneness.
(Prayers of Intercession)

In the spirit of Christ Jesus, whose words I pray.
(Pray the Prayer of Our Savior.)

(Morning)
Now I submit my day to your guidance, my actions to your governance, and my will to your unity of purpose. Amen.

(Evening)
Remind me as I fall asleep of all whose loyal affection has enriched my life and fills me with thanks. Amen.

SATURDAY, JUNE 21
Read Psalm 107:1–3, 23–27 or sing a familiar hymn)
(Reading from Job 38:1–3, 8–11)

(Morning)
Great Sovereign, whose steadfastness endures forever, I know the feeling of being out of control, the anxiety of inhabiting a world that is unresponsive to my command.

(Evening)
Great Sovereign, whose steadfastness endures forever, thank you for your steadying hand over this day, and your sovereign dominion that I receive as love.

It would be frightful indeed, were the forces of the universe dependent upon my feeble powers of supervision. I who cannot even control the weather that browses and blows about my home, much less discern the manner of your laying the foundations of earth—how should I acquire the wisdom to direct the flow of galaxies? Wherefore I praise you for your authority which commands what you have created, requiring that primeval chaos yield to order, and the world shape itself in sympathy with the needs of finite creatures.

(Morning)
As your creation of the world establishes your governance upon it, so your making of this day confirms your authority to govern my use of it.
(Prayers of Intercession)

(Evening)
Your command is ever evident over the storms that afflict my days, making me glad when there is quiet and I am brought to a safe haven.
(Prayers of Intercession)

In celebration of your dominion, therefore, I bow to pray.
(Pray the Prayer of Our Savior.)

(Morning)
I face this day, grateful that the care of the world is not in my hands, but yours who alone has authority to bear it.
Amen.

(Evening)
I go to my rest, thankful "for your steadfast love, for your wonderful works to the children of humanity!"
Amen.

SUNDAY, JUNE 22
(Read Psalm 107:28–32 or sing "Jesus, Savior, Pilot Me")
(Reading from Mark 4:35–41)

(Morning)
God, who even the elements obey, I wake unsure whether this day holds calm or storm, sure only that I must not allow fear to keep me tied to the dock.

(Evening)
God, who even the elements obey, again this day, you taught me that no matter how desperate things appear, my life is in your hands, not the storm's.

Sometimes, my mind resembles your Galilean lake, churned by turbulence that bruises the heart and disables the will. Often my tempests are illusory—the consequence of ambition in a hurry, all foam and bluster, signifying nothing. But others are genuine and threaten real harm to me or to real people I love. Teach me the difference. Still my imaginary gales and restore the calm center of faith. From real dangers, O Savior, deliver me, by the authority that stunned your disciples and muzzled Galilee.

(Morning)
I begin this day newly aware that you do not share my panic at the tempest's arousal, but maintain calm—and instill it in me.
(Prayers of Intercession)

(Evening)
One more plea I make: to be mindful never to rate faith as less real, because unseen, than breakers.
(Prayers of Intercession)

Thus with confidence, as one for whom you subdue the sea, I pray.
(Pray the Prayer of Our Savior.)

(Morning)
Let this creed frame my day: So Christ be in my ship, I dread no storm, but ride the breast of peace. Amen.

(Evening)
Lay me to rest, Sovereign Majesty, secure in the knowledge that your mercy will secure safe passage to every distant shore. Amen.

MONDAY, JUNE 23
(Reading from 2 Samuel 1:1, 17–27)

(Morning)
Ever-present God, we are blessed that even in times of despair, grief, or sorrow, you are with us.

(Evening)
Ever-present God, as we prepare to close this day, we are able to shut our eyes with confidence.

Omnipotent, omniscient, and everlasting God, it is unto you, our God, the God of David and Jonathan, Ruth, and Naomi, that we pray. We have come to you in this time of distress, grief, and sorrow because we know that you listen to our pleas and that you act to relieve our suffering. Come here and bring your healing balm. Come here and allow your Spirit to wrap us in your love, that we might find with you the strength that we need for this journey. Through your power, we can rise from our despair. With your love, we can walk through sorrow. In your presence, we can move through grief.

(Morning)
Your Spirit comes to us to comfort, direct, and guide us.
(Prayers of Intercession)

(Evening)
We are grateful that you have walked with us throughout this day.
(Prayers of Intercession)

Because we are assured that throughout the night and day God's angels watch over us, we can be at peace.

(Morning)
Thank you for not forsaking us or turning away from us in our time of need. Amen.

(Evening)
We surrender ourselves and our spirits unto your tender, loving care. Amen.

TUESDAY, JUNE 24
(Reading from Psalm 130)

(Morning)
Trusting God, I rise with thanksgiving for this day.

(Evening)
Trusting God, thank you for your abiding presence of peace and joy.

God, there are many times when we become impatient. We feel that you are neglecting us and not providing us with answers and blessings as you should. We dare to feel forsaken and rejected, even though the evidence of your love is before us. We allow our desires to blind us. We cry out, demanding that you move on our behalf—right now. Teach us to pray, O God. Teach us to be faithful to you and your Word and will for us. Allow us to sing with the saints of older times, "I will trust in God. I will trust in God. I will trust in God, until I die." And then grant us the courage to live our faith accordingly.

(Morning)
I will praise you and bless your name today.
(Prayers of Intercession)

(Evening)
Thank you for watching over me, my family, friends, and loved ones.
(Prayers of Intercession)

God is my light and my salvation; whom shall I fear? God is the stronghold of my life; of whom shall I be afraid?

(Morning)	(Evening)
I will confer with you before moving to implement my decisions. Amen.	Now I will rest in your care until you grant a new day. Amen.

WEDNESDAY, JUNE 25
(Reading from Lamentations 3:23–33)
(Sing "Great Is Your Faithfulness")

(Morning)
Precious God, good morning. As I greet you anew this day, I am reminded of your constant love and care of me.

(Evening)
Precious God, for your faithfulness, I bow down with thanksgiving and gratitude.

God of love, mercy, and grace. It is my privilege to come before your presence, once again. And in doing so, I must acknowledge that you have been faithful to me. You have been with me, watching over me, loving me, and providing for me since the beginning of my time. Thank you for blessing me with family and friends. Thank you for your amazing grace, which has covered my faults and my sins. Thank you for all that is good and right in my life. And thank you for moving with me through those things that attempt to destroy my joy. I give your name praise, glory, and honor. I give myself back to you. I pray that I may be used to bless your world and your people.

(Morning)
I rejoice that you have provided me another opportunity to share my life with you and to enjoy your creations.
(Prayers of Intercession)

(Evening)
As we close this day together, I rejoice in you and your Spirit.
(Prayers of Intercession)

Our God never sleeps nor slumbers. God constantly watches over us, making safe our path.

(Morning)
Thank you for the blessings I enjoy. Thank you for my family, friends, and loved ones. I pray for your love to surround them this day. Amen.

(Evening)
Thank you for loving and caring for me. Amen.

THURSDAY, JUNE 26
(Read Psalm 30)

(Morning)
God of power and might, I thank you for another day of grace and love.

(Evening)
God of power and might, I am ready to lie down and rest.
My joy is complete with your love.

A wonderful change has come over me. God has changed me. Now I am free. Almighty God, you who created me from the very dust. Christ Jesus, you who are called a battle ax, shelter from the storm, and a rock in a weary land. Holy Spirit, you who are known to be a comforter and a counselor. You have heard my petitions and have answered my prayers, and so I must give thanks to you. Thank you for removing the ache in my heart. Thank you for never leaving me, even as I considered leaving you and never calling your name. Thank you for restoring my spirit unto yourself. Thank you for walking and talking with me and breathing breath into my soul. I rejoice in your love and care. You are all that I need.

(Morning)
I am mindful that my condition has changed.
My change has come with the strength I have found in you.
(Prayers of Intercession)

(Evening)
I thank you for this day and all that you have done on my behalf.
(Prayers of Intercession)

There is still a balm in Gilead that is able to calm, soothe, and relieve our troubled state.

(Morning)
I bless your name and ask you to bless others as well. Amen.

(Evening)
Your grace has been more than sufficient. Thanks, God. Amen.

FRIDAY, JUNE 27
(Reading from 2 Corinthians 8:7–15)

(Morning)
Generous God, I am amazed at the way you continue to bless me.

(Evening)
Generous God, for your many blessings and benefits, I give thanks.

"God is a good God; God is a great God! God has moved so many mountains out of my way. God is a wonderful God!" Because you are a wonderful God, we rejoice and offer you our praise and gratitude. Because you are our God, we offer our lives and our loyalty. Because you have loved us and not withheld your best, we offer unto you all that we are now and all that we shall ever become. We pray that you will find us acceptable for use in building your realm. We pray that you will find us malleable enough to be useful in completing your work on the earth. Our desire is to give back that which you have offered us in such abundance. We have more than we need; our cup does overflow. Direct us that we extend your love and bounty to others.

(Morning)
I find that, day by day, your gifts multiply.
(Prayers of Intercession)

(Evening)
For the many provisions you grant. I give thanks.
(Prayers of Intercession)

As we have received of God, let us praise God and give back to God, that God's name might be blessed throughout this earth.

(Morning)
You have blessed me so abundantly. Show me how to bless others on your behalf. Amen.

(Evening)
For your unmerited favor and grace, I praise you. Amen.

SATURDAY, JUNE 28
(Reading from Mark 5:21–43)

(Morning)
Loving God, we give thanks for your love which moves to relieve our condition.

(Evening)
Loving God, your love has brought us through another day.

God, you have blessed us with your love. Your mercy and grace have protected us, even during times that we were unaware of the danger that threatened us. Your love has been a source of power and comfort, peace and joy to us. We have known your Spirit to move in intercession for us as did Jairus for the sake of his child. We are grateful for your intervention in our lives, for you have upheld us when we would have fallen. We pray that as we follow Christ, we might model behavior that signifies our love for you. Allow us to be intercessors on your behalf here on earth. Grant that we love one another as you have loved us. Amen.

(Morning)
For love that cares more for other than for self, we thank you.
(Prayers of Intercession)

(Evening)
Your love embraced us and carried us safely through dangers and snares.
(Prayers of Intercession)

There is no force equal to the power of love.

(Morning)
Give us the same love for one another that you have evidenced for us. Amen.

(Evening)
Your love is what has sustained us. Amen.

SUNDAY, JUNE 29
(Reading from Mark 5:21–43)

(Morning)
Courageous Savior, I thank you for boldly taking on flesh for my sake.

(Evening)
Courageous Savior, this has been another day wherein you have blessed me.

God, there are times when you require that we take on boldness. We must be willing to acknowledge our shortcomings and our need for healing and wholeness, as did the woman with the issue of blood. We pray for the wherewithal to move through and in spite of the opinions of others, that we might reach out to you and receive that which is needed. There are times when we are too mindful of public opinion, convention, and restrictions. Help us to gain the boldness that we need to make a difference, not only in our own lives but in the lives of your people. And then, when it has been said and done, remind us to praise you and not ourselves.

(Morning)
I thank you for boldly standing on the side of justice and righteousness.
(Prayers of Intercession)

(Evening)
Thank you for modeling behavior that is acceptable.
(Prayers of Intercession)

Courageously trust in God, knowing that God ever cares for you and desires your well-being.

(Morning)
Remove my fears and my timidity that I might stand with you and act on your behalf. Amen.

(Evening)
Bless me that I may be a blessing and further your work here on earth. Amen.

MONDAY, JUNE 30
(Read Mark 6:1–13)

(Morning)
O God, who sent Jesus to teach in his hometown synagogue, unsettle my tendency to want things to remain as they are and to reject those who speak your Word in my presence.

(Evening)
O God, who sent Jesus to teach in his hometown synagogue, let me be disturbed at my own unbelief, which was so evident in my unwillingness to speak your name among friends and strangers today.

Astounder of the sitters in comfortable pews, may I not be like the people of the synagogue at Nazareth, the wavering disciples, and Jesus' querulous family. May I not be like those who cannot handle the amazing words of grace that come from the mouth of your Child. Help me to cast out the demons of racism, sexism, and division and be a voice for unity in our cities.

(Morning)
When the opportunity presents itself today, may I speak for you, O God, even if others take offense at my words.
(Prayers of Intercession)

(Evening)
Did I speak a word today that led people to think I uttered wisdom, O God?
(Prayers of Intercession)

Sing or read "Won't You Let Me Be Your Servant."

(Morning)
O God, whose Child, Jesus, said we would do greater things than he, may I do deeds of power today. Amen.

(Evening)
Forgive the rejection of others that I perpetrated today by not seeing you in them. May I rest knowing that you alone will never reject me or anyone else in this world. Amen.

TUESDAY, JULY 1
(Read 2 Samuel 5:1–5, 9–10)

(Morning)
Anointing God, anoint my ears, my eyes, and my lips today, that I may hear your voice, see you in others, and speak good words for you.

(Evening)
Anointing God, may I remember tonight the good words I spoke, confess the bad words, and be assured of your hand upon me.

God of the tribes of Israel who anointed David king, may your strengthening hand be with me as it was with David, who served you faithfully yet failed you miserably; and who to the end of his life was still your anointed, despite his sins. I ask, O God, that the leaders of this country and of all the world know that they can be anointed by you, learn your ways, and staunchly do what you have set before us for the good of all humanity. May I keep the promises I have made and be faithful to the covenants that you have made with all people.

(Morning)
May I know all people as my bone and flesh today.
(Prayers of Intercession)

(Evening)
Dear God, what things did I do this day that broke my promise to you?
(Prayers of Intercession)

Sing or read aloud "O for a Thousand Tongues to Sing."

(Morning)
As I go as one anointed to be among your people. May I speak and act for loving justice. Amen.

(Evening)
I know, O God, that tonight my bed is a refuge, and I seek your blessing in my sleep, that I may rise tomorrow anointed by the peace you give me. Amen.

WEDNESDAY, JULY 2
(Read 2 Corinthians 12:2–10)

(Morning)
Granter of visions and thorns, may my past experiences of your presence be daily, living reminders of your vigor in my life.

(Evening)
Granter of visions and thorns, may I be solaced in coping with thorns in my flesh, and may this night be a healing time for me.

O God, whose omnipotence humbles us in our boasting, I yearn that my life may not become so preoccupied in bragging about my accomplishments and my deeds done in your name, that I foil the possibilities to be an effective witness for you. At the same time, may I not become so despondent about my weaknesses that I am rendered incapable of fulfilling all that I can do to love my neighbors. I know that as I live in the way of Jesus' weakness I am strong. May weaknesses, insults, hardships, persecutions, and calamities—to me, to my friends, and to all people—work for good.

(Morning)
Do not let me become an insufferable boaster or complainer this day, O God.
(Prayers of Intercession)

(Evening)
I thank you for the times today I focused on others and not my own problems.
(Prayers of Intercession)

Sing or read aloud "Come O Fount of Every Blessing."

(Morning)
May I not become too elated today. Help me to discover that I have thorns that I have not realized. Amen.

(Evening)
May tonight be a time when my own flesh is restored, and may my dreams be filled with vision of paradise. Amen.

THURSDAY, JULY 3
(Read Ezekiel 2:1–5)

(Morning)
Sender of prophets to rebellious people, stand me on my feet and stand before me as I speak truth to power in my nation.

(Evening)
Sender of prophets to rebellious people, may I know when I sleep that your Spirit goads me whether awake or asleep.

O God, who stood Ezekiel up on his feet and sent him to the people of Israel, send prophets to us in our nation. We know we are a rebellious people and use your name to defend violence. We fail to see how what we do hurts poor people in other countries struggling with their own rebellions. We need you to confound our impudence and stubbornness. As I watch fireworks tonight and celebrate our nation's independence tomorrow, may it be your spirit that enters into me. May I not be dismayed but hopeful that we will be a people of God in this country.

(Morning)
May I hear the prophetic words that may be spoken in my presence today.
(Prayers of Intercession)

(Evening)
May the martial exuberance of fireworks tonight in our nation turn us from violence as a way to resolve differences.
(Prayers of Intercession)

Sing or read aloud "We Would Be Building."

(Morning)
May I not be afraid of any briers and thorns that may come to me today because I try to be your prophet. Amen.

(Evening)
Prepare me for the gatherings, events, and parties that will be part of my holiday tomorrow. Amen.

FRIDAY, JULY 4
(Read Psalm 48)

(Morning)
O God of the earth and skies, how beautiful for spacious skies, amber waves of grain, and the majesty of purple mountains is this nation among nations.

(Evening)
O God of the earth and skies, may my evening be a time of quiet recognition that you are the God of our country, forever and ever.

I ponder your steadfast love in our world, O God. You who set before your people in Jerusalem a place to honor your name. As I go about my country and look at the homes that line the streets; ride the subways or fly the airways; squint at the gleaming alabaster cities; admire the gothic cathedrals and country churches; drive the interstate highways, the back roads, and the festering city streets, O God, may I never forget that all this is yours. And may I honor your name by telling all generations that we can be a city set upon a hill when we trust you.

(Morning)
May I know myself as a citizen of the people of the covenant brought out of Egypt.
(Prayers of Intercession)

(Evening)
God, help me to remember and confess the times I forgot you, your ways, and did not do justice to your justice.
(Prayers of Intercession)

Sing or read aloud "America the Beautiful."

(Morning)
May every word I speak today be a word of steadfastness, love, and strong testimony to your justice in our nation.
Amen.

(Evening)
May I sleep tonight certain that you are the God of all people everywhere.
Amen.

SATURDAY, JULY 5
(Read Psalm 123)

(Morning)
My eyes look to you, O Sovereign God, for you regard the low estate of your people, especially those who bear the scorn of the proud and the wealthy.

(Evening)
My eyes look to you, O Sovereign God, so that when I retire tonight I may know that your mercy has been with me and upon the millions of your people who suffer and are held contemptible by the rich.

Merciful God, may I be an instrument of mercy in this world, where too many people look to the hands of their masters and mistresses for whatever aid they may deign to give out. May all people be able to live out their own lives with dignity, freed from dependence on the relief of the powerful and mighty. May our nation be a gracious people, merciful in our dealings with the world and open to the independence of others.

(Morning)
May I be an agent today to affirm the dignity of poor people
and people held in contempt.
(Prayers of Intercession)

(Evening)
Cleanse me of the contemptible ways in which I behaved today
by putting others down.
(Prayers of Intercession)

Sing or read aloud "In Christ There Is No East or West."

(Morning)
I lift up my eyes, O you who are enthroned in the heavens! Amen.

(Evening)
May your mercy rest upon me and upon all who seek to be at peace this night.
Amen.

SUNDAY, JULY 6
(Read Mark 6:1–13)

(Morning)
Sender of your servants into the world, send me into the world with a consuming mission to call people to repentance.

(Evening)
Sender of your servants into the world, help me to sleep this night in the peace of knowing that I am trying to live a repentant life.

Provider of all I need to take into my life. Wherever I go in this world, whether into the city or countryside, may I go as one sent upon a mission by Jesus himself to preach repentance and to cast out the demons that infest our spirits and our society. May I go without feeling the necessity to avail myself of all of the accoutrements of success, such as expensive electronic devices, lavish meals, large grants, and posh churches. Instead may I meet people face to face and speak a loving word of faith that can cast out the tormenting demons, the unclean spirits, and heal those who are sick.

(Morning)
Prepare me this day for the times when people will reject me when I try to speak for you and be a disciple of Christ Jesus.
(Prayers of Intercession)

(Evening)
If I slammed a door in the face of someone today who tried to reach out to me, forgive me.
(Prayers of Intercession)

Sing or read aloud "Just as I Am without One Plea."

(Morning)
May I be willing to risk the displeasure of those who reject your Word. May I shake the dust off my feet and never quit because of rejection. Amen.

(Evening)
God of healing and controller of demons, be with me tonight, that I may rest assured that there are many in this world sent on a mission to proclaim your way. Amen.

MONDAY, JULY 7
(Read 2 Samuel 6:1–5)

(Morning)
Lifegiver, for this new day and the promise it holds, I praise you.

(Evening)
Lifegiver, I give thanks to you, Holy One, for the sounds and the movements of your Spirit this day.

I give thanks for your Word and listen for your guidance. Dancing mightily before you, God, the people of Israel brought the ark to Jerusalem. Joyous was the music they offered as your gathered community. Teach me to dance and sing, mightily, your praises each day, that all whom I encounter may catch a glimpse of the joy it is to be yours.

(Morning)
I pray this morning for my family, myself, and the needs of others.
(Prayers of Intercession)

(Evening)
Much has happened today. Be with me as I reflect on the ways I used the voice you have given me and pray for those who join with me in the intimate dance of life.
(Prayers of Intercession)

And now with a song in my heart, I pray.
(Pray the Prayer of Our Savior.)

(Morning)
May your song and dance guide me throughout this day. In your name. Amen.

(Evening)
Grant my body, mind, and soul rest and restoration. In your name. Amen.

TUESDAY, JULY 8
(Read 2 Samuel 12b–19)

(Morning)
God of all blessings, I joyously arise to a new day, a gift from you.

(Evening)
God of all blessings, I have been blessed this day by your abundant love
and am ready to rest in you.

I give thanks for your Word and listen for your guidance. Blessings where showered on those who honored you, God, while your anger was visited upon the one who was anxious to possess you. It is so tempting to want to keep you to myself, as if I could. Show me the way to receive your love and share it with others, so that we all may know your blessings.

(Morning)
This brand new day, I lift in prayer those in special need of your blessing.
(Prayers of Intercession)

(Evening)
I give thanks for the wonders experienced this day and pray for those
who cannot recognize the blessings of life.
(Prayers of Intercession)

Assured of your love for all your children, I pray.
(Pray the Prayer of Our Savior.)

(Morning)
May my thoughts, words, actions, and deeds this day serve to express the blessings you have given me. In your name. Amen.

(Evening)
Bless me with peace as I sleep. In your name. Amen.

WEDNESDAY, JULY 9
(Read Ephesians 1:3–14)

(Morning)
Loving Parent, what joy it is to awake as your chosen child to this new day.

(Evening)
Loving Parent, with peace I come to the close of this day knowing whose I am.

I give thanks for your Word and listen for your guidance. As a tender father and a nurturing mother, you have chosen me to be your child. Through the life, death, and resurrection of my brother, Jesus, you have adopted me into your family, that I may share in the riches of Christ's glorious inheritance. I can be an ungrateful and spoiled child. Forgive me when I am tempted to squander the abundance of my inheritance by seeking my will rather than yours. Mark me with the seal of your Holy Spirit, that I may always know to whom I belong.

(Morning)
Before the rush of the day, I pause to pray for these personal needs and the needs of others . . .
(Prayers of Intercession)

(Evening)
Hear me as I give thanks for all that has taken place this day and pray for my sisters and brothers in Christ.
(Prayers of Intercession)

Knowing that I am yours, I pray.
(Pray the Prayer of Our Savior.)

(Morning)
Send me now, as your own, into this new day. In your name. Amen.

(Evening)
And now I rest in the promise of my inheritance obtained through Christ. In your name. Amen.

THURSDAY, JULY 10
(Read Amos 7:7–15)

(Morning)
Justice Seeker, thank you for the rest of the night and the opportunities
of a new day.

(Evening)
Justice Seeker, weary from a day of seeking, may I receive rest
and refuge in you tonight.

I give thanks for your Word and listen for your guidance. You called Amos away from his flock to be a prophet to your people Israel. They refused to hear and to heed your call to justice. In your anger, you separated the people from their comfort, their land, their families, their very lives. Yet in the unfathomable power of your forgiveness, you restored the fortunes of your people. Break open my ears, my heart, and my lips that I may hear, embody, and shout your call to be a justice seeker.

(Morning)
I pray this morning for my personal needs and the needs of all
who thirst for justice.
(Prayers of Intercession)

(Evening)
As I reflect on my thoughts, words, and deeds this day, sit with me.
Hear my prayers for those with whom I have been just and unjust today.
(Prayers of Intercession)

Embolden me to seek the way of righteousness as I pray.
(Pray the Prayer of Our Savior.)

(Morning)
Guide me along the path of justice today, I pray in your name. Amen.

(Evening)
Blessed are you, God of justice. May I rest in your peace tonight. In your name. Amen.

FRIDAY, JULY 11
(Read Mark 6:14–29)

(Morning)
O Just One, the ways of life and death are set before me once again.

(Evening)
O Just One, I come to the end of the day in continuing need of your guidance.

I give thanks for your Word and listen for your guidance. The words of judgment you spoke through John the Baptizer angered and perplexed Herod. Yet Herod protected John from those who would harm him, for he knew John was a righteous and holy man. John's death came as a result of Herod's misguided regard for his oath. Be with me, God, when the demands of family, friends, and colleagues, mixed with my own pride, threaten to override my best judgment. Give me strength to discern and follow your will in choosing life over death.

(Morning)
This morning, I pray for family, friends, and colleagues.
(Prayers of Intercession)

(Evening)
I ask your special presence, God, as I review the choices made this day
and pray for the needs of acquaintances and strangers.
(Prayers of Intercession)

As your forgiven child, I pray.
(Pray the Prayer of Our Savior.)

(Morning)
I go into this day confident that you will guide me in your way. In your name. Amen.

(Evening)
Now may I sleep enfolded in your embrace. In your name. Amen.

SATURDAY, JULY 12
(Read Psalm 85:8–13)

(Morning)
Bountiful Provider, how good it is to greet this new day in a place called home.

(Evening)
Bountiful Provider, restoring God, it is time to seek rest in you.

I give thanks for your Word and listen for your guidance. How often, O God, have you forgiven me and my forebears and restored us again to a new place. You set your vision before us. Love and faithfulness, righteousness and peace come together in your shower of salvation. Once again there is a cry for restoration ringing throughout the land. I stand among your people in need of forgiveness. Let your word of peace be heard. You give what is good, so our land and lives may overflow with blessings.

(Morning)
I pray for those who are homeless, the church, and myself.
(Prayers of Intercession)

(Evening)
Help me to learn from today's encounters to be more loving tomorrow.
I pray for those close to me and those still far away.
(Prayers of Intercession)

With renewed hope in your salvation, I pray.
(Pray the Prayer of Our Savior.)

(Morning)
Being restored, send me out to live and share your vision this day. In your name. Amen.

(Evening)
I sleep with gratitude in your comfortable embrace. In your name. Amen.

SUNDAY, JULY 13
(Read Psalm 24)

(Morning)
Creator God, I awake with the joy of being part of your creation.

(Evening)
Creator God, I settle into the quiet of your night.

I give thanks for your Word and listen for your guidance. How vast and wondrous, O God, is the cosmos you have brought into being. All of creation is yours and sings your praises. Help me to seek that which is true when I am tempted toward falsehood. May I be granted clean hands and a pure heart so your blessing will rest upon me.

(Morning)
Seeking your face, I pray for the needs of others and myself.
(Prayers of Intercession)

(Evening)
Show me where I was false today and hear my prayers for family, friends, and colleagues, and these special needs . . .
(Prayers of Intercession)

As a grateful member of your family, I pray.
(Pray the Prayer of Our Savior.)

(Morning)
Come into my life this day and send me out to serve. In your name. Amen.

(Evening)
Shine your face upon me and let me rest with peace. In your name. Amen.

MONDAY, JULY 14
(Read 2 Samuel 7:1–14a)

(Morning)
O God, builder of houses, I awake eager to rush off and accomplish today's tasks; but this morning, I pray, bring me around to face you even more eagerly.

(Evening)
O God, builder of houses, thank you for helping me make my day a great one.

God, I also want to build you a house like King David's. A house in which to hold you; a place to which I can retreat and know that you are there. Quickly I would begin, but you take my impulses and turn me around with your words to King David: "I will build a house for you and for all my people. I will make your name great." You stopped David as you stop me now with such promises and big dreams. I would not have hoped this much, but you show me your own eagerness to build me up.

(Morning)
As I begin this day, I pray especially for those who rush into it,
thinking only of what they can do.
(Prayers of Intercession)

(Evening)
As evening winds down, I see how much you accomplish, O God.
(Prayers of Intercession)

Truly, it is not what I can do for you, God, but what you can do for me.

(Morning)
Send me out, God, to build with you,
not for you. Amen.

(Evening)
Let me rest in your house, O God.
Amen.

TUESDAY, JULY 15
(Read Psalm 89:20–37)

(Morning)
God, your love follows me throughout this day. Help me follow you.

(Evening)
God, you are my rock. You help me endure and last. You honor me,
when I thought it was I who was to give to you. Thank you, God, for such life.
Show me how to be a rock to others.

O Rock of Salvation, you make me strong. You support me and stop those who would harm me. With oil you anoint me and lift me up, when I would lie hunched over and afraid. As your hand reached out to King David to exalt him, you stand ready—vigilant—to bring me to your love and to your heights, where I, too, will be established; where I, too, will last when I had feared I only would pass away.

(Morning)
In all that I do today, let me carry on your work.
(Prayers of Intercession)

(Evening)
Thank you, God, for a day filled with your love and promise.
I especially remember . . .
(Prayers of Intercession)

Call out to me, God, when I forget you and remind me of your promises, so that I will cling to these and not to the gray, shifting shapes of struggles.

(Morning)
I bring before you all those who need your rocklike strength. Amen.

(Evening)
You are my rock on whom I lay down to rest. Thank you for such peace. Amen.

WEDNESDAY, JULY 16
(Read Jeremiah 23:1–6)

(Morning)
God of safety, I have not seen how I can be safe in you,
but I know this is what I want.

(Evening)
God of safety, thank you for keeping me safe this day in all these ways . . .

When I feel safe in you, God, then I can guide my children even when they resist. When I feel safe in you, God, then I can feel pain at the war in Bosnia, the killings in our cities, the decline in jobs. When I feel safe in you, God, then I can stand up for what is right—at home, work, church, my community, even when everything around me tries to distract or tear apart. When I feel safe in you, God, then I can lead others to you instead of scattering them and leaving them alone to fight overwhelming battles. When I feel safe in you, God, then I can come back again and again to hear your words of comfort and challenge.

(Morning)
God, help me to feel safe in you.
(Prayers of Intercession)

(Evening)
I feel safe in you, God, yet even more aware of the ways
in which I still am scattered and therefore disperse others.
(Prayers of Intercession)

When I feel safe in you, God, then I can hope that together we all can build a better world.

(Morning)
Send me out safe in you, able to care for others as you care for me. Amen.

(Evening)
I lie down to rest in your safety, God. Thank you for receiving me. Amen.

THURSDAY, JULY 17
(Read Psalm 23)

(Morning)
Christ Jesus, I awake already not feeling well; the knot in my stomach, the pain in my head.

(Evening)
Christ Jesus, we praise you for this day, your day, a new day of breathing with you.

Weakened and drained I come to you, Christ Jesus. You are the only one who can help. Your hand caresses my head, resting in your lap. I let go into your care. As on a gentle sea I drift, buoyant and upheld by you. All my worries, all my concerns float away from me. All that is left inside of me is your name. Your beautiful name, Jesus. I breathe in JE and breathe out SUS: Je-sus, Je-sus, Je-sus. How still I feel, yet oh so awake. My breath breathes Je-sus; my heart beats Je-sus; my voice speaks Je-sus; over and over, Je-sus.

(Morning)
Slowly I feel myself able to greet the day, your day, Jesus.
A day of breathing you in and breathing you out.
(Prayers of Intercession)

(Evening)
I pray for all those who are weakened and drained.
May they feel you lifting them up above their worries.
(Prayers of Intercession)

You fill my empty spaces, and I overflow with your love for me. Thank you, Christ Jesus, thank you. Praise you, God, praise you.

(Morning)
May my breath become one with yours, Jesus. Amen.

(Evening)
Good night, Jesus. In my sleep may I breathe you in and breathe you out, so that I may rise with you on my mind and in my heart. Amen.

FRIDAY, JULY 18
(Read Ephesians 2:11–22)

(Morning)
O Body of Christ, I awake and see you so wonderfully made. I praise you.

(Evening)
O Body of Christ, I return to you, humbled by the challenges
of changing my habits.

Often have I heard your words, O God, that you dwell within me and all others, turning our simple, human bodies into your marvelous temple. But these words of truth have remained just that—words. Yet now, you ask me, as you asked the Gentiles, to live out your words and become your temple. Immediately, I see a wall within me, standing straight and strong. "Me? A temple of your Spirit? How can I be?" To be a temple, I cannot live the way I am: working too many hours, eating unhealthy food, not exercising, wasting time watching TV. "Your temple? Far from it." I am an alien in this holy body you have given me. I forget I belong to your household.

(Morning)
My God, my God, already I see how difficult my work will be—these habits rest
hard and sure, layer upon layer. Help me.
(Prayers of Intercession)

(Evening)
I want to give up trying, but even more I want to give back to you, O Christ.
(Prayers of Intercession)

Knock down this wall inside me, O Christ. Show me how to take away the bricks, one by one, so that I may be your temple and you may be—finally— my God.

(Morning)
Send me out with the grace and the will
to be your temple. Amen.

(Evening)
Thank you, Christ, for your love. It will
help me rise anew tomorrow. Amen.

SATURDAY, JULY 19
(Read Mark 6:30–34)

(Morning)
God, I wake up, but I would rather sleep.

(Evening)
God, another long day—a day of giving to others the little I have inside.

"Come with me by yourself to a quiet place and get some rest." How wonderful it is, O God, for you to invite us to rest. Like Jesus' disciples, I, too, find myself coming and going with so many demands on me. Eagerly, I come away from these unending tasks and look only to the simple, single task of rest. But it is not so simple. My mind races away with thousands of details: projects unfinished, people wanting my attention, books I would love to read, friends I haven't seen, and the fear—they will all be here when I return. I settle into the details of rest. My lungs gulp in air five times and crash over in waves of yawns, over and over. They roll through me as if a storm had been gathering and now can let go; and then, before the yawns can even subside, the tasks break in.

(Morning)
Christ Jesus, when I am tired, help me be compassionate with others.
(Prayers of Intercession)

(Evening)
Teach me to rest enough in you so that I overflow with your love.
(Prayers of Intercession)

How could you go on Jesus, when you were still tired?

(Morning)
Show me places of rest in the midst of my busy day. Amen.

(Evening)
Thank you, for this time of rest. I give myself back to you. Amen.

SUNDAY, JULY 20
(Read Mark 6:53–56)

(Morning)
Christ Jesus, healer of all, I awake with a yearning for you.

(Evening)
Christ Jesus, healer of all, I thank you for beginning to heal me.
At first, I wanted to be transformed immediately—made new, with no traces of pain. But now I see that your healing completes itself when I participate.

"And all who touched him were healed." At Gennesaret, sick people ran or were carried to you. They begged and begged you for what they most needed. What a gift, Jesus, to beg. What a gift, Jesus, to ask for what we most need. But what is that? What do I need? Heal me, Jesus, of too much busyness so that I can give my time to you. Heal me, Jesus, of working only to survive so that I can work, instead of thrive. Heal me, Jesus, of resenting people when they ask for help, so that I may serve you through others.

(Morning)
Heal me, Jesus, and all the others who languish in pain. Let us feel you touching our sickness and drawing away its power.
(Prayers of Intercession)

(Evening)
Your love is so great that it flows over us, whether we are healthy or sick.
I give thanks for your love.
(Prayers of Intercession)

Heal me, Jesus, of my tiredness, so that I can feel again that wondrous joy in you.

(Morning)
Send me out with this simple prayer: "Jesus heal me." Amen.

(Evening)
May I rest in your healing power and embrace sleep as that place where health comes alive. In your healing love, I am yours, Christ Jesus. Amen.

MONDAY, JULY 21
(Read Psalm 14 and 2 Samuel 11:1–15)

(Morning)
O God, who knows me through and through, I give you thanks for the chance to greet another day. Stay as close to me as my breath, O God, filling me with your love.

(Evening)
O God, who knows me through and through, thank you for your love living in me today and for your forgiveness if I have betrayed that love in any way.

I am grateful for your Word which illumines my life. By your Spirit, help me to see how David's story connects with my story. God, it would be easy for me to point the finger at David and not recognize my own self-serving desires. After all, I have never plotted to kill someone! Yet, like David, I too want what I want when I want it. I know that Jesus taught us that self-centered thinking can destroy us. I know that even if I don't act on my egocentric desires, just harboring them is enough to separate me from myself, from others, and from you. Forgive me, God. Live in me, and accomplish your purpose even through me, I pray.

(Morning)
Hear me, O faithful God, as I bring before you the concerns I feel as I approach this day.
(Prayers of Intercession)

(Evening)
I pray for forgiveness as I remember those times I love less than I could have today . . . and I pray for those in need this night . . .
(Prayers of Intercession)

"You are my God; I have no good apart from you" (Psalm 16).

(Morning)
May the spirit of Christ flow through me today so that all whom I meet might be touched by love. Amen.

(Evening)
Grant me a restful night held, by your loving embrace. Amen.

TUESDAY, JULY 22
(Read Psalm 145:10–18 and 2 Kings 4:42–44)

(Morning)
God of abundance, you are the giver of all good things.
May I be clothed in gratitude this day.

(Evening)
God of abundance, for all the unexpected ways you provided for me this day,
my heart is grateful.

Open my heart to receive your Word. Open my eyes that I not miss the miracle of your Word becoming flesh today. Dear God, forgive me my failure of imagination each time I say with disbelief, "How can I . . . ?" You are able to do so much more than we can ever conceive or envision. Scarcity does not exist for you. Cast out my fears that I won't have enough money, love, prestige, ideas, time, or whatever. Give me the trust of Elisha, who was able to say, "Give it away and see what God will do." Help me remember that because of you, abundant giver, there will always be more than enough if we but share our resources, our power, ourselves.

(Morning)
Today will bring many unexpected challenges. Be with these people
for whom I pray . . . Enliven my imagination to face the surprises of the day
with your creative love.
(Prayers of Intercession)

(Evening)
What a day you have given me, O God! I rejoice in the ways I saw your abundant
love in action today. Continue to bless those who are in need this night.
(Prayers of Intercession)

Glory to you, O God, who are able to do far more than we can ask or imagine!

(Morning)
May I be surprised by joy and
participate in the sharing of your love
throughout the day. Amen.

(Evening)
Let me rest secure this night, blanketed
by your lavish love. Amen.

WEDNESDAY, JULY 23
(Read Psalm 145:10–18)

(Morning)
Great and good God, my heart rejoices when I think of you this morning.
May an attitude of gratitude fill my being every waking hour.

(Evening)
Great and good God, everywhere and in all things I saw your workings today.
As I prepare to sleep, I overflow with thanksgiving for your loving kindness.

The psalmist sings of your wondrous goodness. Help me to praise you with all that I am. In the early church, candidates for baptism would often dance their way to the baptistery. Jerome called such dancing "spiritual applause." I feel like dancing, like giving you applause, O Gracious Giver. You give us your Word of truth, which can be trusted. You never turn away when we call. If we feel ourselves falling, there you are with outstretched hands to catch us and lift us up again. How can we respond to such constant care and steadfast compassion? We must join the dance of overflowing love!

(Morning)
I begin this new morning by thanking you for . . . May my life be a dance
of praise to you this day.
(Prayers of Intercession)

(Evening)
As I review the day, my heart is especially grateful for . . . Because you promise
to be near to those who call on you, please draw especially close to . . .
(Prayers of Intercession)

**I recall the precept from Hebrew tradition: "When you pray,
do so with all your heart, and all your bones."**

(Morning)
Wherever I find myself today, may my body, soul, and mind be a testimony to your great goodness. Amen.

(Evening)
As my lips now fall silent for the evening and my body is at rest, still may I praise you in peaceful sleep. Amen.

THURSDAY, JULY 24
(Read Psalm 145:10–13 and Ephesians 3:14–21)

(Morning)
Root of every living thing, upon arising I greet you with an openness to receive whatever the day will bring.

(Evening)
Root of every living thing, as the shadows lengthen into night, I am reminded of the mysterious ways that you are at work when we are awake or asleep.

Your love is so vast, O God, there is no way for me to comprehend it. I want to be a part of your plan to extend your love to all people, but I cannot do it without Christ living in me. So come, O Christ, and root me deep in the soil of your love. Ground me in grace, that I might not wither but bear the fruit of your mercy and peace wherever I am planted.

(Morning)
O Fullness of Life, I pray for others who especially need you to work in their lives this day.
(Prayers of Intercession)

(Evening)
Thank you for the presence of your Spirit today, for all the miracles of your grace.
(Prayers of Intercession)

Hildegard of Bingen reminds us that "the soul is kissed by God in its innermost regions."

(Morning)
Who knows what will happen today, O God? May Christ live in me today, so that wherever I am, love will be at work in all that I do. Amen.

(Evening)
May the Spirit of God who dwells within, grace me with the gift of restoring sleep this night. Amen.

FRIDAY, JULY 25
(Read Psalm 145:14–18 and Ephesians 3:14–21)

(Morning)
Source of all life, write your love upon my heart this morning, that I might be a message of healing love for others throughout the day.

(Evening)
Source of all life, the starlit sky helps me remember the many ways I saw your light shining today. Thank you.

The world is torn apart: nation against nation; race against race; class against class; person against person. Ideologies rage. Our inner beings are conflicted. Chaos reigns. Yet your design, O God, is that we all be one in your limitless love. How can the world know of your plan unless we embody it? Come, O Christ, and live in us and in the life of your church. May the fullness of your love begin in me.

(Morning)
O God, by your wisdom, the gates of the morning are opened.
Open my heart to extend your grace to all whom I will meet today.
Hear my prayers for a broken world.
(Prayers of Intercession)

(Evening)
Ruler of all, by whose Word the shadows of evening fall,
help me to release the burdens of this day.
(Prayers of Intercession)

"If I can keep one spirit singing, I shall not live in vain" (Emily Dickinson).

(Morning)
Take the life I lead today and let good come of it. Amen.

(Evening)
Take my life this night and re-create it in Christ. Amen.

SATURDAY, JULY 26
(Read Psalm 145:14–18 and John 6:1–14)

(Morning)
Generous God, your abundant grace makes every morning new.
Take what I can offer this day and multiply it by your love.

(Evening)
Generous God, as I review the day, hear my thanks for the ways in which
you fashioned all that was needed from whatever was offered.

There are so many needs in the world, O God. How overwhelmed I can become, and say, like Philip, "There's not much I can do." Help me to be more like Andrew and look for material with which you can make a miracle. All things are possible with you. But I forget. Reaffirm in me that you need whatever I can bring. It may not be much, but help me lay before you all that I am and all that I have. And help me to know that it is enough.

(Morning)
O miracle-working God, your touch makes this world holy. I pray this morning
for the wholeness of creation and the wounds of the world.
(Prayers of Intercession)

(Evening)
As the hush of evening stills my soul, I think of the day and ask your forgiveness
for any opportunities I may have missed to share your abundant goodness.
I pray also for those with special concerns.
(Prayers of Intercession)

"Blessed are you, O Sovereign God, ruler of the universe, For you give us food to sustain our lives and make our hearts glad" (Jewish blessing).

(Morning)
O Christ, as you took, blessed, and gave the loaves and fishes, now take and give me to be a blessing that others may recognize your love. Amen.

(Evening)
For your grace and generosity this day, I give you thanks. May I be attentive to your miracles, even in my dreams.
Amen.

SUNDAY, JULY 27
(Read Psalm 145:15–21 and John 6:15–21)

(Morning)
God of good surprises, on this the Sabbath day, open my eyes to see your wonder-working ways.

(Evening)
God of good surprises, thank you for all the ways you were present with me today, bringing me unharmed to night's beginning.

Gracious God, how often you come to me saying, "It is I; do not be afraid." And yet I recoil to the self-made prison of my own fears. Bound by worries of all kinds, I lash out at others or build up barriers to protect myself. In Christ you offer us your perfect love, the antidote to our fear. Help me realize that, like the disciples in the boat, I will arrive safely where I am supposed to be by acknowledging your presence and living in your love.

(Morning)
Be with me today, guide me along the way of Christ. Hear me as I pray for others, especially those held captive by fears, real or only imagined.
(Prayers of Intercession)

(Evening)
You have led me safely through the day. Forgive my anxious moments and continue to teach me to trust my life to you. Bless those this night who are in any kind of danger or trouble.
(Prayers of Intercession)

"Jesus, Savior, pilot me over life's tempestuous sea" (Edward Hopper).

(Morning)
Steer my path by your presence and promise of hope. Help me to relinquish my fears and live freely in your perfect love. Amen.

(Evening)
O Christ, I release to you all anxiety and ask you to cradle me this night with your peaceful presence. Amen.

MONDAY, JULY 28
(Read Psalm 51:1–9)

(Morning)
God, we pray, "Come you disconsolate, wherever you languish;
Come to the mercy seat, fervently kneel."

(Evening)
God, we pray, "Pass me not, O gentle Savior, hear my humble cry" this night.

O God, David experienced agony in his soul as he struggled with his sinful nature and turned to you for relief. This psalm places before us the gift of languishing in your silent presence. The apostle Paul reminds us that when we are weak, then you can be strong in us. The experience of struggle and languish can be good for us, emotionally and spiritually as those experiences teach us the meaning of patience and strengthen our reliance upon you. Let us remember that today's unanswered prayer can be tomorrow's blessing in our spiritual growth.

(Morning)
"Here bring your wounded hearts. Here tell your anguish;
earth has no sorrow that heaven cannot heal."
(Prayers of Intercession)

(Evening)
"While on others you are calling, do not pass me by."
(Prayers of Intercession)

Fervently I pray.
(Pray the Prayer of Our Savior.)

(Morning)
God, help me to experience the strength that comes through my struggles with people and issues today. Amen.

(Evening)
O God, when I am too afflicted, comfort me, and when I am too comfortable, afflict me. Amen.

TUESDAY, JULY 29
(Read Psalm 78:23–29)

(Morning)
God of glory, morning by morning I am moved by your faithfulness.
Because of this, I am merciful.

(Evening)
God of glory, you have been so good to me today. I don't serve you as I should;
I don't deserve all of your good, but you are so good to me.

O God, the psalmist in these verses of praise through remembrance assures us that you, our creator and provider, are always faithful to us, even when we are unfaithful to you. The psalmist recalls how you fed the people of Israel abundantly when they were in the wilderness, even though at times they displayed a lack of trust and faith in you. Today we are reminded that our faith connection with you lives through memory and hope. Remembering what you have done for us gives us reason to rejoice as we live this present moment. The spiritual act of remembering also gives us the hope we need for the future. We can live today with sure and certain hope because we have memories of how you brought us through all the yesterdays of our lives.

(Morning)
God, help me to live today with hope, remembering how your faithfulness
helped me yesterday.
(Prayers of Intercession)

(Evening)
Creator God, I thank you for the gifts of memory.
(Prayers of Intercession)

Hallowed be your name.

(Morning)
God, you have provided all that I have needed. Amen.

(Evening)
Creator God, I thank you for the gifts of memory and hope which sustain and strengthen my faith and life every day. Amen.

WEDNESDAY, JULY 30
(Read Ephesians 4:1–16)

(Morning)
God, "I have made my vow to you, and I never will turn back."

(Evening)
God, "great day, great day, the righteous is marching."

The apostle Paul defines the vision of unity in the community between all your people through Jesus Christ. That unity is both a present and future reality of our maturing faith in our Savior. God, Christ Jesus has given us different gifts: some are apostles, some prophets, some evangelists, some pastors, and some teachers. The apostle Paul reminds us that Christ Jesus makes no distinction between the gifts as being greater or lesser. All gifts are essential for equipping the saints and unifying your church. Let us use our different gifts to fulfill the prayer of Jesus—that they may all be one.

(Morning)
"I will go, I shall go, to see what the end will be."
(Prayers of Intercession)

(Evening)
"Great day, God's going to build up Zion's walls."
(Prayers of Intercession)

. . . Your dominion come . . .

(Morning)
God, may the gifts you gave me be used to bring healing and unity in all my relationships. Amen.

(Evening)
God, I thank you for the way other people used their gifts to support me today. Amen.

THURSDAY, JULY 31
(Read Psalm 51:10–12)

(Morning)
God, may your Spirit fall afresh on me this day.

(Evening)
God, your grace and mercy have brought me through today,
and because of you, I am living this moment.

Our spiritual approach for today and every day is to seek to do your will in word and deed. Sometimes that is difficult to do by our own strength and wit. But with you, O God, we know that all things are possible! The psalmist tells us to forget about yesterday and focus today on where you are leading us. We can't do your will without your sustaining and strengthening power and presence with us. Our family and work responsibilities can be met if we approach them with you as our copilot. Our consciousness of your presence is like breathing—natural and essential to sustain life.

(Morning)
God, make me in your image and fill me with your Spirit.
(Prayers of Intercession)

(Evening)
God, I praise you and thank you. Your grace and mercy have sustained me.
(Prayers of Intercession)

. . . Your will be done . . .

(Morning)
God, there is nothing that's going to happen today that you and I can't handle together. Amen.

(Evening)
God, I am not what you want me to be.
God, I am not all that I am going to be.
But thank you, God, I am not what I used to be. Amen.

FRIDAY, AUGUST 1
(Read John 6:24–35)

(Morning)
God, "I woke up this morning with my mind stayed on Jesus.
I woke up this morning with my mind stayed on Jesus."

(Evening)
God, all is ready for your people to join the feast, for the table now is spread.

This passage in John's Gospel reminds us that we should not place our ultimate trust in the temporal realm, but on the eternal reality of you, O God, who can sustain us in this life and the next. John's words tell us that sustainable and trustworthy satisfaction can only be found in Christ Jesus, upon whom you have set your seal. Jesus is the bread of heaven who gives long-lasting, satisfying soul food. Jesus is the fountain of life, and when we believe in him we never thirst for anything. You extend to us, through Isaiah, an invitation to the spiritual banquet of life and eternal life. Jesus, who offers us life and satisfying and soul-saving power, is the bread of life.

(Morning)
"Woke up this morning with my mind stayed on Jesus.
Hallelu, Hallelu, Hallelujah."
(Prayers of Intercession)

(Evening)
"You famishing, you wary, come, and you will be richly fed."
(Prayers of Intercession)

... On earth as it is in heaven ...

(Morning)
O God, may I look to the hills from whence my help comes for satisfaction that endures beyond every situation I face today. Amen.

(Evening)
O God, I thank you for today's bread of life experiences which made Jesus real to me and others. Amen.

SATURDAY, AUGUST 2
(Read Exodus 16:2–4, 9–15)

(Morning)
Loving God, I seek your grace just to live from day to day.

(Evening)
Loving God, thank you for another day that has ended;
and for yet another day to begin.

Sometimes, through complaint, we forget how much you have blessed us. Often we want something more in our lives and our desiring causes us to lose appreciation for what we have. Our consumption-driven culture sends a strong message that more is better. Spiritually we need to struggle and resolve the existential question: "When is enough enough?" When we consider our wants and needs, we should do so knowing that you, God, are solely concerned with our needs—one day at a time. Let us shift our thoughts and prayers away from complaint and want. Instead, let us move toward a strong posture of thanksgiving to you who supply all our needs every day.

(Morning)
"I don't worry over the future, for I know what Jesus said,
and today I'll walk beside him, for he knows what is ahead."
(Prayers of Intercession)

(Evening)
"On our sleep bestowing peace and calmness, too.
Strengthened for tomorrow, praising each new day."
(Prayers of Intercession)

. . . Give us this day our daily bread . . .

(Morning)
God, please give me just one more thing, a grateful heart. Amen.

(Evening)
God, I thank you for your blessings today. Each one met my needs and reminded me that your grace is sufficient. Amen.

SUNDAY, AUGUST 3
(Read Samuel 11:26–12:13a)

(Morning)
O God, "it's me, it's me, standing in the need of prayer."

(Evening)
O God, "there is a balm in Gilead, to make the wounded whole."

"You are the person!" These words pierced David's heart when Nathan confronted him about his sin. David had plotted the killing of Uriah so that he could take Uriah's wife as his own. Before we point the finger of blame at David too quickly, let us consider our own attitudes and actions. You are also the person! I am also the person! Like David, we stand condemned before you, God, by being contrary to your will. Like David, we need to acknowledge and name our sins, seeking your forgiveness. You forgave David. You forgive us when we remember how to pray.

(Morning)
"It's me, it's me, O God, standing in the need of prayer."
(Prayers of Intercession)

(Evening)
"There is a balm in Gilead, to heal the sin-sick soul."
(Prayers of Intercession)

Forgive us our debts as we forgive our debtors, and lead us not into temptation but deliver us from evil. For yours is the dominion, the power, and the glory, forever. Amen.

(Morning)
God, help me to live without judging others too harshly or too quickly. Teach me how to show mercy, granting to others the grace and forgiveness I seek for myself. Amen.

(Evening)
God, may I sleep well with the assurance of knowing that since I have forgiven others, you have forgiven me. Amen.

MONDAY, AUGUST 4
(Read Psalm 34:7–8, 1 Kings 19:4–8, and John 6:48–50)

(Morning)
Gracious God, thank you for your steadfast love, which never forsakes us.

(Evening)
Gracious God, "I will lay me down in peace and take my rest,
for you only make me dwell in safety."

God, Elijah fled from Jezebel to Mount Horeb after having been visited by your divine help. The forty days and forty nights recall Israel's wanderings in the desert under your providential care. Through your prophet, your story climaxes when you spoke, not through the wind, earthquake, or fire, but in a still, small voice. Your grace is timeless. Thus the gap between your transcendence and our humanity is bridged!

(Morning)
Open my eyes, God, that I may see your truth. "Teach me your way . . . and lead me on a level path." Let my heart take courage.
(Prayers of Intercession)

(Evening)
Thank you, God, for the sweet relief of food and rest.
May your angels watch over me this night.
(Prayers of Intercession)

And now I pray as Jesus taught.
(Pray the Prayer of Our Savior.)

(Morning)
Sing praises, all you people. Sing praises to God. Sing praises, all you people. Sing praises to God. Amen.

(Evening)
Sing praises to God. Alleluia, alleluia!
Sing praises to God. Alleluia, alleluia!
Amen.

TUESDAY, AUGUST 5
(Read Psalm 34:4–6, 1 Kings 19:7–8, Ephesians 4:26–32, and John 6:41–52)

(Morning)
Merciful God, cast me not away from your presence,
and put a new and right spirit within me.

(Evening)
Merciful God, restore me to the joy of your salvation,
and uphold me with a willing spirit.

Creator God, I repent of my pretenses and resolve to amend my ways. Recalling your deliverance, O God, the psalmist exults in new life, testifying to others that you "hear," "save," and release those afflicted in body, mind, or estate. Just as the angel ministered to Elijah in the wilderness, the downcast can be restored through your steadfast love: "The angel of God encamps around those who fear God. . . . O taste and see that God is good!" Because we are your people, members of one another, we are admonished to "put away from you all bitterness and wrath and anger and wrangling and slander together, with all malice, and be kind to one another, tender hearted, forgiving . . . as God in Christ has forgiven you."

(Morning)
Thank you, God, for opening my eyes to the light when I had given up hope.
I will look to you and be radiant!
(Prayers of Intercession)

(Evening)
I thank you, God, for your saving help this day. Your Word has fed me.
Grant me now a peaceful sleep.
(Prayers of Intercession)

And now I pray.
(Pray the Prayer of Our Savior.)

(Morning)
Gracious Savior, banish my anger and bitterness. Create in me a clean heart, and put a new and right spirit within me. Amen.

(Evening)
Come, fill my heart with your peace.
All my hope comes from you, O God.
Amen.

WEDNESDAY, AUGUST 6
(Read Psalm 34:1–8, 1 Kings 19:4–8, and John 6:35, 41–51)

(Morning)
O God, Holy Spirit, Truth Divine, touch and fill this soul of mine.

(Evening)
O God, to you I commend my body and soul.
Watch over this house and bless my loved ones.

God, your full hand supplies our need. Your rebellious people were sent manna and quails in the wilderness. You fed Elijah and came to us in the person of Jesus Christ, the living bread. You hear our murmurings! Your very being, the Second Person of the Trinity, sustains the world eternally. Even our faith is your providential gift. Jesus gave his life for the life of the world: "I am the bread that came down from heaven . . . and the bread that I will give for the life of the world is my flesh." "O taste and see that God is good!"

(Morning)
Let us joyfully praise God, for God is kind: for God's mercies will endure,
faithful, ever sure.
(Prayers of Intercession)

(Evening)
"All things living God doth feed; God's full hand supplies their need:
Divine mercies aye endure, ever faithful, ever sure."
(Milton's paraphrase of Psalm 136, adapted)
(Prayers of Intercession)

And now, in faith, I pray for daily bread and the bread of life.
(Pray the Prayer of Our Savior.)

(Morning)
O God, hear my prayer; O God, hear my prayer. When I call, answer me. O God, hear my prayer; O God, hear my prayer. When I call, answer me. Amen.

(Evening)
God is my song; God is my praise. All my hope comes from God. God is my song; God is my praise. All my hope comes from God. Amen.

THURSDAY, AUGUST 7
(Read Psalm 130:1–2, 2 Samuel 18:5–9, and Ephesians 4:25–5:2)

(Morning)
"Holy God, we praise your name; God of all, we bow before you. . . . Undivided God, we claim you . . . while we own the mystery" (Ignaz Franz).

(Evening)
Holy God, "come and fill our hearts with your peace. You alone are holy."

O God, from out of the depths we cry out to you. We, like the psalmist, dare to address supreme reality from human extremity—right where it is, just as it is! Indeed, God, you dwell in a high and holy place, but also with those who are of a "contrite and humble spirit! This "Song of Ascents," chanted by pilgrims gone before me, is for the embattled King David as he ordered his army to "deal gently" with erring Absalom. The story of the latter's death ends with David mourning: "O my son Absalom, my son, my son Absalom! Would I had died instead of you." This wrenching cry still echoes through the ages.

(Morning)
"Come to the Comforter, tenderly saying, earth has no sorrow, that heaven cannot cure" (Thomas Moore).
(Prayers of Intercession)

(Evening)
"Come to the feast of love; come ever knowing, earth has no sorrow that heaven cannot heal."
(Prayers of Intercession)

And now from the depths, I pray.
(Pray the Prayer of Our Savior.)

(Morning)
O God, hear my prayer; O God, hear my prayer. When I call, answer me. O God, hear my prayer; O God, hear my prayer. When I call, answer me. Amen.

(Evening)
God is my song; God is my praise. All my hope comes from God. God is my song; God is my praise. All my hope comes from God. Amen.

FRIDAY, AUGUST 8
(Read Psalm 130:1, Psalm 34:5, 2 Samuel 18:33, Ephesians 5:14, and John 6:47)

(Morning)
Thank you, God, for helping me put away all bitterness, malice, wrath, anger, clamor, and slander.

(Evening)
Thank you, God, for your saving love. May it be reflected in me.

God, we must no longer live "in the futility of our minds . . . alienated from [you]." Through your Child, we can put off our old nature and be renewed in the spirit of our minds. Jesus said: "Everyone who has heard and learns from God comes to me. . . . Who ever believes has eternal life." We, like Elijah, David, and the people of Israel, turned to you for deliverance. All the more can we who have tasted living bread do so. An ancient hymn proclaims: "Awake, O sleeper, and arise from the dead, and Christ shall give you light." Your Child calls all who are weary and heavy laden to rest in him. From out of the depths, I can "look to [you] and be radiant!"

(Morning)
"Send out your light and your truth . . . that they may bring me to your holy hill."
(Prayers of Intercession)

(Evening)
"The day you gave us, God, is ended. . . . Your praise shall sanctify our rest."
(Ellerton)
(Prayers of Intercession)

And now I pray our Savior's prayer.
(Pray the Prayer of Our Savior.)

(Morning)
Live in charity and steadfast love. Live in charity; God will dwell with you. Live in charity and steadfast love. Live in charity; God will dwell with you. Amen.

(Evening)
Thank you, God, for being with me in adversity as in health. My faith looks up to you! Amen.

SATURDAY, AUGUST 9
(Read Psalm 130:3–4 and 2 Samuel 18:5–9, 15, 31–33)

(Morning)
God, surround me in my waking: God in my heart, God in my thinking,
God in my hoping, God in my doing.

(Evening)
God, enfold me in my sleeping: God in my watching, God in my soul,
God in my waiting, God eternally.

God, I know that David's army triumphed over the forces of Absalom, the king's rebellious son. Despite explicit orders to spare him, he was killed. I can feel David's pain as he cried: "O my son, . . . my son, Absalom! Would I had died instead of you." Songs of praise, lament, deliverance, vindication, and supplication are ascribed to this very human hero. Pathos and faith are captured in the plea that Israel "hope in [you], for with [you] there is steadfast love, and . . . great power to redeem." God, here your hopeful assurance transcends abysmal grief. Hear my prayer as you have heard the psalmist: "If you, O God, should mark iniquities, who could stand? But there is forgiveness with you, so that you may be revered."

(Morning)
"If we say we have no sin, we deceive ourselves." O God, I confess I have not
loved you with my whole heart, or my neighbor as myself.
(Prayers of Intercession)

(Evening)
"Anyone in Christ becomes a new person . . . the past is over now and gone."
I believe the good news: In Christ Jesus we are forgiven."
(Prayers of Intercession)

And now I pray.
(Pray the Prayer of Our Savior.)

(Morning)
"Enter God's gates with thanksgiving
for God is good; God's steadfast love
endures forever." Amen.

(Evening)
"My mouth praises you . . . when I
think of you upon my bed, . . . for you
have been my help." Amen.

SUNDAY, AUGUST 10
(Read Psalm 130, Ephesians 4:25–5:2, and John 6:41–51)

(Morning)
God, renew our lives, that we may walk in your world, rejoicing.

(Evening)
God, refresh us this night with peaceful sleep, that we may serve you with joy.

God, saints, living and dead, come from the East and West, North and South, to commune at your table. They ask your Holy Spirit to bless the bread and wine, "that we may be united with Christ and one another, and remain faithful to the tasks set before us." Your Word discloses not only the vital "food" needed for our faith journey ("way-bread" from heaven), but also our host and companion, your Child, Jesus Christ. We are warned of the route's demand—the need to put off our corruptible selves and take on the "likeness of God." The pilgrim "Song of Ascents" cheers us on our way by marking the climb from "the depths" to your city.

(Morning)
"Come we who love God's name. . . . We're traveling through Emmanuel's ground, to greater worlds on high" (Watts).
(Prayers of Intercession)

(Evening)
"You prepare a table for me."
(Prayers of Intercession)

And now I pray our Savior's prayer.
(Pray the Prayer of Our Savior.)

(Morning)
"Let all mortal flesh keep silence; . . . ponder nothing earthly minded, for with blessing in his hand, Christ, our God, to earth descended. Amen."
(fourth-century prayer)

(Evening)
"Thank you, God, for bringing me to this night's rest. "For food and loving care, and all that makes the world so fair." Amen.

MONDAY, AUGUST 11
(Read 1 Kings 3:3–6)

(Morning)
O God, it is a new day, unique in all creation, yet blessed with the memory
of all who have prepared me for the living of this day.

(Evening)
O God, as the day draws to a close, I am united again with those who have gone
before me, blessing me with countless gifts of love that still are mine this day.

I praise you, O God of history, that you have shown great and steadfast love to your servants in every generation. I thank you for those who have gone before me—prophets and apostles who shared your Word so that those who follow might know the way to go; martyrs who gave their lives as a sign of your love, willing to die so that we might know why we live; saints who built the church with Christ Jesus as the cornerstone so that the world might have a witness to your love; and parents and teachers who have nurtured us in the faith so that we might respond to the challenges of this generation.

(Morning)
May the memory of those who have gone before accompany me this day,
inspiring me to faithfulness in all that I do.
(Prayers of Intercession)

(Evening)
As I survey the day just past, I thank you that you have been faithful to me
as you were faithful to all who have gone before me.
(Prayers of Intercession)

**First and last, I thank you for the continuing spirit of Jesus,
who taught us to pray.**
(Pray the Prayer of Our Savior.)

(Morning)
May this day bring me closer to those who have preceded me and closer to you, their God and my God. Amen.

(Evening)
May I now have a measure of the rest you promise to all your people. Amen.

TUESDAY, AUGUST 12
(Read 1 Kings 3:3–6)

(Morning)
God of eternity and God of today, I know that this day will offer an array of decisions and choices, some of which I can anticipate and others I cannot anticipate.

(Evening)
God of eternity and God of the day just past, I pause to recollect the day just past, not merely to despair or rejoice over what has happened, but to note the movement of your Spirit at every turn.

O Perfect Judge, I seek to do what is good and reject what is evil. Before I can do either, I seek—with King Solomon—the gift of discernment, because I know that good and evil seldom announce themselves as such. Often life presents both good and evil in confusing disguises. When I expect to see the good at my right hand, it appears on my left. When I think I have found the evil at my left, it sneaks up at me from the right. I know what I want to do, O God, but show me what I need to do, for Christ Jesus' sake. Reveal what is worthy of my loyalties. Show me both who I am and what you expect me to do.

(Morning)
I thank you that there is no road I might travel this day that you do not accompany me, no challenge that I must face alone.
(Prayers of Intercession)

(Evening)
I thank you for memories that remind me of who I am and dreams that remind me of what I can be.
(Prayers of Intercession)

And so I am emboldened to pray.
(Pray the Prayer of our Savior.)

(Morning)
May I live each moment as eternity in miniature. Give me, in your continued presence, a firm place on which to stand. Amen.

(Evening)
May my heart be enlivened with your presence this night so that I may rise to new and vigorous days. Amen.

WEDNESDAY, AUGUST 13
(Read Psalm 34:9–14)

(Morning)
O God, before every corner of this day is filled with human words,
I seek an openness to your Word.

(Evening)
O God, the day now passing has been stuffed with many words
and precious little meaning.

O Word of God, give me a tongue that bears witness to you. Equip me to say those things that build up: If I encounter injustice, equip my tongue for rebuke; if I encounter suffering, equip my tongue for comfort; if I encounter complacency, equip my tongue for inspiration; if I encounter prejudice, equip my tongue for correction. O God beyond words, help me to leave unsaid those things that tear down: If I am wounded, help me to refrain from using my tongue as a weapon of vengeance. May both my silence and my words speak of you and speak for you.

(Morning)
May the words I speak this day be worthy of being offered to you
in the spirit of prayer.
(Prayers of Intercession)

(Evening)
May the many words spoken this day find their true meaning in the prayers
I now offer.
(Prayers of Intercession)

Hear me now especially as I pray.
(Pray the Prayer of Our Savior.)

(Morning)
O God, may I trace your powerful presence throughout the contours of this day. Amen.

(Evening)
O God, may the silence now enfold me with assurance of your continued presence. Amen.

THURSDAY, AUGUST 14
(Read Psalm 111)

(Morning)
O God, the day is young, but already it is filled with your praises.

(Evening)
O God, as the day ends, I have yet another day's worth of praises to offer.

Eternal God, great keeper of human souls and igniter of the brightest human dreams, I praise you for your unwavering goodness to me and to all your children: for mercies that fall like rain on the just and the unjust; for words of promise that find me at my places of greatest need; for coincidental happenings that, viewed in retrospect, bespeak your gentle leading and your constant care; for your sustaining love that I drink in as easily as I breathe the air; for the silent satisfactions of the heart that I barely take time or care to notice; and, above all and beneath all, I thank you that in Jesus Christ you chose not to remain an anonymous giver, but chose rather to be known in the person of the one who teaches, forgives, and redeems me.

(Morning)
Catch me off-guard this day with some moment of beauty or mystery so that I may be startled into seeing that you are with me everywhere and always.
(Prayers of Intercession)

(Evening)
Thank you for the ways in which the day just past has cracked open reality for me to see your presence there at work, helping me learn again delight in your creation.
(Prayers of Intercession)

May I praise you now in the words Jesus taught us.
(Pray the Prayer of Our Savior.)

(Morning)
May the sun that rises sing your praises and echo through the day. Amen.

(Evening)
May the sun that sets issue a final "amen" to the praises that have resounded through the day. Amen.

FRIDAY, AUGUST 15
(Read Proverbs 9:1–6)

(Morning)
O God, I do not ask that you come near to me, for you are already closer than I dare imagine.

(Evening)
O God, I find your name on my lips because you have placed it on my heart.

There is much in the world and in my life that I do not understand. I seek answers, and you approach me with mystery. I seek certainty, and you ask me to respond with faith. I seek direction, and you offer yourself as the way. I seek understanding, and you declare that knowledge of you is the beginning of wisdom. So, let my restless quest for knowledge begin with you: When I set my sights on things that perish, lift my eyes to the place from which my true help comes. When I am impressed with my own accomplishments, knock me down to size so that I might sense more surely your majesty. And when, for a moment, I catch a glimpse of you, help me to respond with awe and wonder.

(Morning)
Give me the gift of insight this day—the gift of your presence.
(Prayers of Intercession)

(Evening)
Let me recall the ways in which you have been made known to me this day.
(Prayers of Intercession)

I now respond to that presence by offering the prayer that Jesus taught us.
(Pray the Prayer of Our Savior.)

(Morning)
I pray in the name of the One who gives life, shows the way, and is the truth.
Amen.

(Evening)
I pray in the name of the One who gives life, shows the way, and is the truth.
Amen.

SATURDAY, AUGUST 16
(Read John 6:51–58)

(Morning)
Most gracious God, who comes to me with love and mercy,
because I am so slow to come to you, help me to come alive to your presence
at the beginning of this day.

(Evening)
Most gracious God of my days and nights, God of my thoughts and dreams,
you have sustained me throughout my days and the day just passed.

I confess that I spend much of my life on that which does not satisfy. I have sought to feed my soul with many things that leave me empty: with entertainments and distractions that provide pleasure but do not nourish; with earthly success that melts like cotton candy as soon as I taste it; with relationships that skip across the surface of life; with spiritual wanderings that drift with the latest tide. O Living Bread, escort me to the table where I may feast upon the gift you offer, the gift of yourself. There may I receive your life into my life, for it is the food that does not perish, the sustenance that nourishes me for eternal life.

(Morning)
I come to you with a hungry heart, waiting to be filled with your presence,
waiting to be filled with new energy for service.
(Prayers of Intercession)

(Evening)
Your glory has surrounded me this day, and I ask now that my life might give
continued glory to you.
(Prayers of Intercession)

I seek now to feast upon your presence as I pray.
(Pray the Prayer of Our Savior.)

(Morning)
May I live the coming day in confidence and joy, in the manner of Jesus Christ. Amen.

(Evening)
I offer these prayers in the name of the One who sustains me and accompanies me, even Jesus Christ, my God. Amen.

SUNDAY, AUGUST 17
(Read Ephesians 5:15–20)

(Morning)
God, as I stir to the promise of the morning, I await the stirring of your Spirit in this new day.

(Evening)
God, as the evening cloaks the world in stillness, I seek a stillness of heart so that I might recall the ways you have been at work in the day just past.

O God, give me a heart that can learn a melody that comes from you, so that I can offer it back to you as a song of praise. I am surrounded by the appeals and distractions of a clamorous world that is too much with us. In many ways my life is full—too full to be a fitting vessel for your Spirit. My mind is too consumed with seemingly urgent tasks to offer you thanks. My heart is so distracted with the concerns of the day that I do not invite you to give it a touch of eternity. There is in my heart a sweet song of praise. But sometimes I forget the melody, and at other times I simply forget to sing. So, O God, in this moment, empty my heart of all that leads me away from you so that I might be filled with your Spirit.

(Morning)
Even as I anticipate the day ahead, I know that I cannot anticipate fully the ways in which you will be at work.
(Prayers of Intercession)

(Evening)
Help me to recall all the quiet promptings of your Spirit that I was too distracted to notice until now.
(Prayers of Intercession)

Draw me entirely to yourself as I pray.
(Pray the Prayer of Our Savior.)

(Morning)
Go with me, O God, into the world and into this day so that I might discover you there. Amen.

(Evening)
As I entrust this day to you, O God, let my final thoughts be accompanied by the melodies of praise. Amen.

MONDAY, AUGUST 18
(Read Psalm 84)

(Morning)
O God, search me and hear my prayer. I come before you this day asking your guidance and presence in all I do.

(Evening)
O God, search me and hear my prayer. My day has been lived as a prayer to you. Allow me to rest gently in your love and strength.

I sing your praises and wait to hear your voice through prophets and apostles, through friends and colleagues, through all your creation. The psalmist sings songs of the joy of being in your presence and songs of confidence in your strength. I have decisions to make and seek your will as this day unfolds. Help me to remember that the "easy way" is not necessarily your way. I say, with the psalmist, "I would rather be a doorkeeper in the house of my God than live in the tents of wickedness." Allow me to live my life as a prayer to you and await your Word as I walk through each doorway this day.

(Morning)
As I look toward this day, strengthen my commitment to you.
Allow me to see your face in the faces I see.
(Prayers of Intercession)

(Evening)
As I reflect on this day, the decisions I made and the people I encountered,
I thank you for each experience.
(Prayers of Intercession)

And now, with a bold faith, I pray.
(Pray the Prayer of Our Savior.)

(Morning)
As your child, send me now into the world to love and serve you. Amen.

(Evening)
As your child, protect me as I sleep in the comfort of your love. Amen.

TUESDAY, AUGUST 19
(Read Joshua 24:1–2a, 14–18)

(Morning)
O God, search me and hear my prayer. You call each of us to be your servant in the service of others. Guide my service this day.

(Evening)
O God, search me and hear my prayer. I seek you when I am unsure and you answer my cries. Hear my prayers this night.

Each day I wrestle with what it means to make a commitment to you. What choices do I face each day? I wrestle with the gods of consumption and popularity. I wrestle with those things that cause death and division in the body of Christ: racism, sexism, classism, heterosexism, ageism, and all the other "isms" which this society has turned into attitudinal gods. I look to your Word and hear you call to me: "Now if you are unwilling to serve God, choose this day whom you will serve, . . . as for me and my house, we will serve God." The temptation to fall prey to the "isms" is great. Strengthen my commitment to you. Allow me to hear your call to me in all I do this day. You, O God, are my strength and redeemer.

(Morning)
O God, strengthen me this day. Guide my decisions.
Help me face difficult choices.
(Prayers of Intercession)

(Evening)
O God, forgive me where I fell short of your will for me.
Strengthen me for tomorrow.
(Prayers of Intercession)

And now, with a bold faith, I pray.
(Pray the Prayer of Our Savior.)

(Morning)
As your child, send me now into the world to love and serve you. Amen.

(Evening)
As your child, protect me as I sleep in the comfort of your love. Amen.

WEDNESDAY, AUGUST 20
(Read 1 Kings 8:1, 6, 10–11)

(Morning)
O God, I awake with you on my mind and sleep with you in my heart.
Each day brings a new beginning of a life lived to you. Thank you.

(Evening)
O God, I awake with you on my mind and sleep with you in my heart.
This day has been ours together. Thank you.

O God, in the busyness of this day, I am grateful for your presence and the presence of the elders of my community. I am grateful for the advice and counsel I have received over the past years, months, weeks, and days from those around me who are wiser than I. Continue to place people and events in my life that challenge me and help me grow. Continue to open my ears that I may hear from others; my eyes, that I may see an opportunity to bring about justice; my heart, that I might be compassionate and bring about an act of kindness.

(Morning)
Help me to be still this day, surrounded by your cloud,
that I might know you are God.
(Prayers of Intercession)

(Evening)
Shelter me in your holiness. Enfold me in your love and strength.
Protect me this night.
(Prayers of Intercession)

And now, with a bold faith, I pray.
(Pray the Prayer of Our Savior.)

(Morning)
As your child, send me now into the world to love and serve you. Amen.

(Evening)
As your child, protect me as I sleep in the comfort of your love. Amen.

THURSDAY, AUGUST 21
(Read 1 Kings 8:41–43)

(Morning)
O God, search me and guide me. I awake and sing praises to your name. I ask that you make me aware that all I encounter this day will be a part of you. Help me to honor your presence in everyone I see.

(Evening)
O God, search me and guide me. Take me back, O God, to the faith I had as a child. Protect me and those I love this night. Allow me to rest in your love, that I might awaken to your service.

Sometimes I do not recognize your messengers when they come, because they come in forms or through people I do not expect. How often do I refuse to recognize you and your presence in someone who is different from me? The text today talks about hospitality and making the decision to welcome someone who is different. Help me to see you in everyone—friend or stranger. Help me to be open and loving to all. Help me to be a gracious host.

(Morning)
As I look toward this day, I seek to be all you have called me to be
I will welcome the stranger in my midst.
(Prayers of Intercession)

(Evening)
As I reflect on this day, I thank you for the opportunities to welcome and to be welcomed.
(Prayers of Intercession)

And now, with a bold faith, I pray.
(Pray the Prayer of Our Savior.)

(Morning)
As your child, send me now into the world to love and serve you. Amen.

(Evening)
As your child, protect me as I sleep in the comfort of your love. Amen.

FRIDAY, AUGUST 22
(Read Psalm 34:15–22)

(Morning)
Taste and see that God is good! Happy are all those who take refuge in God!
I praise you, O God, in the heat of this August day.

(Evening)
Taste and see that God is good! Happy are all those who take refuge in God!
I praise you O God, in the cool breeze of this night.

O God, I try to do what is right. I am not perfect, but I try to live according to your Word. I get into trouble when I forget to turn to you in times of trial and indecision. I get into trouble when I try to rely on my own strength and not yours. As I go through each day, let my decisions be made after asking: "What would God have me do in this situation? Are my actions ones that will promote kindness, justice, and peace? Is this decision for the good of the whole?"

(Morning)
O God, guide me this day as I turn to you and seek your face.
(Prayers of Intercession)

(Evening)
Thank you for one more day to enjoy the beauty of all your creation.
(Prayers of Intercession)

And now, with a bold faith, I pray.
(Pray the Prayer of Our Savior.)

(Morning)
As your child, send me now into the world to love and serve you. Amen.

(Evening)
As your child, protect me as I sleep in the comfort of your love. Amen.

SATURDAY, AUGUST 23
(Read Ephesians 6:10–20)

(Morning)
O God, I am weary. Dress me in the armor of your love this day.
Guide my feet, give me strength.

(Evening)
O God, I am weary. As I prepare for rest, wrap me in a shroud
of your protective love.

God, sometimes I feel as though I am fighting a losing battle. I try to do what is right, and I get ridiculed by family, friends, and colleagues. I turn to your Word and find comfort and challenge. I sing the songs of the faith, but sometimes they seem empty platitudes in the midst of a society that has forgotten your name. I read your Word for today, and it tells me to "put on the whole armor of God so that I might be able to stand against the wiles of the devil." Give me strength, dear God, to stand for that in which I believe. Give me courage to do all that I know to be right and then simply stand—stand firm.

(Morning)
Protect my heart this day.
(Prayers of Intercession)

(Evening)
Protect my spirit this night.
(Prayers of Intercession)

And now, with a bold faith, I pray.
(Pray the Prayer of Our Savior.)

(Morning)
As your child, send me now into the world to love and to serve you. Amen.

(Evening)
As your child, protect me as I sleep in the comfort of your love. Amen.

SUNDAY, AUGUST 24
(Read John 6: 56–69)

(Morning)
I have come to believe and know that you are the holy One of God.
I come to you an empty vessel, rested from the night's sleep
and ready to be filled with your plans for me today.

(Evening)
I have come to believe and know that you are the holy One of God.
This day has been filled with your presence. I have seen you in the faces
of friends and strangers.

Sometimes your Word is hard to understand and hard to accept. Some of your teaching causes those who want to follow you to go away empty. They turn away because the commitment is too hard to make. Choices, commitment, difficult decisions, discernment—that is what this week has been about. Jesus never promised that being a Christian meant my life would be easy. Commitment is difficult to come by in these days. Commitment means requirements, demands, opportunities, and privileges. Help me to live my commitment to you.

(Morning)
O God, I am available to you. I know that you and I will face
all commitments together.
(Prayers of Intercession)

(Evening)
I felt your Spirit in the warm August breeze and the cool water.
(Prayers of Intercession)

And now with bold faith, I pray.
(Pray the Prayer of Our Savior.)

(Morning)
Send me now into the world with healing love, so that all may know you are the Holy One. Amen.

(Evening)
I have known your creation in the wildflowers and the bees. Please remind me again tomorrow that you are with me always. Amen.

MONDAY, AUGUST 25
(Read Song of Solomon 2:8–13)

(Morning)
Revealing, inviting, nourishing God, at the beginning of this new day,
I am conscious of your healing strength and rest during the night.

(Evening)
Revealing, inviting, nourishing God, at the end of the day, I review the activities and events that have occupied my attention. Where I have slighted another, forgive.

Holy mystery beyond all metaphors, you reveal and give of yourself in surprising ways and forms. You invite me to stop, listen, and discern your holy presence while involved with the ordinary and the routine events of this day. In the midst of my rushing and busyness, you appear, in a diversity of forms, providing new and fresh gifts which nourish both my spiritual and physical life. May your holiness surround my life each hour of this day. May you grant me fresh strength and faith for each of the opportunities that presents itself this day.

(Morning)
During each hour of this day, keep me alert to your abiding presence and peace.
(Prayers of Intercession)

(Evening)
The evening shadows have fallen. My activities must cease. Help me to seek rest.
Teach me about care of self.
(Prayers of Intercession)

In boldness, I dare to pray.
(Pray the Prayer of Our Savior.)

(Morning)
I ask for your continual and constant presence in and about my life, through each hour of this day. Amen.

(Evening)
May my heart, mind, and body now rest. Enable me to place all things confidently in your care. Amen.

TUESDAY, AUGUST 26
(Read Psalm 45:1–2, 6–9)

(Morning)
Ever-giving God of plentiful gifts, you have birthed and nourished me with abundance. Teach me how to be more thankful.

(Evening)
Ever-giving God of abundant gifts, I have toiled this day, and I have grown tired. I have given freely of myself, and more was needed. Bless my efforts.

Before any thing was, you, beautiful God, were. You know all of your creation individually. You know my name. You knew me even as I was being formed in my mother's womb. You nourished me and gave me existence. You, holy, creating God, gifted me with a part of your very self. You give me daily breath and bread. You give me a mind that can think and reason. You give me a heart that can feel and care. You give me hands and feet, skills and opportunities. In holy freedom, you invite me to come closer into the circle of divine intimacy. Hold me close by your side through the hours of this day.

(Morning)
Help me to see the extraordinary in the midst of the ordinary and routine. Help me to know the source of all enduring blessings.
(Prayers of Intercession)

(Evening)
When I drifted from your presence this day, there were unexpected markers that pointed me back.
(Prayers of Intercession)

In boldness, I dare to pray.
(Pray the Prayer of Our Savior.)

(Morning)
You have gifted me with an abundance of blessings. Teach me how to better use these gifts, that I may be a blessing to others. Amen.

(Evening)
I thank you, merciful God, for these moments of recollection and reflection. I ask for your continual and abiding presence in my life. Amen.

WEDNESDAY, AUGUST 27
(Read Deuteronomy 4:1–2, 6–9 and Psalm 15)

(Morning)
God of wisdom and strength, help me to be attentive this day to your holy Word. By the manner in which I live, strengthen me to make goodness attractive.

(Evening)
God of wisdom and strength, I have experienced the involvement of your presence in my life this day. Keep me ever alert and watching for your surprise visits.

You invite me to follow in your path of honesty and goodness to self and to neighbor. You provide me with clarity of thought of ageless wisdom. You teach me about goodness. You teach me to refrain from evil and to speak the truth within my life. You give me specific direction in the aid and care of others. Your path gives strength and stability. Walking your holy path provides me with truth for my life and care for my neighbor. Help me this day not to stray from your path. And when I lose my way, I pray that there will be a signpost that calls me back to your path of ageless wisdom.

(Morning)
In the midst of busyness, I pause to recall those strategic points in my life where honesty and truthfulness empowered me to make good decisions.
(Prayers of Intercession)

(Evening)
For blessings received and forgotten, and for blessings that came and went unnoticed, I ask for forgiveness.
(Prayers of Intercession)

In boldness, I dare to pray.
(Pray the Prayer of Our Savior.)

(Morning)
In each of the paths that I must walk this day, stay near to my heart and soul. Give me a conscience that is alert and mature. Amen.

(Evening)
At the end of day, my trust is in you, mighty God; grant me peace of mind and restorative rest. Amen.

THURSDAY, AUGUST 28
(Read James 1:17–21)

(Morning)
Birthing, gifting, nourishing God, grant me time and quiet this day,
that I may be attentive to my soul. Bless my mind, that my heart may feel.

(Evening)
Birthing, gifting, nourishing God, your holiness reaches out to me
and invites me to come closer into the realm of divine intimacy.

Before I breathed my first breath, before my eyes could see, your holy presence was already active in my life. You gave of yourself to me, and I knew it not. Your divine imprint was on my life even before I came to recognize it. Before my birth, you were watching over, guarding, nourishing, and caring for my life. In the midst of the speed and noise of this day, teach me to pause and to recall the blessings that I have received. In the remembering of past blessings, teach my soul to stand ever at attention—always alert for fresh blessings that come in the form of surprise and wonder. I offer words of heartfelt thanksgiving.

(Morning)
Beyond any deserving, you have given me blessings upon blessings. Teach me this
day how to use all that I am: body, mind, and soul to foster peace and love.
(Prayers of Intercession)

(Evening)
Throughout this day, you have journeyed with me. You have been friend and
companion. You have invited me to new levels of understanding.
(Prayers of Intercession)

In boldness, I dare to pray.
(Pray the Prayer of Our Savior.)

(Morning)
This day keep me mindful of time, and my use and abuse of it. Teach me how to make time to pray. Strengthen me to live as I pray. Amen.

(Evening)
As I prepare for sleep, I place aside all activities, stresses, and anxious concerns and leave them in your care. Renew my body and soul while I sleep. Amen.

FRIDAY, AUGUST 29
(Read James 1:22–27)

(Morning)
Ever-present, involving, liberating God, at the beginning of this new day,
I seek your holy presence and watchful care about my whole being.

(Evening)
Ever-present, involving, liberating God, help me to recollect all of the events,
activities, and individuals that have touched my life this day.

Merciful God of peace and justice, you look not on the outward appearance of any, but see and judge all by the intent within the individual's heart. In all of the arenas of life, enable me to clarify my own intentions. Grant me grace, that I may discern your whole-making Word. Teach me anew this day how to translate my understanding into deeds. Help me to discover new ways and means of putting my faith into action. Transform all that I have been into new deeds of human compassion and service to others in your holy name.

(Morning)
I pause for perspective and reflection. Draw me close to your side.
(Prayers of Intercession)

(Evening)
Now at the close of day, I put aside all of my labors,
and seek rest and restorative sleep.
(Prayers of Intercession)

In boldness, I dare to pray.
(Pray the Prayer of Our Savior.)

(Morning)
Teach me how to better respond to all that I know. May my faith be reflected in my deeds. Amen.

(Evening)
Throughout the watches of the night, watch over and keep me safe from harm's way. Amen.

SATURDAY, AUGUST 30
(Read Mark 7:1–9)

(Morning)
Living God of honesty and vitality, I am awakened by the sights and sounds of nature. Morning light awakens my soul.

(Evening)
Living God of honesty and vitality, the evening shadows have fallen on this day, and my labors must cease. Grant me peace.

You invite all of your creation into direct relationship. You bid all welcome, and you extend hospitality to each. You offer holy ways of living with and among one another. You give of yourself to me. And in perfect freedom, you allow me to choose how I shall live in relationship with others. Teach me how to see beyond my own small traditions. Aid me in the task of affirming and celebrating the goodness and honesty in all others. Teach me more about community and commitment. Help me to affirm my beliefs without degrading the religious views of others. May there always be honesty and vitality to my faith.

(Morning)
I am conscious of your holy presence, actively inviting me into divine intimacy.
(Prayers of Intercession)

(Evening)
On all of my activities of this day, I seek your benediction.
(Prayers of Intercession)

In boldness, I dare to pray.
(Pray the Prayer of Our Savior.)

(Morning)
Enable me to look within for quiet. Help me to be ever alert and attentive to your beckoning whispers. Amen.

(Evening)
As I have labored with my whole heart and mind, now grant my body rest. Amen.

SUNDAY, AUGUST 31
(Mark 7:14–15, 21–23)

(Morning)
God of inward purity, enable me to feel, see, and know this new day as a gift given in trust. Be my constant companion and soul guide.

(Evening)
God of inward purity, aid me as I prepare for sleep, recollecting those points of grace where I have been blessed.

Great and magnificent God, you are pure holiness. You invite me to come into your all-inclusive circle of wholeness and health. You reveal and give yourself to me. You teach me the way of peace. You teach me how to be honest with my soul and how to have a good heart. You teach me of the sacredness of inward things, and you invite me to be one of your disciples. You provide me with hope that is real. You promise to be my faith companion and to walk with me.

(Morning)
Holy God, you have watched over me while I did not know of it.
Enable me to make this new day a gift to you.
(Prayers of Intercession)

(Evening)
Grant to me this night restful sleep and fresh dreams that will empower me for the new day.
(Prayers of Intercession)

In boldness, I dare to pray.
(Pray the Prayer of Our Savior.)

(Morning)
Help me to recognize you and to affirm your holy presence by my actions with all whom I encounter this day. Amen.

(Evening)
As you have blessed my work, bless my sleep. Amen.

MONDAY, SEPTEMBER 1
(Read Proverbs 22:1–2, 8–9, 22–23)

(Morning)
Just and righteous God, I awake facing a day filled with opportunities to be kind, generous, and loving.

(Evening)
Just and righteous God, I want to rest tonight knowing that I have been kind to every person I have met today.

I am thankful for your words which strengthen and guide me. You speak to me, God, in your admonitions in Proverbs. God, you called attention to the importance of a good name. In my relationships with others, you make me aware of my responsibilities to all those I meet. You make me aware of my opportunity to show justice to all those with whom I come in contact. You make me aware of the need for sharing my food with those who are less fortunate. Help all of us to understand the significance of our obligation to others, so that by sharing our goods with all we may come to know that we are members of your family.

(Morning)
As I look forward to this day, I pray for these personal needs of mine as I work with others . . .
(Prayers of Intercession)

(Evening)
I need you as I think of this day and pray for those who are close to me. May those who are estranged from me know I care.
(Prayers of Intercession)

And now I pray.

(Morning)
I know you will be with me as I meet this day. Help me to live my best this day. In your name. Amen.

(Evening)
Now I can sleep because I have peace in my heart. In your holy name. Amen.

TUESDAY, SEPTEMBER 2
(Read Psalms 125)

(Morning)
Gracious God, I wake up to a day filled with possibilities for infinite good.

(Evening)
Gracious God, I want to rest in the knowledge that I have trusted you to guide me to do my best.

God, thank you for the Word, and for the messages that encourage me. I listen as you speak your message from the psalms to me. God, thousands of years ago, you reassured the psalmist that those who trusted you would be surrounded by your presence. You assured the psalmist that wickedness would not prevail and the righteous ones would be fortified. We also beg for good things for those who do good and behave uprightly. The speaker believes that the wicked will be punished for their crooked ways. I believe that peace will be mine because I will trust you, God. Show me the way of goodness and love towards others.

(Morning)
As I look forward to this day, I think of others who have problems where I may offer help.
(Prayers of Intercession)

(Evening)
As I think of this day, I pray that I will have helped other persons. I pray for wisdom to see the needs of others.
(Prayers of Intercession)

As your child, I pray.

(Morning)
As your child, I ask strength and courage from you to face the challenges of the new day. In your name. Amen.

(Evening)
May I have peace in my heart as I rest during the night. May sleep bring strength. In your holy name. Amen.

WEDNESDAY, SEPTEMBER 3
(Read Isaiah 35:4–7a)

(Morning)
Glorious and majestic God, this new day holds infinite possibilities for thanksgiving.

(Evening)
Glorious and majestic God, I want to sleep tonight knowing that I was truly thankful for the blessings of today.

I praise you, God, for your words that give sustenance and strength to a fearful heart. All of us are like pilgrims in a strange land, and you in Christ opened unto us a new and vital way of living. Life is still difficult, but we, as pilgrims, are safe in your hands. With your arms beneath us, we are secure. Your wondrous loving care sustains us even when life threatens to stifle us. The joy and gladness of a living faith is the possession of every believer. Teach me to trust your guidance during the difficult and strangling times of life. Help me to show others that you will support us during the difficult times, that you will never leave us.

(Morning)
As I look forward to a new day, I pray for a close walk with you, God.
(Prayers of Intercession)

(Evening)
As I think of this day, I pray for a closer walk with you, not only for myself, God. I want a closer walk with you for my friends.
(Prayers of Intercession)

And now, with trust as your child, I pray.

(Morning)
As your trusting child, help me to show others your love and care for each one. In your name. Amen.

(Evening)
Now I am safe from the cares of the world. May blessed sleep be given to me. In your holy name. Amen.

THURSDAY, SEPTEMBER 4
(Read Psalm 146)

(Morning)
Caring and loving God, my first thought this morning is my need for your strength to meet today's challenges.

(Evening)
Caring and loving God, I think of the challenges of the day and I know you, God, were with me.

God, I praise you today as I seek to do your will. I know that people cannot always be trusted, but you can always be trusted. As creator of heaven, earth, and sea, you show justice for the oppressed and you feed the hungry. God, you set the prisoners free, and you open the eyes of the blind. You love the righteous, but you bring the wicked to ruin. God, you will reign forever, and I will praise you forever. You do wonderful things for the widow and the orphans, and you lift up those who are downtrodden. Teach me to be like you as I live among other persons.

(Morning)
As I begin my day, I pray for my need to be like you.
I will keep your goodness to people in mind.
(Prayers of Intercession)

(Evening)
Be with me as I think of those who praise you as I do.
I ask that those who do not express praise be touched by your goodness.
(Prayers of Intercession)

And now, with trust as your child, I pray.

(Morning)
May I praise your name so others will be touched to praise you, too. In your name. Amen.

(Evening)
Now I rest in your arms. May I sleep in peace as I praise you. In your holy name. Amen.

FRIDAY, SEPTEMBER 5
(Read James 2:1–13)

(Morning)
Caring and merciful God, I face a day filled with possibilities for caring for others.

(Evening)
Caring and merciful God, I want to rest in you tonight
as a caring and merciful person.

I praise you for words that challenge and heal me. You speak to me through words found in Christ Jesus. Your servant James gives words of wisdom regarding our relations with others. He shows us that you are no respecter of persons and we should follow your example. We are admonished to love our neighbors as we love ourselves. But if we show partiality to persons, we are disobedient to you, O God. God, guide me today so that I will not show partiality to anyone, because breaking the law of love that Jesus taught by showing partiality makes one guilty. Teach me to do justly to others and so to be a hearer and doer of the Word. Then I can expect God's mercy.

(Morning)
As I think of the new day, I pray that I will do to others as I would expect others to do to me.
(Prayers of Intercession)

(Evening)
As I think of the day, may I know that I have shown no partiality.
(Prayers of Intercession)

And with confidence as your child, I pray.

(Morning)
As your forgiven child, take care of me help me to be caring to everyone I meet. In your name. Amen.

(Evening)
May I find blessed peace as I sleep. In your holy name. Amen.

SATURDAY, SEPTEMBER 6
(Read James 2:14–18)

(Morning)
Loving and caring God, this morning I have opportunities to express my faith to others.

(Evening)
I want to rest in you tonight with confidence that I have shown my faith to others by my works.

I praise the words of James that challenge me to show my faith to others. I read again the words that show me that I express my faith by the work I do. When I became a Christian, I repented of my sins, I confessed Christ Jesus as God, and I died to my selfish desires. I show others my faith by the way I live my life as I interact with others. As I live this day, may I be aware of the needs of others. If I have the resources to meet those needs, may I give unsparingly to meet those needs. Help me to remember that faith without works accomplishes nothing. Teach me to remember that a living faith is always evidenced by deeds.

(Morning)
As I look forward to this day, I pray for insight to see the personal needs of others.
(Prayers of Intercession)

(Evening)
Be with me as I think of the events of the day. I want to think that I was aware of the personal needs of others.
(Prayers of Intercession)

And now with confidence, I pray.

(Morning)
As your child, help me today. Help me to show my faith by the works I do. In your name. Amen.

(Evening)
I rest in your arms. May I have restful sleep. Thank you for your love. In your holy name. Amen.

SUNDAY, SEPTEMBER 7
(Read Mark 7:24–37)

(Morning)
Loving Jesus, today I will think of you as you healed a person of another faith.

(Evening)
Loving Jesus, I want to think of how I have shown the concern you would have shown to persons of another faith.

God, your Child, Jesus, showed that persons had more value in his eyes than customs of separateness and exclusiveness. Jesus had a meeting with a woman of another faith. She requested healing for her daughter. Because she was obviously a person of need and faith, Jesus responded to her need and healed the child. When Jesus instantly and perfectly healed a person who could not hear or speak, the crowd was amazed. Jesus called for silence about who had healed and what he had done. Even as Jesus insisted on secrecy, dear God, the healed man proclaimed more greatly what Jesus had done for him.

(Morning)
As I look forward to this new day, I will think of how Jesus valued other persons.
(Prayers of Intercession)

(Evening)
As I think of the events of the day, may I know that I have considered other persons as important, even though they did not hold my beliefs.
(Prayers of Intercession)

And now with confidence as your child, I pray.

(Morning)
As your forgiven child, help me to show loving concern for every person I meet. In your name. Amen.

(Evening)
May I rest in your arms in peaceful sleep. Thank you for your love and care for me today. In your holy name. Amen.

MONDAY, SEPTEMBER 8
(Read James 3:1–12)

(Morning)
Ever-loving God, who sent your Child to be the Word among us,
I greet this week aware of the power of words.

(Evening)
Ever-loving God, whose tender words of forgiveness bring mercy into our lives,
forgive me for ways my tongue has betrayed me today.

"God, gracious word beyond words, let the word we hear be in the words we choose, the words we use, and join in chorus the words of those whose song and speech tumble walls of sterile silence and meaningless noise, in the name of Christ."

(Morning)
God, source of all that is good, bridle my words that could bring pain. Quench my fiery words that inflame anger. Pilot my babbling conversations. Tame my poisonous barbs. Remind me that everyone I talk about today
is made in your image.
(Prayers of Intercession)

(Evening)
Relieve my agony over words I did not bridle. Release me now from the flames of anger I fanned, even within myself. Guide me into a port of peace,
free from the babble of the day. Cleanse my mouth and thoughts.
(Prayers of Intercession)

Now I bless your name.
(Pray the Prayer of Our Savior.)

(Morning)
Give my words your blessing as I respond to others today. Amen.

(Evening)
I rest in the assurance of your love spoken through Jesus, the Word among us. Amen.

TUESDAY, SEPTEMBER 9
(Read Isaiah 50:4–9a and Psalm 116:1–9)

(Morning)
Gracious and righteous God, you speak through the silent dawn and the noisy day. Whisper! Shout! Let me know that you are calling me and are hearing me.

(Evening)
Gracious and righteous God, I give thanks for the way your voice drowned out conflicting sounds of the day.

God, like the psalmist, I give thanks for those times when my voice evoked your presence, when your hand snatched me from destruction that was of my own making, when my step was halted before the abyss, and when death passed me by. You, gentle as a loving father, wiped away my tears. I can truly say, "I am in the land of the living." Like the writer in Isaiah, I celebrate times when I did not rebel against you, when I turned the other cheek, and when I suffered gladly for your sake. You, strong as a protective mother, helped me confront the enemies of your reign. I need not be ashamed or guilty.

(Morning)
Strong and loving God, I thank you and pray that others may hear your voice.
(Prayers of Intercession)

(Evening)
Loving and strong God, I give thanks for your presence in the lives of all who need you to wipe away tears.
(Prayers of Intercession)

In gratitude, I pray Jesus' prayer, which "sustains the weary with a word."
(Pray the Prayer of Our Savior.)

(Morning)
Throughout the day, may my actions show my thanksgiving. Amen.

(Evening)
Free from cares and tears, I rest in the assurance of your presence. Amen.

WEDNESDAY, SEPTEMBER 10
(Read Psalm 19:1–6, 14)
(Sing or read one of the great hymns praising God for creation)

(Morning)
Life-giving Spirit, as I begin the day, let the words of my mouth and the meditation of my heart be acceptable to you, my rock and my redeemer.

(Evening)
Spirit-giving Life, as I end the day, let the words of my mouth and the meditation of my heart be acceptable to you, my rock and my redeemer.

Many and great, O God, are your works! The psalmist declares that the heavens tell your glory with the sun's light from morning to night, proclaiming your handiwork over all the land. The message of your glory fills the earth without a word being uttered. All nature gives you glory! I pause to give name to ways I have experienced your glory: my favorite places to watch the sun running its course; breathtaking views I have seen; and amazing people I have known who give glory to you.

(Morning)
As the sun begins its circuit today, I pray for the world, that your glory will not be destroyed.
(Prayers of Intercession)

(Evening)
As the sun ends its circuit today, I pray for the world, that your glory will not be destroyed.
(Prayers of Intercession)

I also give you glory through the prayer Jesus taught.
(Pray the Prayer of Our Savior.)

(Morning)
As I go through this day, help me give you glory through the choices I make. Amen.

(Evening)
As I reflect on this day, I rest in the glory of your creation. Amen.

THURSDAY, SEPTEMBER 11
(Read Psalm 19:7–14)
(Sing or read "Great Is Your Faithfulness")

(Morning)
O Sun-abiding One, let the words of my mouth and the meditation of my heart
be acceptable to you, my rock and my redeemer.

(Evening)
O Star-abiding One, let the words of my mouth and the meditation of my heart
be acceptable to you, my rock and my redeemer.

Holy God, our loving Creator, close to us as breathing and distant as the farthest star, I acknowledge times when my soul has been restored by your Word. I rejoice that your unchanging testimony makes it easier for me to understand the purpose of your universe. I give thanks that your fair judgments bring joy to my heart and your clear commandment to love one another opens my eyes to right living. Because your precepts are faithful, fair, and right, they are valuable and sweet to me. I listen now for ways to carry out your commandment.

(Morning)
As the day unfolds, O Holy One, I pray for the life-giving force of your rule
to live by.
(Prayers of Intercession)

(Evening)
As night enfolds me, O Holy Trinity, I give thanks for the life-giving security
of your commandment.
(Prayers of Intercession)

Hear me now as I pray that your will be done.
(Pray the Prayer of Our Savior.)

(Morning)
As I entrust myself to your world, give
me strength for today. Amen.

(Evening)
As I release myself to sleep, give me
bright hope for tomorrow. Amen.

FRIDAY, SEPTEMBER 12
(Read Proverbs 1:20–33)
(Sing or read "Immortal, Invisible, God Only Wise")

(Morning)
Eternal God, companion of all who seek you, and seeker of all who turn away from you, as morning calls me to the busy places of my life, let me heed wisdom's voice.

(Evening)
Eternal God, companion of all who seek you, and seeker of all who turn away from you, as I turn from the busy places of my life, grant me serenity as I reflect on today and prepare for tomorrow.

May I learn from the woman wisdom to identify the voice of God in the noise of the workplace. May I separate the voice of God from the voices that call me to get ahead at any cost. May I not scoff at the call to care for others as I care for myself. May I not relish the simple way things have always been done. May I not foolishly talk rather than listen. May I not be satisfied with my own cleverness. I acknowledge that I have not always chosen wisdom but have lived with the whirlwind of calamity and the storm of panic. Hear now as I confess the causes of my distress and anguish.

(Morning)
As I go through this day, help me give you glory through the choices I make.
(Prayers of Intercession)

(Evening)
As I reflect on this day, I rest in the glory of your creation.
(Prayers of Intercession)

May I continue to be open to new wisdom from familiar words.
(Pray the Prayer of Our Savior.)

(Morning)
Open me, Wise and Raucous Companion, to a day of listening, stretching, and heeding. Amen.

(Evening)
Now I rest secure and at ease in the knowledge of God's wisdom. Amen.

SATURDAY, SEPTEMBER 13
(Read Mark 8:27–33)

(Morning)
Eternal Parent, will you understand if my answers seem to be those
of an impatient child?

(Evening)
Eternal Parent, I give thanks for the certainty of Jesus the Christ,
no matter how childish my understanding of things divine.

How can I answer, "Who do you say I am?" Will I, like Peter, be chastised for giving a human answer—saying the right word without understanding what it means? Others name Jesus: beautiful savior, precious one, friend, redeemer, compassionate lover, sovereign, light of the world, Emmanuel, morning star, suffering servant, child of Mary, child of God, the Christ. But, who, I am asked again, is Jesus for me? Give me, I pray, an answer that has meaning as well as truth. Turn the familiar Bible stories into stories with meaning for my life and for the oppressed people of our world. Provide an image for those around me who have never met Christ Jesus but have seen the church. Help me!

(Morning)
As I pause before the day's activities, help me meditate again on an image of Jesus
as I quietly picture Jesus walking toward me.
(Prayers of Intercession)

(Evening)
I give thanks for the image that I have carried with me today, and I pause now
to meditate on that image of Jesus.
(Prayers of Intercession)

Surrounded by the image of Jesus, I pray.
(Pray the Prayer of Our Savior.)

(Morning)
May I carry the image of Jesus near my
consciousness today. Amen.

(Evening)
I rest in the assurance of Jesus' life,
death, and resurrection. Amen.

SUNDAY, SEPTEMBER 14
(Read Mark 8:34–38)
(Have a cross in your place of meditation)

(Morning)
Merciful God, on this day, we set aside to worship you.
I give thanks for your offering of meaningful life.

(Evening)
Merciful God, at the close of this day, I continue to worship you as I pray for life.

I pray to be able to follow Jesus, even to the cross, in the promise told by those first disciples that "those who want to save their life will lose it, and those who lose their life for Jesus' sake, and for the sake of the gospel, will save it." I ask your presence in the lives of people around the world who are struggling with actual death, chains, walls, fear for their lives, and doubt about tomorrow. Grant us all the wisdom to find life in you and the courage to work for justice.

(Morning)
Give me discernment to recognize the way of the cross and courage to choose life today.
(Prayers of Intercession)

(Evening)
I give thanks for the life offered to all who choose Christ's way.
(Prayers of Intercession)

Recognizing that the way of the cross is your will, I pray.
(Pray the Prayer of Our Savior.)

(Morning)
Today, let me not be ashamed to follow Jesus. Amen.

(Evening)
Tonight, I rest in the assurance of Jesus' gift of life. Amen.

MONDAY, SEPTEMBER 15
(Read Psalm 1)
(Reading from Proverbs 31:10–18)

(Morning)
O righteous and wise God, I rise today realizing I have much to accomplish, but trusting that I will be led by the wisdom of your Word. I thank you, Source of my wisdom, for your Word that calls me into righteousness.

(Evening)
O righteous and wise God, I seek you as I rest tonight. My peace comes from meditation on your Word. Continue to guide me with your wisdom.

God, your Word makes known to me the many tasks of the capable wife. She is trusted by her husband and she completes her tasks with skill. She is strong as well as wise. She is as rare as precious jewels. God, for me it is not easy to be capable, competent, and constant in well doing. It is not easy to work with willing hands when the work is repetitive and sometimes uninspiring. However, I know that the capable wife gains her wisdom and strength from you. I seek your wisdom today in all that I do.

(Morning)
As I prepare to begin my day, I pray for those who are overwhelmed by their many tasks.
(Prayers of Intercession)

(Evening)
Hear my prayer for those who might take the wrong path.
(Prayers of Intercession)

Now, I pray, gird us with your wisdom so that we may walk in your paths of righteousness and prosper in all that we do.

(Morning)
God, send me now strengthened with your wisdom so that I might take the path of righteousness. Amen.

(Evening)
I thank you for the peaceful sleep that comes because I trust that you watch over the righteous. Amen.

TUESDAY, SEPTEMBER 16
(Read Psalm 1)
(Reading from Proverbs 31:19–26)

(Morning)
Wise and loving God, I rise today confident that your wisdom will guide me
and your love will surround me as I seek to hear your voice.

(Evening)
Wise and loving God, I rest in your Word. Open me to opportunities
to speak with wisdom.

I praise you, my provider, for your Word that calls me into loving relationships. God, your Word shows me that I am to be open to those in need. Your Word says that a capable wife creates a comfortable household for her family, but that she also reaches out into the community through personal works as well as financial contributions. God, I am thankful for how you have prospered me. Help me to yield the fruit of generosity. Help me to show my thankfulness through acts of love. Help me to give up some of my comfort so I might be your presence in the life of those in need.

(Morning)
As I prepare to begin my day, I pray for those who need to know your love.
(Prayers of Intercession)

(Evening)
I pray that your wisdom will abound not only in my family,
but in my community and the world.
(Prayers of Intercession)

**Now, I pray, gird us with your wisdom so that we may walk in your paths
of righteousness and prosper in all that we do.**

(Morning)
Send me, God. Help me to teach
kindness in response to your love.
Amen.

(Evening)
As I meditate on your righteousness,
refresh me with sleep. In your holy
name. Amen.

WEDNESDAY, SEPTEMBER 17
(Read Psalm 1)
(Reading from Proverbs 31:27–31)

(Morning)
Wise and joyous God, I rise today prepared to face a day of challenges as well as one of joy and praise, as I seek your will.

(Evening)
Wise and joyous God, I rest in your Word. Allow me to relax in the joyful knowledge that I have served you.

I praise you, most excellent God, for opportunities to celebrate our service to you. God, your Word celebrates and praises the gifts of a capable wife. Her children celebrate her joyous spirit. Her husband praises her as excellent in all things. She is also praised in her community. But her highest praise comes because she fears you. Sometimes we seek the praise of others more than we seek to serve you. Make us mindful of how easy it is to be deceived by charm and vanity. As we hear others praise us, give us the wisdom to first praise you.

(Morning)
As I prepare to begin my day, I pray for my concerns as well as the concerns of your people.
(Prayers of Intercession)

(Evening)
I pray that all people may come to share in the fruit of our communal hands.
(Prayers of Intercession)

Now, I pray, gird us with your wisdom so that we may walk in your paths of righteousness and prosper in all that we do.

(Morning)
Send me, God. Allow me to experience the joy of your Word. Help me to share your joy with others. Amen.

(Evening)
As I meditate on your righteousness, refresh me with sleep. In your holy name. Amen.

THURSDAY, SEPTEMBER 18
(Read Psalm 54, Jeremiah 1:5–10)
(Reading from Jeremiah 11:18–20)

(Morning)
Righteous and wise God, I rise this morning seeking your help.
You are the upholder of my life, and I seek your will.

(Evening)
Righteous and wise God, my rest comes from resting in your righteousness.
Search my heart for all unrighteousness.

I thank you, Righteous Word, for saving me from danger on all sides. Hear my prayer. God, you have made known to me that I need to trust you more. Jeremiah had to withstand the assaults of many enemies, but he continued to remain faithful to you and continued to prophesy in your name. You told Jeremiah not to worry about what to say—you would put the words in his mouth. You told him not to worry about his enemies—you would be with him. Help me to trust you as Jeremiah did. Give me the words to say to have victory over evil. Help me to know that you are with me. I have committed to you all that I do.

(Morning)
As I prepare to begin my day, I pray for my concerns as well as the concerns
of your people.
(Prayers of Intercession)

(Evening)
I pray that your people will trust in you as their helper
and deliverer from all trouble.
(Prayers of Intercession)

**Now, I pray, gird us with your wisdom so that we may walk in your paths
of righteousness and prosper in all that we do.**

(Morning)
Trusting in you, I receive your wisdom.
Send me now. Amen.

(Evening)
As I meditate on your righteousness,
refresh me with sleep. In your holy
name. Amen.

FRIDAY, SEPTEMBER 19
(Read Jeremiah 11:18–20)
(Reading from Psalm 54)

(Morning)
Righteous and faithful God, hear my prayer this morning. I wake up meditating on your faithfulness. Guide my steps so that I might walk in triumph.

(Evening)
Righteous and faithful God, I rest in the knowledge that you will keep me safe from enemies of all kinds.

I thank you, my helper, for upholding my life. Your words are able to keep me from falling. God, you have saved me in many ways. I realize my enemies aren't always people; they are my own disobedience, my own selfishness, my own lack of love. When I pray to you, hear my voice and help me. You know my heart. I willingly confess my unrighteousness to you, and you are faithful to deliver me from my troubles. I thank you for your goodness. You have helped me triumph over my enemies.

(Morning)
As I prepare to begin my day, I pray for my concerns as well as the concerns of your people.
(Prayers of Intercession)

(Evening)
I pray that you will hear the words of your people. Deliver us from all trouble.
(Prayers of Intercession)

Now, I pray, gird us with your wisdom so that we may walk in your paths of righteousness and prosper in all that we do.

(Morning)
Send me, God. Help me to walk in victory and righteousness. Amen.

(Evening)
As I meditate on your righteousness, refresh me with sleep. In your holy name. Amen.

SATURDAY, SEPTEMBER 20
(Reading from James 3:13–4:3, 7–8a)
(Sing a favorite hymn)

(Morning)
Righteous and wise God, I rise this morning seeking your peace
that comes from walking in righteousness.

(Evening)
Righteous and wise God, my rest comes from resting in your righteousness.
Abide in me.

I praise you, righteous God, for your words of wisdom which lead me to a good life; hear my prayer. God, I seek your wisdom. I want to live a life of gentleness and peace. Your Word tells me I have a choice. I can live a life of earthly wisdom, full of bitterness and lacking in spirituality. Or I can live a life of peace, gentleness, mercy, full of good fruits. God, I seek your wisdom. I submit my will to you and resist the wisdom of the devil. Help me to grow closer to you. Fill me with your presence.

(Morning)
As I prepare to begin my day, I pray for my concerns as well as the concerns
of your people.
(Prayers of Intercession)

(Evening)
I pray that you will guide your people so that we may live the good life
filled with your wisdom.
(Prayers of Intercession)

**Now, I pray, gird us with your wisdom so that we may walk in your paths
of righteousness and prosper in all that we do.**

(Morning)
Filled with your wisdom from above,
send me now. Amen.

(Evening)
As I meditate on your righteousness,
refresh me with sleep. In your holy
name. Amen.

SUNDAY, SEPTEMBER 21
(Read James 3:17–18, 4:1)
(Reading from Mark 9:30–37)

(Morning)
Righteous and wise God, I rise this morning asking that you walk with me and resolve those conflicts that may come about as a result of my pride.

(Evening)
Righteous and wise God, forgive me where I have sown conflict.
Fill me with your peace.

I praise you, God of wisdom. Give me a word today that might bring peace to strife. Hear my prayer. God, you often taught your disciples; your time was short, and there was much that you wanted them to know. This time the lesson was lost on them: They did not understand, and because of fear, they did not ask. They lost their focus on you and began arguing, "Who is the greatest?" They thought they could answer that among themselves. God, we, too, lose our focus. We take our minds off your teachings and allow our pride to overcome us. You know our hearts. You remind us that greatness comes not from pride but from humility; not from conflict but from righteousness sown in peace.

(Morning)
Prepare me this day to pray for peace in my life and the lives of your people.
(Prayers of Intercession)

(Evening)
I pray that your people will seek your teachings and find your peace.
(Prayers of Intercession)

Now, I pray, gird us with your wisdom so that we may walk in your paths of righteousness and prosper in all that we do.

(Morning)
I come as a child. Grant me your wisdom. Amen.

(Evening)
As I meditate on your righteousness, refresh me with sleep. In your holy name. Amen.

MONDAY, SEPTEMBER 22
(Read Numbers 11:4–6, 10–16)

(Morning)
God of patience and understanding, I greet this day with the assurance of your presence. I recognize that anticipated and unexpected challenges await me.

(Evening)
God of patience and understanding, draw me into the assurance of your acceptance and compassion in the midst of my failures.

I find comfort in the stories of scripture which enable me to identify with your children of so long ago. Deliverer God, through Moses, you led your children out of Egypt through the sea, into the wilderness of freedom. You heard your children complain as they were tempted to return to the security of slavery rather than face the uncertainty and hardship of freedom. As Moses vented his frustration over the burdens he carried, you listened and responded. Forgive me for the ways in which I have yielded to the temptation to face my struggles by retreating to old patterns of self-defeating behavior. Free me to bring myself to you and, at the same time, grant me the strength to hear your wisdom for my life.

(Morning)
As I prepare for this day, I pray for strength in my trials and for the same grace in the lives of others.
(Prayers of Intercession)

(Evening)
Grant that I show the same understanding toward those who test my patience as I ask of you.
(Prayers of Intercession)

And now, with confidence as your child, I pray.
(Pray the Prayer of Our Savior.)

(Morning)
As I face the tasks of this day, send me forth with joy and peace. Give me understanding, and patience toward others. In your name. Amen.

(Evening)
Like a child at home, I rest in your gentle arms, loving Christ. Amen.

TUESDAY, SEPTEMBER 23
(Read Numbers 11:24–29 and Mark 9:38–41)

(Morning)
Holy and compassionate God, this day you call my body and heart to be awakened to the new work of your Spirit.

(Evening)
Holy and compassionate God, this day you have chosen unpredictable paths of love.

I acknowledge the ready-made temptation to believe that the ways in which your Spirit moves in my life and in the lives of your people can be predicted. Remind me that when the Spirit fell upon two who were not with the select group of elders, Joshua protested; but in wisdom, Moses rejoiced in your mysterious ways. Like Moses, Jesus knew that those who performed deeds of the Holy Spirit were with God, in spite of great surprise! May I have eyes to see that where there is love, there you are. Forgive me and your people for preconceptions and prejudgments which tend to nail shut the open door of your grace.

(Morning)
As this day unfolds before me, I pray that your Spirit will move through the needs and longings of myself and others.
(Prayers of Intercession)

(Evening)
Move my heart with the compassion of Christ as I reflect on this day and the needs of those I have encountered.
(Prayers of Intercession)

As your child, united with your children everywhere, I pray.
(Pray the Prayer of Our Savior.)

(Morning)
With confidence, I am sent forth to love and serve in the name of God. Amen.

(Evening)
May I rest in peace and sleep, united with Christ, held in love. Amen.

WEDNESDAY, SEPTEMBER 24
(Read Mark 9:42–50)

(Morning)
O God, Loving Parent of us all, as I arise, this day brings for me a thousand opportunities to choose and act.

(Evening)
O God, Loving Parent of us all, this day, through decisions made or deferred, another imprint has been left upon my life and the lives of others.

Sometimes I would rather ignore those words of scripture which speak of the consequences of our choices; consequences sometimes spoken in ultimate terms! "If your hand causes you to stumble, cut it off; it is better for you to enter life maimed than . . ." May I live with the tension of knowing that I do not have to feel ultimately responsible for the universe, but that by your grace the choices I make can "shape lives or break them." Redeemer God, help me to understand salvation as the journey of a lifetime, built through choices made moment by moment, day by day. May I turn from the voices of addiction, greed, and indifference; May I choose the path of faith, hope, and love.

(Morning)
I face this day with hopefulness because your Spirit of life surrounds me and others.
(Prayers of Intercession)

(Evening)
May your forgiveness surround all who have made destructive choices this day. May I have the courage, through your grace, to right the wrong and keep the faith.
(Prayers of Intercession)

With many of your children throughout the world, I pray.
(Pray the Prayer of Our Savior.)

(Morning)	(Evening)
As your free and redeemed child, I go forth to create the day. Amen.	As your forgiven disciple, I now rest in peace. Amen.

THURSDAY, SEPTEMBER 25
(Read Esther 7:1–6, 9–10)

(Morning)
O Holy One, this day you have created challenges for me; some may be great, others small.

(Evening)
O Holy One, at the close of the day, I seek rest for my body, quiet for my soul.

Thank you, beloved God, for the stories of scripture which inspire your people to live selflessly. You gave Queen Esther a heart of compassion for the children of Israel. You gave her the courage to risk a life of well-being and safety by interceding for the salvation of her people. May I, too, have the courage of Esther. Forgive me for those times when fear has wilted my soul and my actions have centered around self-preservation and betrayal. May I so fully trust in you that I am freed to right the wrong, to stand firm where needed, to build bridges rather than walls.

(Morning)
I hold before you the needs of others. May these prayers for those I name join your work of love in their lives.
(Prayers of Intercession)

(Evening)
I recall those whom I have encountered this day, their needs and longings. May I be especially aware of the needs of those to whom I am close.
(Prayers of Intercession)

As your forgiven child, I pray.
(Pray the Prayer of Our Savior.)

(Morning)
This day, may I walk the path of courage, integrity, and compassion. May I be a blessing in the lives of others. In Jesus' name. Amen.

(Evening)
I surrender myself to your safekeeping as the night surrounds me. In your holy name. Amen.

FRIDAY, SEPTEMBER 26
(Read Esther 9:20–22 and Psalm 124)

(Morning)
O Creator of all life, my heart is turned to you as I begin this day.

(Evening)
O Creator of all life, as my day comes to a close, I am aware that the night is filled with the presence of the divine Spirit.

I am filled with gratitude that you are a God of hope and salvation. I find comfort as I read the ancient story of the children of Israel's deliverance from death, through the courage of Esther. My heart, too, is filled with joy as I recall the words of the psalmist: "Our help is in the name of God, who made heaven and earth." Even as your children of old celebrated the joy of new life by praising you, remind me that through you comes all life, healing, and love. May all the seasons of my life be grounded in joy and thanksgiving. May my worship, and the worship of your people, echo the praise of all your creation. Help me to know that in the heart of all creation, sorrow can never be the final word.

(Morning)
As I prepare for this day, may the freeing power of your love be evident in my life.
I remember the special needs of others.
(Prayers of Intercession)

(Evening)
Open my heart and remind me of the numerous gifts of this day.
I give thanks for those whom I name before you.
(Prayers of Intercession)

And now in unity with your children everywhere, I pray.
(Pray the Prayer of Our Savior.)

(Morning)
May this day be alive with love and compassion for all. Help me to be aware of your transforming presence in all my experiences. In the name of Jesus. Amen.

(Evening)
As I lay my consciousness aside in sleep, grant a peaceful night to this child. Blessed are you, O holy God. Amen.

SATURDAY, SEPTEMBER 27
(Read Psalm 19:7–14)

(Morning)
O Beloved Sacred Parent, I realize that as I begin this day, my heart, too, needs to be awakened from sleep.

(Evening)
O Beloved Sacred Parent, I return to you at the close of this day, as a child in the arms of a mother, whose lavish love knows no bounds.

How blessed we are, that the sound of all creation is the heartbeat of your compassion. I praise you that your Word is truly the word of love; the one love that fuels the stars, traces the rainbow across the sky, and fills the lungs of a child newly born. Even as your wisdom inspired the psalmist to meditate on the beauty of divine revelation, may I have ears to hear your whisper of life for me. Help me to realize that nothing happens to me or to others but that your grace is at work, seeking wholeness for your beloved. May I even have the faith to receive the gift, that through me, your Word may be spoken. Let me claim, as Meister Eckhart said, that "[I am] a Word of God."

(Morning)
I prepare for this day, believing that your Word is written across this universe and in the Holy Scriptures.
(Prayers of Intercession)

(Evening)
As I come to rest, I am grateful for your unconditional love and forgiveness. I offer to you the following concerns . . .
(Prayers of Intercession)

And now, with confidence as your child, I pray.
(Pray the Prayer of Our Savior.)

(Morning)
I go forth eager to hear your voice, in its thousand mysterious ways. Amen.

(Evening)
Grant me the rest that I need. May I arise tomorrow, ready to face the challenges of a new day. In your holy name, and in the name of Jesus, and of the Holy Spirit. Amen.

SUNDAY, SEPTEMBER 28
(Read James 5:13–20)

(Morning)
O Loving and Divine Friend, I greet you with affection as this autumn day begins.

(Evening)
O Loving and Divine Friend, as the night wraps around this part of your world, I come to quiet communion with you.

Through stories and the testimonies of others, your Word speaks of the comfort and power of a life of prayer. I read that prayer provides an opening to the deep needs of our hearts and bodies. Help me to be aware of the needs of others, that I may be a window of prayer. Help me, through the Spirit's guidance, speak prayer for others in the quiet of my own heart or in the community of the faithful. May I bring before you the yearnings of my life, with the confidence of a beloved friend. Forgive me for the moments of faithlessness, when forgetting the abundant treasure of your presence, I yield to futility and cynicism. Help me to journey in trust, as a child with a loving parent. Free me for joyful communion with you.

(Morning)
As I prepare for this day, I pray for the needs of others and myself.
(Prayers of Intercession)

(Evening)
I thank you for being close to me throughout this day. I pray for those who are in my life: my family, my friends, my adversaries.
(Prayers of Intercession)

As your child, I pray.
(Pray the Prayer of Our Savior.)

(Morning)
Forgiven and free, I set forth this day. My time with you, O God, is just beginning. Amen.

(Evening)
I let go of my concerns and struggles and rest in your loving embrace. In your holy name. Amen.

MONDAY, SEPTEMBER 29
(Read Psalm 8)

(Morning)
God our Creator, your Spirit has awakened me not only to this day but to life renewed in the majesty of your love.

(Evening)
God our Creator, your love has kept me through the hours of this day.
May it protect and guide my spirit through the night.

Accept my thanks and praise that you consider even my human state worthy of honor. I give glory to you with all creation that in your sovereignty you care for me in my weakness. Loving God, we see the wonder of your creation in the brightening colors of the trees, the shortening days, and in your abiding grace through life's ever-changing scenes. Yet we disregard your presence and reject your love. Forgive us for our unthinking ways which turn from appreciation to exploitation of your gifts. Help us to live with integrity, that our daily walk may give praise and honor to your sovereignty and your love.

(Morning)
As I seek your aid to face the tasks of this day, I offer prayers
for your whole creation, especially suffering humanity.
(Prayers of Intercession)

(Evening)
In this evening hour, I give thanks for your presence during the day.
I pray for fellow travelers who also need the assurance of your presence.
(Prayers of Intercession)

With confidence in your love, I pray.
(Pray the Twenty-third Psalm.)

(Morning)
Now I go forward uplifted and empowered to walk in the light of your divine presence. Amen.

(Evening)
I take my rest confident of your loving care while I sleep, and I rest in the peace of Jesus Christ, my Savior. Amen.

TUESDAY, SEPTEMBER 30
(Read Job 1:1, 2:1–10)

(Morning)
Gracious Redeemer, you bring us through the shadows of night
and evil into life-giving light.

(Evening)
Gracious Redeemer, you travel the roadways of life with us,
shining your revealing light into the places of obscurity.

I praise you, God of love, that your ways, though unfathomable, reveal the greatness of your power and the magnitude of your grace. Omnipotent God, like your servant Job, we seek to live uprightly with integrity and to walk blameless before you. We try to keep faith in you when evil surrounds us and we are afflicted in body and soul. Forgive us when, in our weakness, we curse your name and turn away from following you. Give us strength of will to reject evil and the grace to love and trust you always.

(Morning)
I come in prayer for those who, in the midst of pain, have turned from you
and for all of us who strive to walk your path with integrity.
(Prayers of Intercession)

(Evening)
I pray for all who are experiencing the pain of rejection of your love,
of absence from your body, of loneliness of spirit, of hunger and want.
(Prayers of Intercession)

With confidence in your love, I pray.
(Pray the Twenty-third Psalm.)

(Morning)
Take me into this day in the strength of your power to resist all evil that confronts me. In Jesus' name. Amen.

(Evening)
Be with me as I sleep. May my body and soul be renewed through your love, for you are my God and my all. Amen.

WEDNESDAY, OCTOBER 1
(Read Psalm 26)

(Morning)
God of justice, I awaken with a song of thanksgiving
that proclaims the wonder of your grace.

(Evening)
God of justice, I approach the night secure in your grace
for deliverance from labor to rest and sleep.

I give thanks for your boundless love and your faithfulness. My heart is filled with praise, and I bless your holy name. God of truth and deliverance, in this moment I am sadly aware of the weakness of my faith; yet I trust in you to deliver me. I tell the wondrous story of your love; yet too often, my own actions are unloving. I try to walk in the rightness of my honor; yet my footsteps falter and I stray from your path. Forgive me, I pray. Steady my steps, that I may walk with integrity. Bring us all back to your way, that with truth and justice, we may rejoice.

(Morning)
I pray for all who do not give or receive justice.
Redeem us to love and serve you and one another with truth.
(Prayers of Intercession)

(Evening)
I pray for all those who shared my day and for all anywhere who share my life.
By your grace, grant them justice.
(Prayers of Intercession)

Hear me as I pray in the words you taught.
(Pray the Prayer of Our Savior.)

(Morning)
Go with me into my day. Stay with me, dear God, and with all your people, for we need your guiding hand. Amen.

(Evening)
Grant me peaceful rest and restful sleep, safe in your loving care. Amen.

THURSDAY, OCTOBER 2
(Read Genesis 2:18–22)

(Morning)
Creating Spirit, I praise the dawning of this day,
even as you praised the dawn of creation.

(Evening)
Creating Spirit, I give thanks for the day you gave me and for its many blessings.

Thank you for making me as I am, for allowing me to share the joy of your creation and the evidence of life all around me. In your wisdom, you gave us human beings the opportunity to join with you in the work of creation. In your love, you allowed us the freedom to name ourselves and all that you made. Forgive us, that we have abused the privilege of your love. Forgive me, that I have not truly appreciated and shared your bountiful blessings. Bring us all back to full awareness of your sovereign love, that we might share your love with each other and all creation.

(Morning)
God, I pray for the unity of all people, male and female,
that we might again be one in you.
(Prayers of Intercession)

(Evening)
Dear God, help me and all people to be ever mindful
and give honor to your whole creation and to one another.
(Prayers of Intercession)

With confidence as your child, I pray.
(Pray the Prayer of Our Savior.)

(Morning)
Make this day into whatever is best for me. I pray in the name of Jesus. Amen.

(Evening)
As you rested after each day, may I rest in peace with you this night, my God.
Amen.

FRIDAY, OCTOBER 3
(Read Genesis 2:22–24 and Mark 10:2–12)

(Morning)
Uniting God, I awake with joy, secure in the knowledge that, through your love, I am one in Spirit with all who love you.

(Evening)
Uniting God, I come to the time of rest, tired yet renewed by your Spirit, joined with mine.

I celebrate the unity of spirit that is part of all who know and keep your Word. I rejoice because you make us one with you. With one form and for one purpose, you made us in your likeness. You join us together in units of compassion and concern. You invite us to care for one another and celebrate together in a union of love. Yet, O God, we crave an unjust sovereignty over one another. We find ways to separate ourselves from you and from one another. Forgive us for rejecting your love and the unity it allows. Forgive us for striving to be greater than others and you. Join us with you in the unity of your Holy Spirit.

(Morning)
I pray for those near and dear to me, that together we can be one in love, and for the unity of all people.
(Prayers of Intercession)

(Evening)
Help those who do, to continue the joy of oneness with you, and those who do not, to experience it for themselves.
(Prayers of Intercession)

With confidence as your child, I pray.
(Pray the Prayer of Our Savior.)

(Morning)
I go in your Spirit, God, to be one with your creation this day. Amen.

(Evening)
Stay with me as I sleep this night. Grant me rest, safe in your divine care. Amen.

SATURDAY, OCTOBER 4
(Read Hebrews 1:1–14)

(Morning)
Incarnate Word, I come to this new beginning knowing that as you are,
I too am God's child.

(Evening)
Incarnate Word, in the close of this day, I rejoice that you were made flesh
for my sake.

All glory to you, Firstborn of Creation. O Word made flesh, I praise you, for you are the hope of my salvation. God, you sent Jesus Christ, your Child, to take our lowly state and then to take our sins. You made Jesus sovereign with you, having all power in heaven and on earth, yet taking for our sake the lowliness of human frame. You anointed Jesus with power, yet in your love made him lowly, that we might have power over sin. Forgive us for our rejection of your great love. Forgive us for our yearning to be powerful like you yet unwilling to accept responsibility. Bring us back to our rightful place as your children, that like and through our Savior, we might serve you and one another.

(Morning)
Blessed Savior, make me more like you this day. Bring us all closer to your side.
(Prayers of Intercession)

(Evening)
Christ, I pray for strength and humility for myself, for those I love,
and for all humanity.
(Prayers of Intercession)

With a renewed spirit, I pray.
(Pray the Apostles' Creed.)

(Morning)
Assured of your forgiving love, I go forward to serve you this day. Amen.

(Evening)
With confidence in your saving love, I rest in peace this night, dear Savior. Amen.

SUNDAY, OCTOBER 5
(Read Hebrews 2:5–12 and Mark 10:13–16)

(Morning)
Sovereign One, I awaken once more to your love and grace, assured of your blessing.

(Evening)
Sovereign One, I approach the time of rest, blessed and revived through your love.

I celebrate with joy the gift of grace that you offer through your Child, Jesus Christ. I honor and give glory to my Savior, who acknowledges me with joy. Blessed Redeemer, you welcome with open arms all who with childlike faith turn to you, yet we make excuses to stay away from your side. You invite us to receive freely the love and the grace you offer, but we move far from you. In your sacrificial death, you offer us salvation and life for all time, but we give in to the temptations of this fleeting life. Forgive us, we pray. Free us from sin. Sanctify our hearts to receive you. Loving God, I bring myself; forgive my shortcomings and grant me your grace.

(Morning)
I pray for all who share my life, for Christians everywhere, for all humanity.
(Prayers of Intercession)

(Evening)
I pray for friends and family, loved ones near and far, for your whole creation.
(Prayers of Intercession)

Hear me as I pray in the words you taught.
(Pray the Prayer of Our Savior.)

(Morning)
Bless me and make me a blessing to all this day, my God and my redeemer.
Amen.

(Evening)
Stay with me through the night, grant me rest and peace in sleep, my God.
Amen.

MONDAY, OCTOBER 6
(Read Job 23:1–9, 16–17)

(Morning)
O God of power and mystery, as I embark upon this day, I am aware
that there may be times when I feel isolated from you.

(Evening)
O God of power and mystery, as I come to the close of this day,
continue to dwell with me in the stillness of the night.

I give you thanks, O God, that in my times of isolation and bitterness you are yet near, even as you were to Job. O God, you allowed Job to experience struggle, challenge, and difficulty; and in the midst of the bitterness of his situation, he was moved to question your very presence. He prayed to you for just the ability to plead his case and to argue his cause; yet, O God Most High, you remained silent, though you were there. Remind me this day, abiding One, that you neither leave us nor forsake us, even when we cannot see your face or hear your voice.

(Morning)
And now, Holy One, I pray for all those who stand in need of your blessing.
(Prayers of Intercession)

(Evening)
This day's journey has been fraught with ambiguities and inconsistencies.
Give insight to all who could not see your constant hand in the midst of it all.
(Prayers of Intercession)

**"No, never alone, no never alone you promised never to leave me,
never to leave me alone."**

(Morning)
As I go forth this day, I go with the assurance of your abiding presence. In Jesus' name. Amen.

(Evening)
Now may your promise of perfect peace and rest bring solace, comfort, and refreshing sleep. In Jesus' name. Amen.

TUESDAY, OCTOBER 7
(Read Psalm 22:1–15)

(Morning)
Merciful and wonderful God, I approach this new day rejoicing in the knowledge that you are still good, in spite of my circumstances.

(Evening)
Merciful and wonderful God, yet another day you have allowed me to be called your child, not because I am worthy, but because of your grace.

I extol you, O God, because you command us to praise you in all seasons. Even though sometimes I cry out like the psalmist, "My God, my God, why have you forsaken me?" I, too, must proclaim that "you have kept me from my mother's womb." Sometimes when we consider ourselves and our situation, we, too, must recognize that we are but worms in comparison to your holiness. Help me, O God, to understand that in spite of who I am, I am yours. Teach me not to moan or complain but rather to bring my burdens to you. Bring me to a place where I may always give you thanks and praise.

(Morning)
O God, today I lift up to you those who are among the last, the lost, the least, and the left out. Have them to know of your love from generation to generation.
(Prayers of Intercession)

(Evening)
As I think of your goodness in the lull of the evening, may this day's grace prepare me for tomorrow's new mercies.
(Prayers of Intercession)

"Alas and did my Savior bleed, and did my Sovereign die. Would he devote that sacred head for such a worm as I."

(Morning)
O God, guide me this day toward a humble recognition of your presence in my life. In Jesus' name, I pray. Amen.

(Evening)
As I lie down this night, I can only say thank you for being there when I needed you most. Because of you, I can rest assured of your providential care for me. Amen.

WEDNESDAY, OCTOBER 8
(Read Amos 5:6–7)

(Morning)
God of righteousness and justice, I come today knowing that in you
there is newness of life.

(Evening)
God of righteousness and justice, as I prepare for this night's rest,
I come to praise you for the insights of this day.

I am reminded by the words of Amos that you are not only a God of mercy, but also of justice. Until we seek you, we live only partial lives of artificial fulfillment. Our dreams remain deferred, and our hopes are continually dashed against the rocks. But in you there is life—life abundant and life everlasting, life that finds its fulfillment as we find our oneness with you. Stand with me as I stand for those unable to stand for themselves and as I seek to liberate those whom evil has oppressed.

(Morning)
My desire today is to seek you with all my being. Speak to me now, O God,
your will for my life this day.
(Prayers of Intercession)

(Evening)
It is only by your power that I have done any good today.
(Prayers of Intercession)

Wise people still seek you.

(Morning)	(Evening)
Let me go out this day rejoicing in the life that you have given me. By the name and power of Jesus. Amen.	Let me also seek your presence with me in my rest, in my thoughts, and in my dreams. For your name's sake, I pray. Amen.

THURSDAY, OCTOBER 9
(Read Amos 5:10–15)

(Morning)
O God of truth and right, on this new day, I celebrate afresh the opportunity to choose that which you intend for me.

(Evening)
O God of truth and right, before I rest tonight, I must confess that in many ways I have failed to do this day what is right.

I thank you, O God, that you are a God who loves the truth and rejoices in what is right. Through the prophet Amos, you reproved those who rejected your preachers of old and chastised those who oppressed the poor. Your Word, through Amos, speaks a clear and compelling message to my soul, that I too must turn from evil and seek good. Forgive me when I fail you by neglecting to seek your truth.

(Morning)
I pray today for myself and others who find themselves making wrong choices. I want to live so God can use me, anytime, anytime!
(Prayers of Intercession)

(Evening)
Now that evening has come, may I find assurance of your forgiveness.
(Prayers of Intercession)

I want to live so God can use me, anytime, anytime!

(Morning)
Let my life today be an example of what is good and right in your sight. In the name of Jesus. Amen.

(Evening)
O God, in sleep you create in us anew the ability to be used by you. Grant me that refreshment. In the name of Jesus. Amen.

FRIDAY, OCTOBER 10
(Read Psalm 90:12–17)

(Morning)
God of grace and God of glory, I arise today with a glad song of praise in my mouth, for you are worthy to be praised.

(Evening)
God of grace and God of glory, as I lie down and close my eyes tonight, may I rest rejoicing in your glory.

I praise you because through the psalmists you have said that it is right to do so. I praise you because of the marvelous things that you have done. I praise you because I know that when the praises go up, the blessings come down. I praise you because the light of your countenance is ever about me. Give me a new and glad song of praise that ever may give glory to your name.

(Morning)
As I meditate about your goodness, I pray for those who do not know your joy.
(Prayers of Intercession)

(Evening)
Before I rest, I pray for those for whom sadness obscures hope.
(Prayers of Intercession)

Let my life, O God, praise you.

(Morning)
As I go about this day, let a shout of praise stay on my lips. Through Jesus Christ, our God. Amen.

(Evening)
Now I rest in your presence, where there is fullness of joy. Through Christ Jesus, our God! Amen.

SATURDAY, OCTOBER 11
(Read Hebrews 4:12–16)

(Morning)
All-wise and all-knowing God, today I come filled with awe and wonder
as I think of your knowledge and understanding.

(Evening)
All-wise and all-knowing God, you have been with me this day
through every situation.

You instructed the early Hebrew church of the sharpness of your Word. You told them and us that there was nothing about us that is hidden from you. But you sent your Anointed One from heaven to be our only mediator and advocate with you. Instruct us to come boldly to your throne, because there is one there to intercede on our behalf and one who is bringing our concerns before you.

(Morning)
I begin this day by interceding on behalf of those in need.
(Prayers of Intercession)

(Evening)
I close this day by interceding for those who have crossed my path today.
(Prayers of Intercession)

What a privilege to carry everything to God in prayer.

(Morning)	(Evening)
I go out and about this day knowing that you care about my needs. In Jesus' name. Amen.	As I find my place of rest tonight, there is comfort in knowing that you watch over me, both day and night. In Jesus' name. Amen.

SUNDAY, OCTOBER 12
(Read Mark 10:17–31)

(Morning)
O generous God, on this day, I want to surrender my all to you, afresh.

(Evening)
O generous God, this day has been filled with new opportunities
to give my all to you.

I magnify your name, O God, because in your wisdom, through your Child, Jesus, you have shown us the proper use of material things. So often we—like the rich young ruler—are grieved because you cause us to be freed from our worldly wealth so that we may be rich toward you. You teach us by your Word how difficult it will be to enter your dominion encumbered by our material goods. Release me, eternal God, from the things that bind me and keep me from being your surrendered servant. Remind me, as you did Peter, that you will replenish abundantly all who sacrifice for you.

(Morning)
This day I take time to count my blessings and to give God thanks and praise
as I name each one.
(Prayers of Intercession)

(Evening)
As I prepare for rest tonight, I reflect upon the special ways
you have blessed my life today.
(Prayers of Intercession)

"All to Jesus I surrender, all to Christ I freely give."

(Morning)
God, go with me now through this day, reminding me always of your abundant blessings. In the name of Jesus Christ. Amen.

(Evening)
In the stillness of the night, allow me to enjoy peaceful sleep, knowing that my all rests in you. In the name of Jesus Christ. Amen.

MONDAY, OCTOBER 13
(Read Job 38:34–41)

(Morning)
How could I have lost you? Signs and symbols of your presence
are with me everywhere! I am open again to hear and see.

(Evening)
For all you have given and the insights that came,
now I remember who presides and provides. Thank you, my God.

God, you placed wisdom in these autumn colors of my life and season. Help me to reflect on Job's experience with my own. Like trees blown bare, an ordering of my life becomes clearer. I forsook wisdom—she, who for so long inspired my life when you brought her to me as a gift. Earth's rhythms and hidden cadences show me an order so profound that I am returning to her and to you. You came in mutuality with Job to recall him to faith. I would like answers to your plan for my life. God, are you telling Job and me that there is no plan, but that there is an ongoing ordering of my life which is a part of your creating?

(Morning)
I am going to rage and rave with you today, God. I will need courage to do so, but I need you to come forth from hiding and speak with me for this season of my life.
(Prayers of Intercession)

(Evening)
My God, we did it! I shouted; you pronounced. Such freedom and release.
(Prayers of Intercession)

And now in your grace I entrust my prayer.

(Morning)
My life is in your hands. I thrive in your orderings of my journey. Amen.

(Evening)
Thanks be for your Word unto this day and through this night. Amen.

TUESDAY, OCTOBER 14
(Review Job 38:34–41)
(Read Psalm 104:1–9, 24, 35c)

(Morning)
All glory, honor, and awe be to God! In you, my God,
I will be refined this day by the fire and flame of my daily routine.

(Evening)
All glory, honor, and awe be to God! Rendered to ash were my guilt and shame
by confession and fire; I let go of judgment.

God of judgment for justice, cleanse me by your fire and flame so that I leave judgment to you. I am caught by the psalmist's words, that fire and flame are your ministers. The ending of the song "Amazing Grace" uses the injunction "Let sinners be consumed from the earth, and let the wicked be no more." Does this mean that I, and we, who forget to honor the fullness of your creation, are the sinners and the wicked? Every day I start the morning by building a fire; it is part of my survival. Let it remind me that fire and flame are your ministers. Perhaps my confessions to you are like the logs in my stove. They become ash as I am warmed by their heat. Does your fire and flame minister to me by rendering my confessions into heat, which warms me to life and becomes balm for my day?

(Morning)
God, be fire and flame to my soul so that I may be warmed this day
by the rendering to ash of my confessions.
(Prayers of Intercession)

(Evening)
Let my sin flee by your Word as the waters fled by your rebuke.
(Prayers of Intercession)

Cleanse me to know your meaning, God of my salvation.

(Morning)
Be balm to my heart by the warmth of your flame. Amen.

(Evening)
Keep me warm through the night, that my spirit may be cleansed afresh until the morn. Amen.

WEDNESDAY, OCTOBER 15
(Read Isaiah 53:4–12 and Psalm 91:9–16)

(Morning)
God, to be partners with you in creating is an awesome responsibility! I accept with joy in my spirit. I stand in awe to know that I am a partner and steward of your mysteries.

(Evening)
God, to be partners with you in creating is an awesome responsibility! I accept with joy in my spirit. What a joy and task to have the job of protecting you. My call is to answer and obey. I trust that I have been and done so this day.

God, your prophet Isaiah and your psalmist call me back to know that the time is fulfilled. I am Eve, I am Adam. I am nature and history. Named by you, I am partners with you. Imbue me with the will to serve you fully. Isaiah knew the freedom that comes from cleaving to you. Cleaving seems more personal—I like it. I have been teased for being Christian and scorned by being a minister. Usually I feel defensive and spiteful. How good, how released I have felt the few times I have cleaved to you and simply said yes. I want to learn more about cleaving and be your partner in loving and creating in the world. Teach me more, God. I commit myself this day to cleaving.

(Morning)
When you call, God, I will answer. Awed but not afraid, I will cleave to you.
(Prayers of Intercession)

(Evening)
To deliver you to life is freedom and release;
salvation in immanence even when reviled.
(Prayers of Intercession)

God, my burden is lifted, and my heart is full of love for your revelations.

(Morning)	(Evening)
I am called to succor you. I will be succor as I open to this new understanding of who I am. Amen.	Thanks beyond belief for the experience of knowing you, my God, as a partner. Amen.

THURSDAY, OCTOBER 16
(Review Isaiah 53:4–12)
(Read Hebrews 5: 1–10)

(Morning)
God, teach me more of what it means to be a priest—your ministry of all believers. Made anew by you, I cease my search and answer my call to community.
I rejoice in new life.

(Evening)
God, teach me more of what it means to be a priest—your ministry of all believers. Appointed by your Spirit, I have given myself this day. And I am your servant.

Angel messengers at dawn break into our lives and give us resolutions we cannot make ourselves. Insights, revelations, the Word. They are imps, troublemakers, for they change us into your greeters and servants. And so we serve, take stands, listen, and often forget how to receive as well as give. I am one of these so favored. But I am afraid—not with the fear provoked by danger but with the awe evoked by wisdom, the wisdom that makes me know I will suffer. So I will try to stop and understand rather than leap to fix the suffering—my own and that of others. Jesus' call is not my call. However, fulfilling my call, as he fulfilled his, is being made perfect in you.

(Morning)
I remember those vague images and felt the deep breathing release of resolution as I awoke: an angel messenger at dawn! Thank you.
(Prayers of Intercession)

(Evening)
I am pondering the meaning of my message and my suffering.
I am begotten to fulfill your ordering.
(Prayers of Intercession)

Keep me, that I might know more fully my fulfillment.

(Morning)
Out of my suffering, my loss, my chaos, come a new day, a new order, and a new covenant with God. Amen.

(Evening)
Grace infuses me from the learnings of this day. Thanks be to you, my God, for fulfilling me in your eternal covenant. Amen.

FRIDAY, OCTOBER 17
(Read Mark 10:35–45)

(Morning)
God, you really are right in our midst. Keep coming and waking me.
What is my preparation, my serving you on my path of fulfillment? I am ready.

(Evening)
God, you really are right in our midst. Keep coming and waking me.
These were my experiences . . . My preparation was . . . My fulfillment is . . .
I give thanks for . . .

What made your Child was his knowing and cleaving to you, O God. Christ Jesus fulfilled to perfection his call. How do I follow his norm? Each of us is prepared for our own fulfillment in you. I remember that Jesus said he came to fulfill the law, not to destroy it. The word he used for "fulfill" means to fill a cup to overflowing. Is this what you intend for me, too? I may share in baptism and the cup with Jesus, but my fulfillment is not to be the Christ. It is something else: what? What are the clues, the obvious characteristics? How am I fulfilling these now? Perhaps I am still fighting being a Christian, for I have not yet given myself up fully. It does mean leading and accepting full responsibility for all I am given. In this day, how shall I lead and minister as your servant?

(Morning)
God, make me responsive to your call for my service.
Help me to see and hear the fullness you intend.
(Prayers of Intercession)

(Evening)
God, I tried to be flexible and allow you to transform me.
I feel . . . I learned . . . I know now . . .
(Prayers of Intercession)

Being formed and fulfilled can seem overwhelming. The gift is to let go in God.

(Morning)
God, lead me into my community as a servant this day. Amen.

(Evening)
Your peace is mine. Thank you, God, for fulfillment. Amen.

SATURDAY, OCTOBER 18
(Read Isaiah 53:4–12 and Mark 10:35–45)

(Morning)
God of all creation, what a gift you have given us! For this morning,
I want to reflect on who I am and what being Christian means, through this poem
in each of my meditations.

(Evening)
God of all creation, what a gift you have given us! For this evening,
I want to reflect on who I am and what being Christian means, through this poem
in each of my meditations.

God of all creation, what a gift you have given me! To be born in a time of one globe, one people, one economy, of mixed genes. Cross-fertilized by rituals and food, faith and art, music and media, trade and politics, even terror, war, and death. What chaos, what creativity. Whose am I? You are my God, and I am your person. Alleluia!

(Morning)
Help me to see the plank in my own eye, shared with all people
who refuse to see and hear anew.
(Prayers of Intercession)

(Evening)
Open me to your unconditional love so I may love my neighbors near and far,
here and now.
(Prayers of Intercession)

**As one called to lead in the way of Christ, catch me and guide me
to your wisdom and Word.**

(Morning)
Dear God, wake me to really understand the person who seems most different in my life this day. Amen.

(Evening)
Cleanse my spirit through the night, with dreams configured for my light to see and hear anew. Amen.

SUNDAY, OCTOBER 19
(Read Psalm 91:9–16 and Hebrews 5:1–10)
(Reflect on the week's readings)

(Morning)
God, through the Christ, I come to you. On this Sabbath day, I submit myself to your Word through Christ's spirit.

(Evening)
God, through the Christ, I come to you. Night is folding 'round me, settling all the day. Gently let me know how I have been the way.

In my faith community, I will know more fully your Word and the way of Jesus. Through the seeing and hearing of my neighbors, my faith will be enriched. Sometimes I wonder about the church; then I remember that my faith community is found in and through the church. Jesus' way is the way of which I have so much more to learn. He is the one in whom I have placed my trust. Not the media, not my political party's platform, not my teachers or my workplace, not even my family. The focus is Christ Jesus, the mark is God, and I will keep returning to faith in and through all I experience in my faith community.

(Morning)
God, remind me of my baptism and the words I spoke, so that their meaning becomes fresh this day.
(Prayers of Intercession)

(Evening)
I know that my gifts, life experiences, joys, and sufferings are from you in the way of the Christ.
(Prayers of Intercession)

For scripture that leads me to remember and to ponder, I give thanks and am humbled in faith and community.

(Morning)
God, when I share the cup, infuse me with a focus for my faith. In Christ and in the world. Amen.

(Evening)
Obedience to your Word and way is becoming my freedom and faith. For this gift, I rest in peace and trust. Amen.

MONDAY, OCTOBER 20
(Psalm 34:1–8, 19–22)

(Morning)
God, Strong Deliverer, through the night to this dawn, you brought me.
I awaken grateful.

(Evening)
God, Strong Deliverer, through this day to this time of rest, you brought me.
I come at the end of this day, grateful to you.

The psalmist praised your strength and compassion, for you answered the psalmist's cries—dispelling fear, ceasing shame, healing the brokenhearted, and saving from all troubles. Thank you for moments and days of deliverance in my own life—when you offer courage and forgiveness and lift me from hopelessness—even though fear, shame, and troubles continue. The psalmist knew that afflictions trouble even the righteous. No one has it easy. I draw near to you and seek your presence. Keep me close. Be my refuge. Deliverance comes in the comfort of your arms.

(Morning)
I pray for the troubles in this world, asking for your deliverance.
(Prayers of Intercession)

(Evening)
This night, I call upon you, O God, to deliver those with special needs.
(Prayers of Intercession)

And now, with the confidence of your child, I pray.
(Pray the Prayer of Our Savior.)

(Morning)
O God, together may we go into this day. In your holy name. Amen.

(Evening)
Deliver me through this night, confident of your care. In your holy name. Amen.

TUESDAY, OCTOBER 21
(Review Psalm 34:1–8)
(Read Job 42:1–6)

(Morning)
God, found in the whirlwind and hidden in the grieving heart, there is little certainty about what I face this day. Joy, fulfillment, sadness, or loss may greet me and this world. Will you be with me?

(Evening)
God, found in the whirlwind and hidden in the grieving heart, at the end of this day, filled with joys and sadness, fulfillment and losses, I call out to you.

Job lost his wealth, his family, and his health. He lost it all. Friends tried to explain the losses using theological clichés of the day. No words eased the pain or explained your ways. Pushed to the limit, Job raised his voice and fist to you, calling for you. Like Job and his friends, I have wanted words to answer the "whys" of suffering and loss. I have used empty words to answer the questions. Do not let me settle for words. Give me the courage to raise my voice and fist to you. Come to me. Give me your wonderful and fearful presence. Let me have not the easy answers, but *you*. "I heard of you by the hearing of the ear, but now my eyes see you."

(Morning)
Confident of your presence, I name these concerns . . .
(Prayers of Intercession)

(Evening)
I am grateful for your presence this day, and ask your continuing care this night for these needs . . .
(Prayers of Intercession)

With the confidence of your child, I pray.
(Pray the Prayer of Our Savior.)

(Morning)
Unafraid, I move into this day with you. In Jesus' name. Amen.

(Evening)
Having met you in joy and sadness, I rest confidently in your hands. In Jesus' name. Amen.

WEDNESDAY, OCTOBER 22
(Review Psalm 34:1–8)
(Read Job 42:10–17)

(Morning)
God, who restores all your people, awaken my eyes and heart to you.

(Evening)
God, who restores all your people, night draws near, and I long to be in right relationship with you.

After Job's grief and loss, you restored abundance to him. Friends, fortune, children, and health returned, and he lived out his days to a great age. Job was granted a double portion of your favor. Such a restoration is a strange ending to Job's tale. It's too simple: "Hang in through the tough times and you'll be doubly blessed afterwards." God, that just isn't so. Throughout your world, there is loss upon loss. Rewards for suffering are few. I don't understand. Please promise me something. Restore us. By your grace, give to us what you gave to Job. Bring us back to you, even in the sufferings, healed and loved. Restore a right spirit within us.

(Morning)
I am mindful of these needs this day . . .
(Prayers of Intercession)

(Evening)
I place before you the needs of these persons this night. Restore them . . .
(Prayers of Intercession)

I pray this prayer in the spirit of Jesus.
(Pray the Prayer of Our Savior.)

(Morning)
Send me into this day. In Jesus' name. Amen.

(Evening)
O God of night, I rest in your love. In Jesus' name. Amen.

THURSDAY, OCTOBER 23
(Review Psalm 34)
(Read Hebrews 7:23–28)

(Morning)
Eternal God, I rise this morning to a new day with new possibilities.

(Evening)
Eternal God, at the close of a day of uncertainty, I come now to you.

Change happens all around. In our world, nothing is certain. Leaders come and go, nations advance and fall, religions prosper and fade, and cultures gain power and then disappear. In whom could the Hebrews put their trust? In whom would salvation come? Where do I look for salvation, for hope? For all times, O God, you deliver your people. Through Christ Jesus, we know you and can count on you. "Forever" is beyond my comprehension, but such is your time. Forever may I—may we—trust in you. Forever may I know your salvation.

(Morning)
I pray for the changes that bring despair and fear in my world.
(Prayers of Intercession)

(Evening)
I pray for the changes in the world and in my world that need your eternal care.
(Prayers of Intercession)

With the confidence of your child, I now pray.
(Pray the Prayer of Our Savior.)

(Morning)
Certain of your abiding care, I enter your world this day. In Jesus' name. Amen.

(Evening)
Assured of your unending care, I rest this night. In the name of Jesus. Amen.

FRIDAY, OCTOBER 24
(Read Psalm 126)

(Morning)
Leading and laughing God, awaken me to your goodness and steadfast love.

(Evening)
Leading and laughing God, you have led me through this day to this place and time, alone with you.

Come as you did in the days of exile and restore your people. Come laughter; end the tears. Come shouts of joy; end the weeping in despair. Help me to discover your work in this world—places where recovery occurs, where justice thrives, and where your children laugh unafraid. Thank you. Thank you for the bounty of your care. "God has done great things for us, and we rejoiced!"

(Morning)
I anticipate this day and pray for these special concerns . . .
(Prayers of Intercession)

(Evening)
I am grateful for your goodness, as I recall this day . . .
(Prayers of Intercession)

With joy and conviction, I pray.
(Pray the Prayer of Our Savior.)

(Morning)
Send me into this day with joy. In your holy name. Amen.

(Evening)
Rest comes. My heart is glad in you. In your holy name. Amen.

SATURDAY, OCTOBER 25
(Review Psalm 126)
(Read Jeremiah 31:7–9)

(Morning)
Loving God, who welcomes me home, bless this morning as I awaken and come to you.

(Evening)
Loving God, who welcomes me home, bless this evening as I come to you.

Exiled, taken from a familiar and comfortable place, your people Israel longed to return home. Strong armies conquered them and led them away, but your prophet Jeremiah declared that a remnant of forgiven outcasts—those who were blind, lame, and pregnant—would return. God watch over your children. Though we rebel against you, forgive us and welcome us. Especially watch over your children whom injury, injustice, and bigotry cast out. Gracious God, gather your exiled people. Make us into a just company, a healing remnant, and a compassionate people. Bring us home.

(Morning)
Mindful of those for whom you care, I lift up these concerns . . .
(Prayers of Intercession)

(Evening)
This night watch over, in a special way, these persons and situations . . .
(Prayers of Intercession)

In the shelter of your care, I pray the prayer of Jesus.
(Pray the Prayer of Our Savior.)

(Morning)
In the company of the faithful and your presence, I enter this day. In the name of Jesus. Amen.

(Evening)
At home in you, I rest. In the name of Jesus. Amen.

SUNDAY, OCTOBER 26
(Review Psalm 126)
(Read Mark 10:46–52)

(Morning)
God, who gives sight and voice, open my eyes and slowly awaken me to your light.

(Evening)
God, who gives sight and voice, night approaches. The day draws to a close, and I look for your light.

Bartimaeus called out to you, Jesus. Blind, he recognized you and called you "Son of David." Although there were those who wanted to silence him, he called and called. He was persistent in his cry. And you heard him and gave sight to his eyes—celebrating the insight of his heart. Give me a persistent faith, a stubborn faith, a faith that never stops crying out to you. Heal me. Deliver me. Make me yours. Heal this world. Deliver this world. Make us yours.

(Morning)
I call to you, O God. Hear my prayers for these personal needs and those of others . . .
(Prayers of Intercession)

(Evening)
I call to you, O God. Hear my prayers for these personal needs and those of others . . .
(Prayers of Intercession)

I now pray as Jesus taught me.
(Pray the Prayer of Our Savior.)

(Morning)
O God, keep me awake and watching for your work throughout this day. In Jesus' name. Amen.

(Evening)
O God, I close my eyes and rest in your arms. In Jesus' name. Amen.

MONDAY, OCTOBER 27
(Read Ruth 1:2–22)
(Sing "Jesus Is All the World to Me")

(Morning)
Loving God, there are those to whom I am bound in spiritual friendship.
Help me to nurture that bond this day.

(Evening)
Loving God, the joy of this day you have made has caused my heart to rejoice
and be glad.

I thank you, loving God, for your words that model for me loving, caring, nurturing relationships. Through the story of Ruth and Naomi, may I find greater appreciation for those friends you have given me. Naomi, Ruth, and Orpah were bound together not by blood, but by marriage and the commonality of widowhood. The prevailing cultural norms called for each to return to her father's house, especially since she had no brothers to take the place of her dead husband. Orpah did go at Naomi's insistence. Ruth, however felt such a bond of friendship with Naomi, that she implored Naomi to allow her to stay. Friendship prevailed. Help me, gracious God, to be friend to others as you have been to me.

(Morning)
Creator God, I lift before you this day my concerns for myself and others.
(Prayers of Intercession)

(Evening)
As I remember my day, I ask forgiveness for my failures
and praise you for opportunities.
(Prayers of Intercession)

With boldness and confidence, I now pray.
(Pray the Prayer of Our Savior.)

(Morning)
As Ruth walked with Naomi, send me into the world to walk with others. In your name. Amen.

(Evening)
This night I commit my spirit into your hand. In your name. Amen.

TUESDAY, OCTOBER 28
(Read Psalm 14:6)
(Sing "What a Friend We Have in Jesus")

(Morning)
Loving God, the day dawns, and I am excited about the possibilities of living in your presence.

(Evening)
Loving God, needs I never knew were mine you have supplied. You truly have been my help today.

God, you are my refuge and strength, a very present help in time of trouble. You know my needs even before I ask. I praise you and thank you for supplying those needs. God, you give help to all who need it: widows, orphans, prisoners, the hungry, the blind, the lost. You do not withhold any good thing from your children. Our only response to your beneficence is to praise you. God, sometimes it's difficult to separate my wants from my needs—I need what I want right now! But you have a discerning eye. You are even able to see how the things I want can sometimes be harmful to me. Teach me to put my trust in you and in no one or nothing else. Then I will find happiness, contentment.

(Morning)
Creator God, this day I lift before you my concerns for myself and others.
(Prayers of Intercession)

(Evening)
As I remember my day, I praise you and thank you for all that you have provided.
(Prayers of Intercession)

With boldness and confidence, I now pray.
(Pray the Prayer of Our Savior.)

(Morning)
As the psalmist praised you, I lift my voice, my hands, my heart, that I might praise you and receive from you.
Amen.

(Evening)
This night I commit my spirit into your hand. In your name. Amen.

WEDNESDAY, OCTOBER 29
(Read Deuteronomy 6:1–9 and Psalm 119:1–8)
(Sing "Thy Word Is a Lamp" or another familiar hymn)

(Morning)
Loving God, I awake and greet the day, asking that you would put a song in my heart and a smile on my lips.

(Evening)
Loving God, today I discovered that I must be fully present with you to acknowledge that you alone are my God.

I praise you, gracious God, for your words that give boundaries to my life. I meditate on your statutes, that I might become more fully aware of your great and wonderful love for me. God in heaven, you spoke to Moses, declaring your sovereignty. You invite your people to constantly think about you—sitting and standing, lying down and rising up, going out and coming in. We are to be encompassed round about by you, through meditating on your Word. Loving and compassionate God, you call me to wholehearted devotion to you. Help me to love you with all that I have and with all that I am.

(Morning)
Creator God, I lift before you this day my concerns for myself and others.
(Prayers of Intercession)

(Evening)
As I remember my day, remind me when I was fully with you and when I strayed away.
(Prayers of Intercession)

With boldness and confidence, I now pray.
(Pray the Prayer of Our Savior.)

(Morning)
As I move into my day, may I walk in your law. May I observe it all the day long. Amen.

(Evening)
This night I commit my spirit into your hand. In your name. Amen.

THURSDAY, OCTOBER 30
(Read Hebrews 9:11–14 or John 10:11–18)
(Sing "When I Survey the Wondrous Cross")

(Morning)
Creator God, may the light of your love for me shine forth into my heart today.

(Evening)
Creator God, there is a time to be still, to be silent.
Help me to reflect on my walk with you.

Friends give gifts to one another—expecting nothing in return. Thank you for the gift of life and love through your Child, Jesus. Loving God, you walked with your people, and you gave your statutes, that your people might walk with you. We did not always remain within the standards you established. Thus, you found it necessary to send a mediator to bring us back to you. Jesus became the perfect sacrifice—the precious lamb whose blood sanctifies all humanity. I am awed by the depth of your love. Thank you, thank you, thank you for loving me so much that you gave your Child as high priest and sacrificial lamb for me.

(Morning)
Creator God, I lift before you this day my concerns for myself and others.
(Prayers of Intercession)

(Evening)
As I remember my day, remind me again of how much you love me
and want me to love you.
(Prayers of Intercession)

And with boldness and confidence, I now pray.
(Pray the Prayer of Our Savior.)

(Morning)	(Evening)
Purify my conscience from dead works to worship you, the living God. Amen.	This night I commit my spirit into your hand. In your name. Amen.

FRIDAY, OCTOBER 31
(Read Mark 12:28–34)
(Sing "Thy Word Is a Lamp")

(Morning)
God, the new day comes. Remind me that your Word is as new and fresh as this day.

(Evening)
God, I have no doubt that you have spoken today, but I wonder: Have I heard every word?

Gracious God, I do not want to be far from you and your realm. Help me to hear your Word, that I might be drawn closer. Many came to Jesus to test him, to dispute with him, to engage him in debate. In his presence, they missed the fulfillment of the law. Rather than create a new word for a new day, Jesus showed them your eternal Word, which is good every day. One who came to him had that insight and was deemed "not far from the realm of God." Your Word speaks to me every day, inviting me into closer, deeper communion with you. Forgive me, I pray, when I am willing to contend with you and am not willing to receive you.

(Morning)
Creator God, I lift before you this day my concerns for myself and others.
(Prayers of Intercession)

(Evening)
As I remember my day, help me to be honest with myself in responding to your Word.
(Prayers of Intercession)

With boldness and confidence, I now pray.
(Pray the Prayer of Our Savior.)

(Morning)
In this day, let me be not only one who hears your Word, but one who does it, as well. Amen.

(Evening)
This night I commit my spirit into your hand. In your holy name. Amen.

SATURDAY, NOVEMBER 1 (ALL SAINTS' DAY)
(Read Isaiah 25:6–9, Psalm 24, Revelation 21:1–6a, and John 11:32–44)
(Sing "For All the Saints")

(Morning)
Loving God, when I arose, I remembered my mentors, my role models—
the ones who shaped my faith. I am bound to them eternally.

(Evening)
Loving God, I find strength and comfort in the lives of those
who have put flesh and blood on your Word for me.

Loving God, your home is among mortals. For you to descend, the old heaven and the old earth must be replaced with the new—and the old me must be replaced by a new me. I await my transformation. God, since time began, you have been creating, refining, and fixing, preparing your dwelling place; for our dwelling place is with you and yours with us. Your creation comes full circle. You are Alpha and Omega, beginning and end. To the One who is, was, and is to be, I find my resting place in you. I long for your courts, O God, where I will be one with you, you will be one with me, and I will be joined with all those who have longed for you and loved you. God, let it be soon.

(Morning)
Creator God, I lift before you this day my concerns for myself and for others.
(Prayers of Intercession)

(Evening)
As I recall my day, let me return thanks for all your marvelous works.
(Prayers of Intercession)

With boldness and confidence, I now pray.
(Pray the Prayer of Our Savior.)

(Morning)
As I move into this day, remind me that I am accompanied by a great cloud of witnesses. Amen.

(Evening)
This night, I commit my spirit into your hand. In your holy name. Amen.

SUNDAY, NOVEMBER 2
(Read Mark 12:28–34)
(Sing "We're Marching to Zion")

(Morning)
Loving God, I worship you as I remember that today is a "mini-anniversary" of my Savior's resurrection.

(Evening)
Loving God, this day has been marvelous in my sight—and it is all your doing. I praise you.

Living God, you do not desire sacrifices or burnt offerings. The only sacrifice acceptable to you is a broken spirit. Break my spirit, that in your healing, I may have your Spirit. One among the many who came to Jesus had the proper spirit to receive Jesus. He had learned the lessons from old. Perhaps someone had spoken your Word to him in his sitting and standing, in his lying down and rising up, in his coming and going, so that he was totally immersed in your law, walking in it day and night. This is what brought him to the threshold of the your realm. God of all peoples, we gather in your name today. May we hear your Word as Moses proclaimed it, as Jesus proclaimed it, as it is proclaimed today.

(Morning)
Creator God, this day, I lift before you my concerns for myself and for others.
(Prayers of Intercession)

(Evening)
You've ordered my steps this day. If I have stumbled, forgive and help me to do better tomorrow.
(Prayers of Intercession)

With boldness and confidence, I now pray.
(Pray the Prayer of Our Savior.)

(Morning)
May I walk in such a way that I will be closer to your realm at the end of the day than I was when it began. Amen.

(Evening)
This night, I commit my spirit into your hand. In your holy name. Amen.

MONDAY, NOVEMBER 3
(Read Hebrews 9:24–28)

(Morning)
Christ Jesus, you came once for me to sacrifice your life for mine. By your actions, you offer me so much. I cannot fathom it all. Thank you, dear Jesus.

(Evening)
Christ Jesus, all creation speaks of you. The birds and the animals know you; the trees and the sky see you. Creation is positively a reflection of you.

One day, someone came to take my cares and my wounds upon himself. He took all my mistakes and gathered them into himself. He walked a difficult road with my burdens heavy upon his back, but never once did he complain. He arrived at his destination, and they grabbed him and tortured him; all the while he carried part of me along. When they sentenced him to death, he made sure my burdens were sentenced to death as well. And as he died, my cares, my wounds, and my mistakes all died with him. Now I often think of him, and deep within me I know that he still carries me with him, because deep within me I know that he is alive once more.

(Morning)
You speak to me in so many ways—but I only hear a few.
May today be different so that I may hear you.
(Prayers of Intercession)

(Evening)
I knew today would be a day that I would walk with you again.
Please God, let tomorrow be the same.
(Prayers of Intercession)

Thank you for your powerful pull upon my life, may it never go away.

(Morning)
Today I fear difficulties. I already know I will need you, God. Thank goodness you are here, ready to walk this day with me. Amen.

(Evening)
Today was full of trouble, God. Thank you for taking the weight of my burdens. Give me peace as I sleep and bless me with a new day of promise when I wake. Amen.

TUESDAY, NOVEMBER 4
(Read 1 Kings 17:8–16 and Psalm 146)

(Morning)
O Spirit God, I awake hungry. Grant me your divine food for my hunger.

(Evening)
O Spirit God, I need sleep like the deepest hunger. Fulfill my craving for rest and rejuvenation and for a respite from the risks of the day.

Sometimes I think that "all I have is a handful of flour and a bit of oil." I fail to see that you provide in abundance for me. All around me there is evidence of your creative presence and healing power, and yet I seem to focus on the negative. As you did with the widow in 1 Kings, you do also with me. Wake me up to all the ways you minister to my needs. Give me the ability to see beyond my needs and those of my children alone; cause me to see that I have enough to share with others in abundance. As you said, "The bowl will not run out of flour or the jar out of oil." My heart, my life, will not run out of love or of ways to give to others, because you fill my cup to overflowing.

(Morning)
You are there for those who need you, God. You provide, you bless, you nurture. Empower me to be like you today.
(Prayers of Intercession)

(Evening)
I hunger, as the oppressed of this world always do. Praise be to you, O God, and thank you with all my heart that I can fully trust in you.
(Prayers of Intercession)

Praise be to you, O God, and thank you with all my heart that I can fully trust in you.

(Morning)
Thank goodness I have you to love me, God. Stay with me all day, I pray, and keep me close. Amen.

(Evening)
Life is full of mystery. All I know is that God is with me, no matter what happens. On God I can depend. Praise God! Amen.

WEDNESDAY, NOVEMBER 5
(Read 1 Kings 17:8–16 and Psalm 146)

(Morning)
O God, as I watch the sky turning from night to day, bringing to light all creation, I feel the dawn of your love within my heart.

(Evening)
O God, I feel your promise. Help me to do my part to fulfill this promise.

God, you told Elijah to go to a certain town, where he would have his hunger satisfied. You said, "I have commanded a widow who lives there to feed you." At first, she didn't think she would be able to feed Elijah, but he spoke your Word to her, and then there was plenty of food created from her meager supply. When we are told that you will provide for us, do we expect some miracle to occur in an instant? Often, we must participate in your plan for your provision to come forth. In this story, both Elijah and the widow had roles to play. What are we being called to do in order to help God's provision come forth in this life?

(Morning)
Like Elijah, I, too, can believe in your answer to my needs, while at the same time you will use me to take care of the needs of others.
(Prayers of Intercession)

(Evening)
As we care for one another, we experience your love passing between us like flowing water and burning flame. Flood us and burn yourself into our souls, O God!
(Prayers of Intercession)

I come to you for the answer to my needs, and I reach out for the promise of your love and companionship in my loneliness. Walk beside me, God.

(Morning)	(Evening)
God, you beckon me to discover the promise and the joy of this coming day as I walk its path beside you. Amen.	Good night, dear God. You have walked this day with me. Sometimes I felt strong on my own and sometimes I desperately needed you. I now can rest in comfort and in peace. Bless you, O God. Amen.

THURSDAY, NOVEMBER 6
(Read Ruth 3:1–5, 4:13–17)

(Morning)
O God, the dawning of this new day issues a chance for new and meaningful connection with those whom I love. Will this be a day to discover new life?

(Evening)
O God, as I rest under the warm blanket at your feet tonight, make it possible for me to find comfort in a sense of true belonging.

God, you were present with Ruth. You empowered her. You gave her courage as she chose to leave all that was familiar to her. Instead, she chose to love and to follow her mother-in-law. Naomi, in turn, responded to Ruth's devotion by taking care of her, so that her future bore fruit and she became an important link that led to the coming of Christ Jesus. Thank you, God, for the example of obedience and devotion these two women are to me. I ask that you also empower me and give me courage to obey the call of your Spirit upon my life. I pray that I may respond in devotion to you by bearing fruit and thereby receive your blessing.

(Morning)
This morning, help me to appreciate my family, O God,
and help me to be a loving family member to all your children.
(Prayers of Intercession)

(Evening)
I rest my weary self tonight with gratitude in my heart for the love
and the support I receive from my family. Bless us as we go to sleep tonight.
(Prayers of Intercession)

Cause us to rely on one another and to trust in our family connection to carry us through life with you.

(Morning)
Thank you for making me a part of your family, God. May I be a vehicle of your love to others today. Amen.

(Evening)
Be with my family tonight as each member falls asleep. Please, God, bless your entire family. Amen.

FRIDAY, NOVEMBER 7
(Read Psalm 127)

(Morning)
God, this morning, as I face my day and anticipate the challenges before me, help me to rejoice in my children as you do. I praise you, God, for my children!

(Evening)
God, I give myself to you in my sleep. I know I can be in no better care than this. Fill me with yourself tonight while I sleep, I pray.

Children give us so much. They remind us to be joyful and to catch the wonder of a butterfly. They have energy for life, and they trust and believe. By caring for children, we are strengthened in character and we become more in touch with the essence of life. Children are willing to learn and even to join us in our efforts against what we see as "the enemy." Blessed are the children, and blessed are we because they give us so much.

(Morning)
As the crisp coolness of the night turns into warm light over all the land—
may your love flood my soul, O Holy Spirit.
(Prayers of Intercession)

(Evening)
As the cold dusk returns to the earth and shuts down the day, let me fold up all my cares and hand them back to you to carry, O Holy Spirit, while I sleep tonight.
(Prayers of Intercession)

Bless me, God, that I might be a part of your presence and of your plan.

(Morning)
Without you, Jesus, my life is nothing. What point is there to put forth effort and to care if you are not present? Help me to relax in the strength of your love.
Amen.

(Evening)
This day, I worked hard and put forth a lot of energy and effort toward what I thought was important. Help me now to let go and to trust in you, O God.
Amen.

SATURDAY, NOVEMBER 8
(Read Ruth 3:1–5, 4:13–14 and Psalm 127)

(Morning)
God, I wish to prepare to be my best today! Wash me in the water of purity, help me to put on the perfume of righteousness and dress in the clothes of love. Perhaps I will be as available for relationship with you as Ruth was for Boaz.

(Evening)
God, today I found it easier to go my own way than to give myself fully to your plans for me. Enable me to become more like Ruth.

Naomi was blessed in many ways by the love and devotion of her daughter-in-law. She did not ask Ruth to follow her home to her strange homeland. But after having said to Naomi, "Wherever you go, I will go, wherever you live, I will live. Your people will be my people, and your God will be my God," Ruth proceeded to bless Naomi with her love, her loyalty, her companionship, and then with a grandson. Do we give so totally of ourselves to those whom we love? Do we give ourselves so totally to you?

(Morning)
Perhaps I can be like Ruth and show my love, my devotion, my loyalty, and my companionship to those who need me today.
(Prayers of Intercession)

(Evening)
God, enable me to rejoice in the life I have and not complain about what I do not have. Like Naomi, let me also see you in my present life situation, and find peace and deep satisfaction.
(Prayers of Intercession)

**Be with me and cast out all false gods that I find along the way.
Thank you, God.**

(Morning)
God, like Ruth, I desire to follow you. But I am afraid I have not released the false gods in my life. Please help me to let go. Amen.

(Evening)
Ruth was obedient to Naomi and agreed to do everything she said. Naomi was then able to provide for Ruth, and she was blessed. Provide for and bless me, God. Amen.

SUNDAY, NOVEMBER 9
(Read Hebrews 9:24–28)

(Morning)
Christ Jesus, if I have any doubts about the power of your salvation to cleanse my sins forever, then please send your Spirit to cleanse me of all doubt.

(Evening)
Christ Jesus, as the ancient Hebrew people offered sacrifice to atone for their sins, let me also make amends for mine. But let me be assured of the final forgiving power of your one and only sacrifice, which has brought me forgiveness forever.

O God, Jesus has acted on my behalf, as a high priest would do. He has entered into your very presence to plead my case and to acquire the forgiveness I need. He has provided the offering, the sacrificial lamb, in order that I might be made pure and new in your sight. It was the sacrifice of his own life that he offered. His offering needed only to be given once, and it is sufficient for all eternity and for all people.

(Morning)
Jesus, you have come, lived among my people, suffered and died for me, and entered heaven to bring me forgiveness. I now look to your next coming. I await you, dear Jesus, to carry me home.
(Prayers of Intercession)

(Evening)
Tonight let me rest in peace and in the knowledge that some day you will appear again to bring me with you, so that I, too, can dwell with my God for all eternity.
(Prayers of Intercession)

Through your blood and your body, Christ, you have given me a new life.

(Morning)
Before I start my day, I ask you, God, to forgive me all my blunders and keep me safe within your reach. Amen.

(Evening)
My sins, O Christ, have haunted me today. Please forgive me and cleanse my soul as I sleep, so I will be ready for a fresh start tomorrow. Amen.

MONDAY, NOVEMBER 10
(Read 1 Samuel 1:4–20)

(Morning)
God, my heart is open before you this new day,
trusting in your compassionate presence.

(Evening)
God, for remembering me this day, I thank you with my whole heart.

With an open heart I praise you for your eternal and compassionate remembrance of me. In her deep and silent distress, enduring alone the "shame" of barrenness, the pain of ridicule, and the guilt of apparent worthlessness, Hannah presented herself to you at the temple. As bitter tears flowed from an anxious and vexed heart, she prayed for a child . . . for worth . . . for happiness. Upon receiving words of promise, which she knew in her heart to be true, she returned to her quarters, filled with hope and trust. For God, you would remember her and honor her life with the child named Samuel.

(Morning)
I welcome this day, trusting that all in my soul is known to you, my dear God.
(Prayers of Intercession)

(Evening)
For a day of light and shadow and your goodness in it,
I give you a heart filled with the deepest of gratitude.
(Prayers of Intercession)

"The best name for God is compassion" (Meister Eckhart).

(Morning)
In anticipation of tears and laughter, pain and happiness, I thank you, for in them my soul finds your healing presence. Amen.

(Evening)
For the wiping of my tears and the healing of my troubles, I worship and adore you, O God, this night. Amen.

TUESDAY, NOVEMBER 11
(Read 1 Samuel 2:1–10)

(Morning)
O God, may I sing a new song of praise to you this day,
with a glad and adoring heart.

(Evening)
O God, for a day lived in and through your strength, I give thanks.

I will sing to you Hannah's song, making her prayer and proclamation mine. With a heart filled with gladness, Hannah, being thankful for your strength and victory, knowledge and judgment, celebrated in poem and song your remembrance of her in the day of her deep distress. In poem, she recognizes and proclaims with her whole life that you not only remembered her but remember also the feeble, hungry, poor, low, needy, and faithful ones. God, you know their needs and respond with generosity, raising up those who have been forgotten and neglected. You break the bows of the mighty. You raise the poor from the dust. You lift the needy from the ash heap. God, you will judge the ends of the earth.

(Morning)
In this day I will rejoice in your strength, knowledge, and judgment, O God.
(Prayers of Intercession)

(Evening)
In your goodness I will rest this night, assured of your presence with me,
even in my sleep.
(Prayers of Intercession)

With a heart open to new life, place into your own words this poem and song.

(Morning)
In my waking, I celebrate your goodness for all, especially the downcast, the poor, the needy. And with you, I commit my life to their raising up. Amen.

(Evening)
Now I rest in you, knowing that you will raise me up to new life and commitments. Amen.

WEDNESDAY, NOVEMBER 12
(Read Daniel 12:1–3)

(Morning)
O God, upon awaking this day, I remember that you are my salvation.

(Evening)
O God, in my sleep, may my whole being and all who put their trust in you rest in the promise of your salvation.

God, you have promised to be with us always. In suffering and crises, you are the salvation of all people. God, your promise of everlasting life extends to all who walk in the way of right relationships, even in times of increased evil and oppression. Protection and deliverance from evil will come from you. Shame and everlasting contempt will come to those who do evil. Yet the doers of justice—the lovers of righteousness—will shine like the brightness of the sky and the stars, which are forever and ever. This is your promise, sealed with truth. Let us run always to these words of life, for in you is our salvation.

(Morning)
You are my protector and deliverer. This day I will trust in your protection and deliverance. I will look to you.
(Prayers of Intercession)

(Evening)
As I come to the end of this day, I thank you for leading me into the way of righteousness, of right relationships.
(Prayers of Intercession)

And Jesus said, "I will be with you until the end of age."

(Morning)
May each moment of this day be filled with the brightness of eternal life. May eternity be near to me and to all who love your ways of true justice and peace. Amen.

(Evening)
In the hours of my sleep, seal in me and in all your people everywhere your words of life. Amen.

THURSDAY, NOVEMBER 13
(Read Psalm 16)

(Morning)
O God, how wonderful you are! In you I will take refuge this day.

(Evening)
O God, this night while I sleep, I trust that your counsel will continue to instruct my heart in your ways of goodness and life.

God is the shepherd of my life and all my ways. God, you feed and lead us. You restore and renew us. You watch over us and wake us up to new life each morning. You walk with us. You prepare for us the cup of wholeness and the path of life. I will bless you. I will keep you before me always. I will be glad and rejoice in you. I will delight in all your pleasures. I will know the fullness of the joy you give to all the faithful ones who live with one another as you live with us. We shall not be moved from this path of life.

(Morning)
Your goodness this day will be my fill. You are my inheritance; in you my life is made whole and blessed. Thank you, O God.
(Prayers of Intercession)

(Evening)
I now rest my body in the wonderful security of your presence throughout the night.
(Prayers of Intercession)

Sing a song or hum a tune that stirs in your soul the watchful presence of God over your life.

(Morning)
Upon waking, I delight in your counsel, path of life, and pleasures. Today I will follow in these, knowing that in you I am secure. Amen.

(Evening)
I give thanks for the pleasures of your divine presence stirring in me as I prepare for a night of restoring rest and peace. O God, you are good, and my soul knows this. Amen.

FRIDAY, NOVEMBER 14
(Read Hebrews 10:11–14 [15–18])

(Morning)
O loving Holy Spirit, this life of Jesus make mine today.

(Evening)
O loving Holy Spirit, be the presence this night that sanctifies my heart, soul, mind, and body.

Prepare me now, O Spirit of the Living One, for these words of life and true meaning. In vain we look for ways of living that leave us empty and without meaning. Yet this need not be how we live. There was a life lived with integrity that is now the way of life for all. This life is Jesus! Jesus, you offered your life, heart, soul, mind, and body. Before they came to take it and nail it to a tree, you gave it back to God. You laid it down in love for us, with the power that comes from above—the power of love, of compassion, of fearlessness, of forgiveness, and of a holy life. Nothing can remove sins and make whole as this life can; yes, this way of life, the only way to live. I know this life and power to be also in you.

(Morning)
This morning I pray, O God, for a clean heart, a heart cleansed with Jesus' life. Make me one with you, as he was.
(Prayers of Intercession)

(Evening)
I will rest this night by your right hand, for in it I am set apart for your way of life and love.
(Prayers of Intercession)

All day, contemplate on the way of life Jesus showed the world.

(Morning)
Today may my life sanctify and set apart for you all that I touch and all that touches me. Amen.

(Evening)
May the meditations of my heart and the thoughts of my mind, even now as I lay down, be made whole by your Spirit. Amen.

SATURDAY, NOVEMBER 15
(Read Hebrews 10:19–25)

(Morning)
O God, this morning I praise you for your faithfulness with me and the whole world. You do not waver with us. Thank you.

(Evening)
O God, for a day filled with your faithfulness, I now thank you.
This night I will rest secure in it.

We approach with confidence, for we are called and given strength to persevere in friendship, confidence, intimacy, Christ's life, openness, a true and sincere heart, your house, full assurance, faith, a cleansed conscience, confession, hope, love, good deeds, togetherness, and encouragement, as we see the day dawning. May we approach you, O God, and one another with friendship, confidence, intimacy, Christ's life, openness, a true and sincere heart, full assurance, faith, a cleansed conscience, confession, hope, love, togetherness, courage, and with all that comes from the fiber of your being. For you have a great priest in your house, whose name is Christ Jesus.

(Morning)
You give me confidence, O Spirit, to enter into your presence.
I worship you with my whole being.
(Prayers of Intercession)

(Evening)
Cleanse my conscience and heart of all that is not pleasing in your sight this night,
and sprinkle me with your purifying presence.
(Prayers of Intercession)

Practice love and good deeds today.

(Morning)
Sprinkle my heart clean this morning, and make the confessions I now declare true and pure in your presence. Amen.

(Evening)
For the strength to persevere this day and this night, I give you my deepest thanks, offering to you my heart, mind, soul, and body, for your service of deeds of justice and kindness. Amen.

SUNDAY, NOVEMBER 16
(Read Mark 13:1–8)

(Morning)
O God, teach me this new day what really is great and glorious in your sight.

(Evening)
O God, as the end of this day arrives, draw me again to you
and your purpose for me.

Open my eyes, O God, and show me what lives forever. What will survive when all is said and done—when the end appears? What has eternal value? "Not one stone will be left here upon another; all will be thrown down." Stones and buildings do not have eternal permanence. But there is a temple that when destroyed is raised up again in three days. Oh how wonderful it is when our bodies are restored, built up again, by your power and presence, O God. When war, enmity, strife, earthquakes, famines, destroy life and shatter all hopes, your divine purpose still remains. In the end, neither evil nor the might of the nations will prevail. You will judge all things, destroy what makes for rubbish, and save what makes for eternal life.

(Morning)
I awake to you and your greatness. Keep me from being led astray from your truth:
My life is your temple; all of life is holy.
(Prayers of Intercession)

(Evening)
The wars I heard about today have worn me down. O God, have mercy upon us
and bring to an end all that destroys life.
(Prayers of Intercession)

God is the Alpha and the Omega, the beginning and the end.

(Morning)
Give birth to me anew today and teach me not to fear the might of the nations and what makes for war. Teach me your divine purpose: respect for all who breathe the breath of life. Amen.

(Evening)
When all of life fades, may I come to you filled not with shame but with confidence in your eternal love. Amen.

MONDAY, NOVEMBER 17
(Read John 18:33–37)

(Morning)
O God, show me your truth, as I move through this day. Let me be able to decipher truth from deception and realize that anything that is not truth is not from you.

(Evening)
O God, thank you for showing me the way today, for keeping me mindful of truth, which is good because it is of God.

There is something powerful about truth. No matter how big a lie may be, it is never more potent than truth. And no matter how far away the truth seems to be at a given moment, it will surely rise, like grass pushing up through ground that has been frozen. Jesus told Pilate that he was born in order to bear witness to the truth, and Pilate asked Jesus, "What is truth?" Pilate learned, as did the world, that the truth about Jesus was that death could not destroy him.

(Morning)
Help me today, God, to celebrate the truth that I am your child, and that no situation, no person, no lie, can change that.
(Prayers of Intercession)

(Evening)
Did I seem a little more joyful today, God? Please, forgive me if I believed more in the power of negativity than in the power of you.
(Prayers of Intercession)

Awaken early in the morning and listen to the sounds of truth.

(Morning)
As I go through this day, God, help me to hear your confirmation and affirmation of me as your child. Amen.

(Evening)
I say "amen" to the truths about me, about my life, about your desires for my life. I say "amen" because I trust the truth. Amen.

TUESDAY, NOVEMBER 18
(Read 2 Samuel 23:1–7)

(Morning)
God, I began this week asking you to reveal truth to me.

(Evening)
God, I want to stop remembering all the lies that I have believed about myself and rest in the truth about myself. Give me confidence, O God.

When we are small, we go through awful times when our peers, our parents, our teachers begin to tell us things about ourselves. It's too bad, because when we are young, so many of the things people say about us are not true. We must, like David, rest in the confidence of knowing your truth in order to get past the backpack of lies we carry. David was confident enough to say that your Spirit spoke through him, and that confidence let David know beyond the shadow of a doubt that you were with him and would always reveal truth to him.

(Morning)
This day, please reveal your truth about me to me.
(Prayers of Intercession)

(Evening)
Make my house stand firm with you so that our covenant may be pleasing in your sight.
(Prayers of Intercession)

"Make my house stand firm with God."

(Morning)
Forgive my doubt, God, as I struggle to let loose of the lies I believe about myself and search for the truth about myself that you offer. Amen.

(Evening)
Make my house stand firm with you, O God, like David's did, and please help me to tell you my desires in truth. Amen.

WEDNESDAY, NOVEMBER 19
(Read Psalm 132:1–12)

(Morning)
O God, I am trying to learn your truth and to rest in that truth.
Please let me know that you are with me.

(Evening)
O God, if I pray with a wavering spirit, then my prayer is not of truth
and the blessings cannot come. Fix my spirit.

David was no saint; he was an adulterer, a liar, and a murderer. But David had an undying belief in your truth, precious God. This allowed him to have the power that his enemies claimed. David also had a covenantal relationship with you, allowing him to talk to you and to be able to hear when you answered. The result for David was a life of blessings—in spite of his lies, his adultery, his murderous act. The biggest blessing of all was David's change from a man given to major mistakes and wrong turns to a man directed by you.

(Morning)
As you swore to David, O God, please let me know that you hear me and that my prayers are getting through to you. I, like David, promise you that I will keep all the promises I make to you.
(Prayers of Intercession)

(Evening)
Help me to hear your voice over the voices of my enemies. God, you told David that you would shame his enemies. Please protect me, even when I fail to keep the promises I have made to you.
(Prayers of Intercession)

Yahweh, remember David and all the hardships he endured.

(Morning)
Please remember the hardships I have already endured, O God, and the ones I have yet to face today. Renew my spirit of covenant with you. Amen.

(Evening)
Now the day is over. Please show me if I have kept my promises to you, and hear my thanksgiving that you have kept me and preserved me. Amen.

THURSDAY, NOVEMBER 20
(Read Psalm 132:13–18)

(Morning)
God of love, sometimes I don't feel special. Help me to believe that I am special and have been chosen by you.

(Evening)
God of love, if I concentrate too much on my enemies and their words, I fall. Help me to close my ears to them and to open my spirit to you.

The whole notion of being chosen by you is hard for us to understand, especially since so many of us feel like nobody—not even you—could or would want us. The lie is that we are that awful; the truth is that we realize that you have a love that is unconditional. It is soothing, ever present, and healing, and can work miracles. You do not require perfection; you require belief, repentance, and obedience. You will bless us if we turn to you, and you will bring to shame our enemies, those who try to disturb us and torment us.

(Morning)
Unclog my ears today, God, so that when bad news comes and tries to defeat me, I hear the Good News even louder.
(Prayers of Intercession)

(Evening)
If I gave too much credence to my mistakes and to the memory of those who hurt me, forgive me, O God.
(Prayers of Intercession)

I want my life to change; I want to stop living under the power of lies and live in the comfort of truth.

(Morning)
Unclog my ears today, God, so that I can receive the comfort of knowing that I am in your care. Amen.

(Evening)
If I listened to the thundering drums of my past burdens, forgive me, O God. Amen.

FRIDAY, NOVEMBER 21
(Read Daniel 7:9–10)

(Morning)
O God, with my earthly eyes, I see evil and I give it power. On this day, help me put evil in perspective.

(Evening)
O God, I am trying to believe that earth really doesn't have a situation that heaven can't handle. It's hard, because the evil around me is so great. Show me your power.

Evil is so pervasive. It slides into our lives and hovers over us; it taunts us and torments us and haunts us. It laughs, too, because we who say we believe in you squirm and duck under its presence. Evil laughs because we give it false power. So what's the truth? There is no evil that cannot be overcome. That's good news, necessary news, for us who struggle with evil every day.

(Morning)
I cannot see your Spirit, and so sometimes I give evil more power than it is due. On this day, help me to put evil in perspective.
(Prayers of Intercession)

(Evening)
I tried, O God, to hold on to you today.
(Prayers of Intercession)

There is no evil that cannot be defeated.

(Morning)
O God, do I dare believe that you can take control of this situation that's running my life and killing my spirit? Help me to trust your power so I may be released from the grip of evil! Amen.

(Evening)
Increase my desire to know you so that I may believe more in your love, grace, mercy, and power over the evil in my life. Amen.

SATURDAY, NOVEMBER 22
(Read Psalm 93)

(Morning)
Majestic God, open my eyes today so I may really see how majestic you are. I have been guilty of taking your presence for granted. Change that today.

(Evening)
Majestic God, thank you for allowing me to be receptive to you. I realize, after concentrating on your majesty today, that you are truly worthy to be praised.

This psalm reminds us of your majesty. You are the one who created the world—a world so firm it cannot be shaken. You are the one to whom rivers lift up, to whom the winds listen as they stir up into tornadoes and hurricanes. You are the one who makes the thunder crash and the lightning flash. Now, if you can do all these things and more, why do we think that you are not responsible for the blessings or successes in life?

(Morning)
Open my eyes today so that my praise of you and for you becomes something that spills out because of the awesomeness of your power.
(Prayers of Intercession)

(Evening)
I rest tonight confident that all power is in your hands.
(Prayers of Intercession)

I realize that something is missing ... and that something is always God.

(Morning)
O God, my God, how excellent is your name in all the earth! I praise you for all that you are, all that you have made, all that is, and all that is to come.
Amen.

(Evening)
I rest tonight confident, knowing that my life is in your hands. Amen.

SUNDAY, NOVEMBER 23
(Read Revelations 1:4b–8)

(Morning)
O God, after a week of struggling with the truth of your truth, help me leave this week with a clearer and more comfortable understanding of how powerful your truth is!

(Evening)
O God, I may not yet have it all together, but I am working toward it. Your truth in my life is what I need, and I will continue to seek it.

The measure of any prophetic declaration comes in the fulfilling of the Word. We have said throughout this week that your truth is more powerful than the world's lies. How do we know it? You are Alpha and Omega—that is truth. You are more powerful than evil—that is truth. You hear us—that is truth. You love us, in spite of our weaknesses and shortcomings—that is truth. God, you will always be there—that is truth.

(Morning)
Immerse me today, O God, in the desire to learn you and learn of you.
(Prayers of Intercession)

(Evening)
I praise you, O God, for all that you have done. You are the focus of my life, and I love you. Amen.
(Prayers of Intercession)

God will always be there.

(Morning)
Increase my faith this day. Amen.

(Evening)
You are the focus of my life, and I love you. Amen.

MONDAY, NOVEMBER 24
(Read Psalm 126 and sing or read "For the Beauty of the Earth," verse 1)
(Reading from Joel 2:21–27)

(Morning)
Creating and healing God, I rejoice at the gift of the sunrise which awakens the earth to life and growth and renewal.

(Evening)
Creating and healing God, I praise you for the world of nature, through which you embrace the human family with goodness day and night across all time.

I am mindful today, O God, through the witness of Joel, of times of plenty and want, of seasons of harvest and drought. God of all creation, you formed us in your likeness from the lifeless dust of the earth. Each one of us shares so much in common with the creation that you made and pronounced good. Merciful God, forgive me when I treat the earth and its creatures as though they were foreign to me. Open my heart to the woundedness of nature, sometimes caused by my hand and my greed, and teach me how to celebrate earth's healing when you restore its abundance.

(Morning)
Today, O God, show me my kinship with the earth and all living things so that I may honor you by loving all that you have made.
(Prayers of Intercession)

(Evening)
As night descends and this day becomes a memory, fill me with resolve to remember what today has taught me about being dust formed in your image.
(Prayers of Intercession)

And now, with confidence, as one made by you, I pray.
(Pray the Prayer of Our Savior.)

(Morning)
As I receive this new day from you, grant me a gracious heart toward those near and far who will share it with me. Amen.

(Evening)
To you, O God, I give this spent day. Forgive my failures, confirm my faithfulness, and grant me rest with peace. Amen.

TUESDAY, NOVEMBER 25
(Read Psalm 126)
(Sing or read "Great Is Your Faithfulness," verse 1)

(Morning)
God of my hopes and my dreams, I welcome dawn with the confidence
that your grace is stronger than my fears and richer than all my imagining.

(Evening)
God of my hopes and my dreams, I treasure the signs of your presence today
in people awakened to newness of life by your love.

I am grateful to the psalmist, dear God, for the courage to speak to you about life's sorrows and joys in one breath. It is so tempting to complain to you when my dreams are smashed on some rock of disappointment. It is so easy to forget you when my dreams become realities that even my neighbors see them as blessings from you. If others see in my life great things that you have done for me, forbid that I should overlook your goodness toward me. Grant me, O God, integrity of heart to thank you for your blessings. You are the giver of all gifts.

(Morning)
Show me today the way of gratitude and fill me with dreams
of a more just and compassionate world.
(Prayers of Intercession)

(Evening)
As night turns the page of yet another day and gratitude fills my heart
O God, touch my mouth with laughter and my tongue with joy.
(Prayers of Intercession)

And now, with gladness, I pray.
(Pray the Prayer of Our Savior.)

(Morning)	(Evening)
Make me an advocate today, loving God, for those who know misfortune and have forgotten how to dream. Amen.	This day is now beyond dreaming, dear God, but its unfulfilled hopes touch my pillow with intimations of tomorrow. Amen.

WEDNESDAY, NOVEMBER 26
(Read Psalm 126 and sing or read "Sweet Hour of Prayer," verse 1)
(Reading from 1 Timothy 2:1–7)

(Morning)
God, who hears the prayers of all people, I ask for wisdom not to begin this day without first turning to you and dedicating my life to your glory.

(Evening)
God, who hears the prayers of all people, I know that this day is not rightly ended until it is gratefully returned to you with confidence in your mercy.

I am moved, O God, by the letter to Timothy and its appeal for prayer on behalf of all people. I claim to be a follower of your Christ and to know the place of prayer at the center of Christ's life for others. With Timothy, I need to be reminded that prayer is a ministry not only for my own benefit but for the good of others, especially for those who are hostile to the good news of Christ. Teach me the way of prayer. When I am empty or confused, let your Holy Spirit intercede for me with sighs too deep for words. Forgive me when I remember other things in my praying but forget to say thank you for persons, for others, for everyone made in your likeness and image.

(Morning)
As my life is touched by others today, O God, whether friends or strangers, may they find sanctuary in my prayers offered to you.
(Prayers of Intercession)

(Evening)
Today, O God, I know that I have entertained "angels unawares" in people touched by your grace.
(Prayers of Intercession)

And now, with humility, I pray.
(Pray the Prayer of Our Savior.)

(Morning)
There will be only one day like this day, O God. Keep me open to your presence in each person I meet. Amen.

(Evening)
Praying for everyone, dear God, is not easy. At day's end, this I know with new joy: The cloud of witnesses is closer than I thought! Amen.

THURSDAY, NOVEMBER 27 (THANKSGIVING DAY)
(Read Psalm 126 and sing or read "Now Thank We All Our God," verse 1)
(Reading from Matthew 6:25–33)

(Morning)
God of seedtime and harvest, I greet this morning knowing that your steadfast love preceded the dawn and that you will provide for the day that opens at your command.

(Evening)
God of seedtime and harvest, I celebrate the close of this day, brought to fullness by your grace, with gratitude for gifts uncounted and undeserved.

In Matthew's Gospel, I listen for wisdom on the lips of Jesus and hear timeless truth in familiar words that are always new. Why do I strive so feverishly, O God, for things that do not last and do not ultimately matter? If birds, flowers, and grass in the wild flourish with your care, why do I pretend that everything depends on me? Save me from the ingratitude of believing that on my own, alone, I am more than a shadow of what you call me to be. Free me from the illusion of self-sufficiency. Show me the joy of putting first things first, of seeking you and your reign above all else, and of finding in your righteousness amazing grace.

(Morning)
Save me from the arrogance of a thankless heart and use me this day to bring thanksgiving to the lives of others.
(Prayers of Intercession)

(Evening)
Thank you, God, for this special day of prayer and feasting in a land still in search of justice and peace.
(Prayers of Intercession)

And now, with gratitude, I pray.
(Pray the Prayer of Our Savior.)

(Morning)
On this Thanksgiving Day, God of all creation, teach me again that I do not live by bread alone but by every word that comes from you. Amen.

(Evening)
Your reign, O God, by Christ's promise, is in our midst. I have seen a glimpse of it this Thanksgiving Day. Let not my sleep dull my memory of its splendor.

FRIDAY, NOVEMBER 28
(Read Psalm 25:1–3 and sing or read "O Come, O Come, Emmanuel," verse 1)
(Read Jeremiah 33:14–16)

(Morning)
God of promises that await their time, I do not know what this day holds for me
but I know that you hold both me and the day.

(Evening)
God of promises that await their time, as this day fades into night,
I see the power of your promises that do not fade or fail.

As Advent season approaches, I yearn for the faith of Jeremiah and find in his words of promise and waiting hope beyond what is seen. How can it be that Jeremiah, imprisoned, condemned by religious leaders and certain of his nation's defeat, speaks of your promises? I am in awe of those who face unimaginable burdens without surrendering to them. Help me to live a faith that says to the world: "The day of God's promises is surely coming." Awaken in me, O God, a vital sense of expectancy, lest I miss the signs of your promises fulfilled. Deliver me from indifference and dull expectation, that I may see in the Child of Bethlehem the righteous branch who has promised to come again at the close of history.

(Morning)
Hold me close throughout this day so that I may recognize
your promises unfolding.
(Prayers of Intercession)

(Evening)
My day has been full of so many things. Grant me a discerning heart
to sort out the wheat from the chaff.
(Prayers of Intercession)

And now, with expectation, I pray.
(Pray the Prayer of Our Savior.)

(Morning)
Make me more than a passive observer of your grace. Fill me, dear God, with contagious expectancy. Amen.

(Evening)
At day's end, I rejoice that waiting for your promises touches me with their power even before they come. Amen.

SATURDAY, NOVEMBER 29
(Read Psalm 25:6–7 and sing or read "O How Shall I Receive You," verse 2)
(Read 1 Thessalonians 3:9–13)

(Morning)
Loving and gracious God, I am blessed by this new day and ask for the grace to live it as a child of your love.

(Evening)
Loving and gracious God, I come to the close of this day amazed by your love in a violent world perplexed by gentleness.

God, through the life of Paul, you challenge my timid notions of love and all my comfortable assumptions. If love is as important as I think it is, surely I need to say with Paul, "I love you" more and more. Paul assures the Thessalonians that they are loved before he invites them "to abound in love for one another and for all." Free my lips to speak words of heartfelt love before I expect others to be loving. With Paul, show me the way of love that embraces all, so that when Christ greets me in any human being, my heart will be a place of welcome.

(Morning)
Touch me today with compassion for all who feel excluded
and pressed to the margins of life.
(Prayers of Intercession)

(Evening)
As this day ends, I thank you for all who have loved me,
even when I have not loved myself.
(Prayers of Intercession)

And now, with renewed love, I pray.
(Pray the Prayer of Our Savior.)

(Morning)	(Evening)
Let not this day pass, O God, without my love including in its circle someone who is alone. Amen.	Forgive me, O God, where I have left unsaid today a single word of love that belongs to another. Amen.

SUNDAY, NOVEMBER 30
(Read Psalm 25:8–10 and sing or read "Watcher, Tell Us of the Night," verse 1)
(Read Luke 21:25–36)

(Morning)
God of justice and mercy, grant me a readiness of heart to live this day
in covenant with you as life's surprises unfold hour by hour.

(Evening)
God of justice and mercy, in the requiem of this day, teach me a readiness
for the end of all my days begun, continued, and fulfilled in you.

The words of Jesus do not pass away. O God, they both trouble and bless the contrite of heart. It is so easy to pay attention to nature's calendar of earth's times and seasons. If only, dear God, I could grasp the signs of your judgment and mercy. Your reign is already real and powerful in the ministry of Christ Jesus. Forgive me for praying for your reign to come when I am too preoccupied to notice that it is already here.

(Morning)
Free me, dear God, from my indifference to your presence
in a world that you love enough to save.
(Prayers of Intercession)

(Evening)
I thank you, God, for caring for me and the world, even when I forget you.
(Prayers of Intercession)

And now, with hope, I pray.
(Pray the Prayer of Our Savior.)

(Morning)
Prepare my heart today for the coming of the Child of Bethlehem that I may be your child forever. Amen.

(Evening)
Your reign come, O God, on earth, in me, this night and forever. Amen.

MONDAY, DECEMBER 1
(Read Malachi 3:1–4)

(Morning)
Ancient God of new beginnings, awaken my soul to perceive your coming.
May I seek your face in each person I meet today.

(Evening)
Ancient God of new beginnings, still your purifying fire burns
as night embraces the earth.

Blessed are you, God, whose words open a path between my heart and yours. Open my eyes, ears, mind, and soul to the words you speak through your prophet Malachi. God of the ages, you call us in this season to prepare a way, to make a space for the one who comes again and again. But how can we, creatures of dust, withstand the burning of your glory and the passion of your presence? Remind me, O God, that you who dwell in splendor also love our humble places and that you who knows my inward spaces desires to dwell therein.

(Morning)
As I look to this day, I offer these prayers to you.
(Prayers of Intercession)

(Evening)
In the evening quiet, bless me as I remember this day and the people
who revealed your presence.
(Prayers of Intercession)

And now with gratitude I pray.
(Pray the Prayer of Our Savior.)

(Morning)	(Evening)
May I journey with you this day, preparing a path for you as I go. Amen.	Enfold me in your dark embrace. I rest in you this night. Amen.

TUESDAY, DECEMBER 2
(Read Luke 1:68–71)

(Morning)
God of the generations, the light of this morning brings memories of your faithfulness from age to age.

(Evening)
God of the generations, in these hours of nightfall, I wait with you, remembering your goodness to me.

Faithful God, how can I keep from singing of your redeeming love and saving grace? As I listen to the canticle of Zechariah, I join with him and all generations who have known your faithfulness. God, you struck Zechariah speechless when he dared to question you about the things to come. How, then, am I to stand before you, filled as I am with questions and uncertainty? Perhaps I, too, need Zechariah's gift in this season—to be quiet, so that I may remember your story and know that answers will come from the silence even as new life comes from old age.

(Morning)
In this time of quiet, I hold these questions out to you . . .
(Prayers of Intercession)

(Evening)
Bless me as I remember the answers you have provided me along my journey.
(Prayers of Intercession)

With gratitude for your faithfulness, I pray.
(Pray the Prayer of Our Savior.)

(Morning)
Remembering your mercy to every generation, I enter this day with thankfulness. Amen.

(Evening)
Even as the earth turns in the darkness, I turn to rest in your peace this night. Amen.

WEDNESDAY, DECEMBER 3
(Read Luke 1:72–75)

(Morning)
Merciful God, by your compassion, you have brought me to this day.
In thankfulness, I give myself to you.

(Evening)
Merciful God, may the prayers of my heart be a pleasing offering to you this night.

Generations have told of your saving mercy, O God. As I listen to these words of Zechariah, may I discern the service to which you call me. You remind us, God, that every act of service freely chosen is a radical affirmation of hope, a sign that not by the hands of our enemies, not by the chains of our oppressors, not by the threats of tyrants, not by the wounds of the past, and not by our fears of the future will your people be held. It is you, God, who captivates our hearts, holding us with fingers interlaced in a gentle and fierce love.

(Morning)
Safe in your hands, I pray for those who long to know your freeing touch.
(Prayers of Intercession)

(Evening)
Bless me, God, as I reflect on my journey through this day.
(Prayers of Intercession)

Bless me now as I pray.
(Pray the Prayer of Our Savior.)

(Morning)
Mindful of your saving mercy, I offer myself in service to you this day.
Amen.

(Evening)
Keep me in your heart, so that even my sleep may be an offering to you. Amen.

THURSDAY, DECEMBER 4
(Read Luke 1:76–79)

(Morning)
God of every time and season, from the shadows of this night I emerge,
thankful for this new day.

(Evening)
God of every time and season, remind me of your presence
as the shadows enfold the earth once again.

Bearer of light, companion in darkness, I thank you for your words that reveal to me your path of peace. There are many kinds of darkness: the darkness that comes when fear obscures our path; the darkness of the womb, where life waits to be born; the darkness enfolding the seed, nourishing it to emergence. There is darkness that engulfs us, seeking to convince us that we are alone; and there is darkness that reveals the touch of one who journeys with us. But no darkness is without you, who dazzles even in the dimness of our sight.

(Morning)
As the earth receives the sun's warmth, receive these prayers, gracious God.
(Prayers of Intercession)

(Evening)
As I prepare for rest, I hold these people in the light of your love.
(Prayers of Intercession)

Remembering your faithfulness in every hour, I pray.
(Pray the Prayer of Our Savior.)

(Morning)
May I bear your light to each person I meet this day. Amen.

(Evening)
One with the silence, at peace with the darkness, I dwell in your love all through this night. Amen.

FRIDAY, DECEMBER 5
(Read Philippians 1:3–7)

(Morning)
God who calls us together, as I greet this day, I remember those
who have journeyed with me in love and in grace.

(Evening)
God who calls us together, may the presence of your love and the memories
of your faithful people keep me company in these evening hours.

I thank you, God, for those who have held me in their hearts. Speak to me through these words written to the beloved community at Philippi. I am here, God, because of those who have loved me into your presence, those who have held me in all my fears, and those who have loved me beyond all the barriers. Freed by your grace, may your people so love one another with a passionate and compassionate partnership that we may bring forth the Christ anew, in this and every season.

(Morning)
As the sun rises in the waiting sky, so I lift these prayers to you.
(Prayers of Intercession)

(Evening)
Bless me as I pray for these people, that they may know your peace in these hours.
(Prayers of Intercession)

I offer you now the prayer passed on from generation to generation.
(Pray the Prayer of Our Savior.)

(Morning)
Bless me this day as I work with you to
bring forth your new creation. Amen.

(Evening)
Draw your rest-filled hand across my
face and hold me in your heart
throughout this night. Amen.

SATURDAY, DECEMBER 6
(Read Philippians 1:8–11)

(Morning)
God of love and longing, I greet this day thankful
for your extravagant love toward me.

(Evening)
God of love and longing, in these evening hours I remember the care
you show for me through your people.

As Paul loved and cared for his friends, even more do you long for your people, O God. May I feel your tenderness toward me as I ponder Paul's words to the Philippians. Prison walls could not contain Paul's love for his friends. And this is how you work, amazing God—with a longing that breaks down the walls, blows open the doors, wears away the stones, washes over the desert, renews your creation and cries out, "Glory! Come to the harvest!"

(Morning)
As I look to this day, I hold out these prayers to your loving, transforming hands.
(Prayers of Intercession)

(Evening)
Even as you hold me in your love, I hold these people in my heart
and pray for them.
(Prayers of Intercession)

And now, with hope, I pray.
(Pray the Prayer of Our Savior.)

(Morning)
Remembering your love and goodness
toward me, may I extend your embrace
to those I meet this day. Amen.

(Evening)
Wrap me in the folds of your darkness
and hold us all in peace throughout this
night. Amen.

SUNDAY, DECEMBER 7
(Read Luke 3:1–6)

(Morning)
Forgiving God, fill my gaze with the wonder of your presence.

(Evening)
Forgiving God, may I perceive your path before me even in the shadows of this night.

God of creation, you long to restore your earth. Bless my own imagining as, with Luke, I remember Isaiah's vision of a new creation. What do you mean, God, by offering visions of filled valleys, of flattened mountains, of straight-shot roads and easy paths? It all seems a terrifying sameness from a God who has blessed creation with difference and variety. Perhaps the vision means not that all will be made easy and the same, but rather that all will be made plain and that no one will be above another. All flesh will stand on level ground and we will meet one another's gaze as we wait for you with wonder.

(Morning)
As I greet this day, I pray for all who wait.
(Prayers of Intercession)

(Evening)
Bless me, wait with me, as I reflect on this day and look to tomorrow.
(Prayers of Intercession)

With hope and with longing I pray.
(Pray the Prayer of Our Savior.)

(Morning)
Send me, God, renewed by a vision of your new creation. Bless my hands and my heart, that I may help prepare a path for you in this and every season. Amen.

(Evening)
Wait with me in these evening hours and throughout this night. Bless this flesh, this soul, this night, that I may dream of your new creation and help bring it to birth. Amen.

MONDAY, DECEMBER 8
(Read Luke 3:7–14)

(Morning)
Divine Wisdom, thank you for a new day with new opportunities, new experiences, new demands, new choices. Help me to let go of yesterday and embrace this new day with courage, enthusiasm, and commitment.

(Evening)
Divine Wisdom, the day is now past. Bless my faithfulness, forgive my failures. Let me rest in the blessed assurance that I am yours and you are mine.

Almighty God, examine my life and my fruit today. Let my repentance be more than guilty or remorseful feelings. Let my repentance lead to sharing with the destitute, honesty in business, and contentment with my wages. Let me not be content that my name is on a church roll. Let me be content knowing that my actions are pleasing to you.

(Morning)
At the beginning of this new day, guard my lips, lest my words offend you; guide my feet, lest I go in the wrong direction; clear my path, lest I stumble along the way; purify my thoughts, lest I imagine vain things; sanctify my motives, lest I deceive myself.
(Prayers of Intercession)

(Evening)
Now I lay me down to sleep, entrusting myself to you all night long.
(Prayers of Intercession)

Lead me not into temptation, but deliver me from evil.
(Pray the Prayer of Our Savior.)

(Morning)	(Evening)
Let the words of my mouth and the meditation of my heart be acceptable in your sight all day long. Amen.	Guard me in the silence of this evening. Watch over me through the night. Keep me in the center of your love. Amen.

TUESDAY, DECEMBER 9
(Read Zephaniah 3:14–20)

(Morning)
Triumphant God, I claim the promise of your presence at the beginning of this new day. Help me hold on to that promise all day long.

(Evening)
Triumphant God, as you have been with me all day, you will not leave me during the night. I close my eyes for sleep, now, knowing that I rest in your watch care.

Triumphant God, you have revealed yourself to your children as a victorious warrior. When I feel discouraged, I need that image. When I feel defeated, I need that image. When I feel distraught, I need that image. When I feel inadequate, I need that image. Help me to see you today as a victorious warrior in my life; unafraid, resolute, courageous, and brave. When I am weak and timid and unsure, let my thoughts return to that image. Then I will be steadfast and strong.

(Morning)
Christ Jesus, lover of my soul, let me enjoy your divine embrace all day long and in the assurance of your love, let me embrace others.
(Prayers of Intercession)

(Evening)
Wonderful Counselor, as you did for the psalmist, counsel me also during my sleep. Let me awaken in the morning rested and wiser.
(Prayers of Intercession)

With confidence I pray.
(Pray the Prayer of Our Savior.)

(Morning)
O God of new beginnings, I delight in the rebirth of day. Give me courage to live this day in its fullness. Amen.

(Evening)
Help me, Heavenly Guide, to sort, and sift, and process all the events of the day. During this night, stir together the different events, experiences, and emotions of the night. Keep me in the center of your love. Amen.

WEDNESDAY, DECEMBER 10
(Read Zephaniah 3:16–17)

(Morning)
O God, strengthen my hands with hope today. Let me face each new demand unafraid and with confidence.

(Evening)
O God, the deeds of today are past. The deeds of tomorrow are seeds yet to be planted. Give me quiet rest so that I may arise in the morning with new strength to plant in hope of a full harvest.

Almighty God, I have known the paralysis of fear and hopelessness in times of pain and confusion and distress. But I hear your words that say, "Do not let your hands fall limp." Rescue me from "limp hands" and the emotional paralysis that robs me of vitality. Let me know today that you "are in my midst." And if I forget, give me helpful reminders.

(Morning)
Help me to lay aside the garment of sleep and take up the garment of wakefulness. Help me to embrace this new day with energy and enthusiasm.
(Prayers of Intercession)

(Evening)
Cleanse me, O God, and I will be clean. Still me, and I will have rest.
(Prayers of Intercession)

In boldness I pray.
(Pray the Prayer of Our Savior.)

(Morning)
Good morning, God. I trust in the goodness of the morning because you are good. Lead me in your goodness all through the day. Amen.

(Evening)
Let my bed be a meeting place for my soul and your Spirit. In this place of holiness, give me pleasant sleep, insightful dreams, sweet peace, and renewing rest. Amen.

THURSDAY, DECEMBER 11
(Read Philippians 4:4–7)

(Morning)
O God, let this be a day of rejoicing, not because everything that will happen today is good, but because I know there is good, regardless of what happens.

(Evening)
O God, as this precious day comes to a close, accept my thanks and praise for another day of life. Give me the gift of quiet rest and a calm heart.

God of joy, if Paul could rejoice in prison, then help me to rejoice in the privileges of freedom that I enjoy today. When I am feeling discouraged, help me to rejoice. When I am feeling sorrow, help me to rejoice. When I am feeling depressed, help me to rejoice. When I am feeling overworked and undervalued and taken for granted, let me remember prison words of praise, "Rejoice in God always, and again I will say, rejoice!"

(Morning)
The night has passed, the day has come. Blessed be the name of God.
(Prayers of Intercession)

(Evening)
Almighty God, let your strong arms surround me, your eternal love enfold me, your watchful eye guard me all night long.
(Prayers of Intercession)

Rejoicing, I pray.
(Pray the Prayer of Our Savior.)

(Morning)
As I open my eyes to a new day, open my heart to receive your Word of guidance, instruction, inspiration, and conviction. Amen.

(Evening)
As the shadows of the night surround and envelop me, I am reminded that night is not gloomy to you, and I am glad. Be with me through the night— an ever-seeing eye. Amen.

FRIDAY, DECEMBER 12
(Read Philippians 4:5)

(Morning)
Dear Heavenly Parent, I greet this new day as an opportunity to continue my life journey. Today when I face conflict, give me patience. When I face confusion, give me clarity. When I face restlessness, give me peace.

(Evening)
Dear Heavenly Parent, I rest tonight knowing that I am your child.
Use my dreams to instruct and correct me.

Immanent God, your Word reminds me that you are near. But sometimes you seem so far away. Remind me of your nearness all during the day: during my conversations; during my decision making; during my commute; and during my time with the family. Be nearer to me than my own breath, and at the end of the day, I will give you thanks.

(Morning)
Divine Wisdom, you have counseled me to number my days so that I might gain wisdom. Let me treat this new day as a day that counts.
(Prayers of Intercession)

(Evening)
Replace my restlessness with your rest, my anxiety with your peace, my activity with your stillness, so that I can sleep all night long.
(Prayers of Intercession)

In the company of your presence, I pray.
(Pray the Prayer of Our Savior.)

(Morning)
In the stillness of the dawn, I am aware of my weakness. Help me to claim your strength so that I can face this day with courage. Amen.

(Evening)
The day is over. A page in my life book is finished. I rest tonight anticipating continuing the journey tomorrow. Amen.

SATURDAY, DECEMBER 13
(Read Isaiah 12:2–6)

(Morning)
O God, in this moment of worship, put a song in my heart and on my mind so that I can sing to you all day long. Let this be a day in which I can give an answer to others for the hope that lies deep within me.

(Evening)
O God, I close my eyes to sleep, knowing that you never slumber or sleep. With that calm assurance, I rest now in peace.

Source of eternal life, I come to this time of worship, that I might draw water from the springs of salvation. Like fresh artesian wells, let your life overflow in me today. Quench the thirsty, parched, dry places in my soul with your refreshing presence. Like a tree planted by springs of water, let my life be a blessing and a witness to others around me.

(Morning)
Creator of the Light, as the light of day dawns,
let me live in the light as you are in the light.
(Prayers of Intercession)

(Evening)
In the stillness of this night, help me to be still.
Still my thoughts, fears, and worries, that I might rest.
(Prayers of Intercession)

With everflowing streams of love, I pray.
(Pray the Prayer of Our Savior.)

(Morning)
God of the new day, help me to accept all the new beginnings of my life with the same hope as I accept this new day. Amen.

(Evening)
Place your loving arms around me during this night and protect me from all harm. Amen.

SUNDAY, DECEMBER 14
(Read Philippians 4:4–7)

(Morning)
Creator God, on this Sabbath day, give me such a sense of your presence that my worship will continue long after the services of my church are past.

(Evening)
Creator God, just as I prepare for sleep, help me to lay aside the worries and cares of the day, that I might be "anxious for nothing."

O God, I hear the words of your servant that call me to be anxious for nothing. But I am anxious—anxious for my health; anxious for my career; anxious for my family; anxious for my future. I want to let go of my anxiety and receive your incomprehensible peace. But I don't know how. Lead me today into new ways of thinking so that my anxieties may be overwhelmed by your peace.

(Morning)
At the break of this new day, I give you thanks for all that is good.
I also give you thanks for difficulties.
(Prayers of Intercession)

(Evening)
All that did not get done this day, I commit to you this night. Let me awaken with new resolve to complete the tasks that await me in the morning.
(Prayers of Intercession)

With assurance, I pray.
(Pray the Prayer of Our Savior.)

(Morning)
As the branch abides in the vine, let me abide in you this day. Let your light, life, and love flow through me to all that I meet. Amen.

(Evening)
As I bow to sleep, bless those that I cannot bless, touch those that I cannot touch, help those that I cannot help, be near those that I cannot be near, comfort those that I cannot comfort. With confidence that you hear my prayer, let me rest in peace. Amen.

MONDAY, DECEMBER 15
(Read Micah 5:3–5a)
(Read or sing "Come, O Long-Expected Jesus")

(Morning)
O God of peace, the promise of this new day is a reminder of the freshness of your love. I face this day filled with expectancy.

(Evening)
O God of peace, I seek the peace that a night of rest affords.

You alone are to be praised, for you find in the smallest portions of your creation, opportunities to bring peace to a troubled world. With care, you found one on the margin of society whose womb you blessed with your divine and human presence. You chose Bethlehem, a small town, for the birth of a ruler. I praise you in your divine wisdom. You call me to remember again and again that a ruler who is to bring divine peace experiences first the newness of birth and of being small, before growing up to be a shepherd.

(Morning)
In silence, I pray for those who also wait to experience again
the glory of your coming.
(Prayers of Intercession)

(Evening)
Comfort me and all those who face the evening, longing for much-needed rest.
(Prayers of Intercession)

Teach me always to pray as you taught your disciples.
(Pray the Prayer of Our Savior.)

(Morning)
Alive with praise for the day foretold, I pray for those surrounded by walls of oppression. Free them so that they, too, will know the peace that you offer. Amen.

(Evening)
Filled with your love, I seek the peace that this night of rest will bring. Amen.

TUESDAY, DECEMBER 16
(Read Psalm 80:1–7 and Luke 1:47–55)

(Morning)
O God of the One who comes, the day foretold is at hand,
and I leap into this new day filled with excitement.

(Evening)
O God of the One who comes, as night approaches,
I wait for the silence that provides calmness and rest.

Blessed are you, God of Israel, you have looked favorably on your people, and what a joy it is to be among those who will experience again your salvation! What love you have shown in choosing a woman to carry the precious child in her womb! You have fulfilled your promise that the least among us will be blessed. I feel with Mary the leaping of the unborn child in the womb. This assures me that my sins are forgiven and your mercy endures forever.

(Morning)
The light of this day is only a foretaste of the light that signals the arrival
of the Savior.
(Prayers of Intercession)

(Evening)
As night draws near, I know that the light that hovered over Mary will shine again
and brighten your promised new day.
(Prayers of Intercession)

Sing or read the Magnificat.

(Morning)
I enter this day without fear, reminded that you alone are God. Hear my prayer for my family and all who have special needs this day. Amen.

(Evening)
I sit in shadows, and yet I know that your light will shine through, even as I sleep. Amen.

WEDNESDAY, DECEMBER 17
(Read Hebrews 10:5–10. Pause for a period of silence before reading today's meditation.)

(Morning)
Gracious and loving God, I arise this day, ready to do your will. I arise knowing that I have been sanctified, through Jesus the Christ, whose advent I now await.

(Evening)
Gracious and loving God, I come to the end of this day, admitting that even as I desired to do your will, I was tempted to take matters into my own hands. Forgive and free me, so that I might sleep in peace.

I am confronted with fear, anxiety, and misgivings—fear that my human pride will overshadow the humility that you desire of me; anxiety that your promised light will reveal what I have hidden; and misgivings about ways that the world has turned your Advent into a time of economic exploits and superficial frivolity. Forgive me for these earthly concerns, and help me live into this day, truly ready to do your will.

(Morning)
Even as I face my own concerns, I lift before you the names of those I know who seek to do your will and need your healing power. I lift up . . .
(Prayers of Intercession)

(Evening)
Thank you for the freedom that your forgiveness provides.
(Prayers of Intercession)

With confidence, I pray the prayer that Jesus taught his disciples.
(Pray the Prayer of Our Savior.)

(Morning)
I move boldly into this day, committed to do your will, for I am surrounded by the light of your love. Amen.

(Evening)
Grant me a restful night, so that I may awaken to the light of your face. Amen.

THURSDAY, DECEMBER 18
(Read Micah 5:2–5a and Luke 1:39–55)

(Morning)
O God of promise, morning has broken, and I am ready to share the goodness of your coming with all who will listen. Guide my feet in the way of peace.

(Evening)
O God of promise, I face the night with joy. I have experienced the blessedness of expectant memory.

Like Elizabeth, I know that the life that leaped in Mary's womb was the promised Savior. I leap into this day with joy, remembering that the world will again be blessed by one who dispels gloom and removes anguish and oppression. By the Spirit's power, my heart rejoices in the majesty of your name, for you look with approval on the lowliness of a servant. I am empowered to serve, to feed the hungry, to break the chains of those who are bound in oppression. I am empowered to avoid seeking to be rich, for I know that you will bring down the high and mighty. Have mercy upon me, O God.

(Morning)
I await your strength, for I am among the kindred flock.
(Prayers of Intercession)

(Evening)
Be with me and all these little ones who labor expectantly at the end of this day . . .
(Prayers of Intercession)

Lift up the names of those for whom I pray.

(Morning)
I pray for the world, that all may realize that the reign of God is near. Grant that peace will fall on all who are walled in by warring spirits. Amen.

(Evening)
By your tender mercy, O God, grant me restful sleep until the dawn from on high breaks upon me. Amen.

FRIDAY, DECEMBER 19
(Read Psalm 80:1–7)
(Reading from Psalm 80:1–7)

(Morning)
God of mercy, I was awakened by the quietness of the dawn,
which announced the beginning of another day.

(Evening)
God of mercy, thank you for the quiet time of prayer that you allowed me this day.

In the silence of this moment through which your glory shines, I hear again the words of the psalmist. You, O God, are creator, sustainer, and shepherd of the universe. You have protected and guided your faithful followers throughout the stormy past. Yet trouble still confounds us, and I am concerned about the future. I sing your praises, I bow before you in prayer, but my prayers often seem to go unheard. I join with others at worship and in the work of the church, and we are told that we are not meeting the needs of the people. Renew your church and revive your servants.

(Morning)
Stir up in me this day a new vision, so that I might provide a tiny spark
to ignite a flame within my own community of faith.
(Prayers of Intercession)

(Evening)
Turn not your face away from me as I seek comfort in prayers that were answered.
(Prayers of Intercession)

I wait in silence for your commissioning.

(Morning)	(Evening)
Restore me to newness of life so that my rejuvenation will inspire others to receive with enthusiasm the long-awaited Christ. Amen.	I rest securely, knowing that you have not deserted me, nor any of your people who earnestly seek to be restored. Amen.

SATURDAY, DECEMBER 20
(Read Micah 5:2–5a, Hebrews 10:5–10, and Luke 1:39–55)

(Morning)
O God of justice and liberation, I was aroused with questions this morning: "Am I free if anyone is in bondage? Does my freedom force others to be in bondage?"

(Evening)
O God of justice and liberation, rest is needed,
for I have struggled with thoughts that have pained me.

Holy God, as I anticipate your promised coming in Jesus the Christ, I want to identify with the lowly, but I prefer to walk with the powerful, for I do not want to be trodden upon. I want to be among those who are hungry, but I eat often and have not felt serious hunger pangs. I want to identify with those who champion the poor, the oppressed, and the despised, yet I work hard to avoid fitting into those categories. I do not want to be scattered with the proud, but pride often gets in my way.

(Morning)
Help me to remember your mercy, O God
according to the promises made to our ancestors.
(Prayers of Intercession)

(Evening)
I pray for those whom I have harmed, and those from whom I am estranged.
(Prayers of Intercession)

Remembering the words of Mary, your humble servant, I pray.

(Morning)
Forgive me for any desires that I have to be among those whom God would scatter, bring down, or send away empty. Amen.

(Evening)
My soul magnifies the Christ, and my spirit rejoices in a loving and forgiving God. Amen.

SUNDAY, DECEMBER 21
(Read Micah 5:2–5a, Hebrews 10:5–10, and Luke 1:39–45)

(Morning)
God of love, I offer myself to you this day in devotion and service.

(Evening)
God of love, hear your servant's prayer and grant me a night of rest,
so I may awaken renewed and energized to love and serve you.

Praise and thanksgiving are offered to you alone. You established a new covenant with your people, replacing human laws with divine love. Because of your love for me and all humankind, you fulfilled your promise to send a shepherd who would demonstrate authentic servanthood. I offer myself to you in devotion and service. Because of your love for me and all humankind, you provided salvation through one who would die, that we might have life more abundantly. I offer myself to you in devotion and service. Because of your love for me and all humankind, you brought peace to a troubled world. I offer myself to you in devotion and service.

(Morning)
Loving God, in anticipation of the advent of Jesus, I will extend myself in love.
(Prayers of Intercession)

(Evening)
I pray for others who need to experience your love.
(Prayers of Intercession)

With confidence in your love, I pray as Jesus taught his disciples.
(Pray the Prayer of Our Savior.)

(Morning)
I pray for those in need of love and healing. Surround me with your love, and enable me to be an instrument of your peace. Amen.

(Evening)
As I sleep, help me to know that the time is near for the blessed coming of Christ Jesus, your love made visible. Amen.

MONDAY, DECEMBER 22
(Read Psalm 96)
(Readings from Isaiah 9:2b–5 and John 1:1–9)

(Morning)
Creator God, open my eyes so that I may see your light in all that surrounds me.

(Evening)
Creator God, as I rest, I thank you for your ever-abiding presence with me throughout this day.

I often become so preoccupied with the duties of the day that I have little time to notice your light. It may have been that way for Mary and Joseph. Their journey to Bethlehem was long and frustrating, filled with disappointments and setbacks. Even though they were carrying the light of the world, they, too, may have lost sight of that promise. O God, I want to believe that light shines through gloom, that the trees of the forest have reason to sing, that the burdens of the oppressed have been broken. But often my sight is so focused on my day-to-day chores that I grow unaccustomed to the brightness of your light. Let me live into your presence this day in all that I do.

(Morning)
I lift before you others who are especially in need of your loving presence.
(Prayers of Intercession)

(Evening)
God, bring to mind those people and events that offered your light to me this day.
(Prayers of Intercession)

As Jesus has taught his disciples, I pray.
(Pray the Prayer of Our Savior.)

(Morning)
I move into this day ready to receive all that you have for me. Amen.

(Evening)
God, even as I sleep, your light continues to shine, offering hope and new life. The shadows will never overcome it. May I rest in that promise. Amen.

TUESDAY, DECEMBER 23
(Read Psalm 96)
(Reading from Titus 2:11–14)

(Morning)
Spirit of hope, this day let me wait for your blessings.

(Evening)
Spirit of hope, I relax my mind and thoughts and rest in your abiding presence.

You come to me in a familiar song, in the waves of the sea, in the coolness of the breeze, in the voice of a friend. You come to me in the mighty act of incarnation. You call me to live out my life in relationship to others the way you relate to me. The only way I can do this is to wait for your blessed Spirit of hope. Forgive me when I fail to wait; forgive me when I am too impatient; forgive me when I choose to go it on my own. Thank you for your love, which forgives and calls us again and again to be your people.

(Morning)
As I wait in silence for your Spirit which empowers me,
bring to mind those people and events for which I need to pray.
(Prayers of Intercession)

(Evening)
Remind me, O God, of those moments I rushed ahead today
and failed to rely on your strength.
(Prayers of Intercession)

**I will let silence come close to me and settle in and around me
as I become aware of the blessed Spirit of hope.**

(Morning)
I go from this place full of hope knowing that salvation wholeness is available to all. Amen.

(Evening)
Let me rest through the night, confident of your loving grace. Amen.

WEDNESDAY, DECEMBER 24 (CHRISTMAS EVE)
(Read Psalm 98)
(Reading from Luke 2:1–14)

(Morning)
Divine Savior, as Mary approached Bethlehem, she was full of new life.
So let me see all the possibilities of new life within this day.

(Evening)
Divine Savior, on this holy evening in which we celebrate your entry
into our world, I praise you and relax in your presence.

Let this familiar story come alive with new meaning for me and all who hear it. Jesus, you were nestled in the womb of a young, unwed girl. You were born in a backyard barn and laid in the feeding pen of animals. Your first visitors where smelly strangers who spoke of angels in the sky. You are a God of the unexpected. You show up in the most unlikely places. I have heard this story many times, yet I forget that you continue to come to us over and over again in those unforeseen people and places of my everyday life. Forgive me when I simply pass them off as mere distractions or interruptions in my schedule.

(Morning)
You have come to me through so many people and events.
Let me name them now before you as an offering of thanksgiving.
(Prayers of Intercession)

(Evening)
As Mary and Joseph settled into this night so long ago, reflecting on their day,
so let me remember the ways in which you offered yourself to me
throughout this day.
(Prayers of Intercession)

**God, you delight in revealing yourself to me and all the world.
May the surprise of your presence bring us joy and peace!**

(Morning)
Creative God, let me enter into my day full of joy and anticipation. Amen.

(Evening)
Loving Jesus, as the warm womb embraced you so long ago, so surround me with your warmth and love this night. Amen.

THURSDAY, DECEMBER 25 (CHRISTMAS DAY)
(Read Isaiah 52:7–10)
(Reading from John 1:10–14)
(Sing "Joy to the World" or another favorite hymn)

(Morning)
Creator God, give me voice to sing and peace that overflows,
for CHRIST IS BORN!

(Evening)
Creator God, as I settle into this night, let me rest easy into your presence.

O loving God, you come and dwell among us. When we try to comprehend the Word made flesh we become lost in the wonder and love of it all. So we simply rest in that reality, relinquishing the need to put words of explanation to the truth of your incarnation. You have pitched your tent with us, and we live and breathe in your presence. We know your coming is not only for our sakes but for the healing of the nations. You bring wholeness to all who are broken and peace to all whose lives are torn by war and strife. So this day, as we remember with joy your birth, we also lift to you all who are oppressed and burdened by poverty and systems or situations that seek to keep them down.

(Morning)
Be born anew this day in my life, the lives of my family, my friends far and near,
my church community, my country, all who are oppressed, the world.
(Prayers of Intercession)

(Evening)
Remind me of those who are in need of an extra measure of your grace.
(Prayers of Intercession)

"And the Word became flesh and lived among us."

(Morning)
Let me joyfully live this day in your presence. Amen.

(Evening)
As the glow of your love surrounds me this night, let me rest in your loving embrace. Amen.

FRIDAY, DECEMBER 26
(Read Psalm 148)
(Readings from Isaiah 9:6–7 and Luke 2:15–20)

(Morning)
Bringer of Peace, let the rhythm of this day be one that would be pleasing to you.

(Evening)
Bringer of Peace, let me end my day full circle in praise of you.

It seems we do much of our celebrating and singing before the fact, but what happens now? For the shepherds, the time for singing was just beginning as they left the manger scene. The psalmist is so full of joy that the words seem to shout, "There's more, more that I want to say." But to tell you the truth, God, praise is not always an easy thing for me. You are praiseworthy—I know that in the depths of my being. But it's the "how-to" of praising that sometimes trips me up. So today I offer my praise modeled after Mary. In stillness, let me treasure and ponder the mystery of you.

(Morning)
Wonderful Counselor, quiet my soul, that I may contemplate the beauty
of your presence.
(Prayers of Intercession)

(Evening)
Everlasting Father, in the place where no words are needed,
bind up my day into your care.
(Prayers of Intercession)

**As silence opens up like an old friend longing to share a secret,
I will bring to God those people and events for which I have concern.**

(Morning)
Mighty God, let this time with you empower me to be with others. Amen.

(Evening)
Sustaining Mother, nestle me close to your breasts, that I may rest in your embrace through the night. Amen.

SATURDAY, DECEMBER 27
(Read Psalm 148 and Hebrews 1:1–12)
(Reading from Colossians 3:12–17)

(Morning)
God, as I awake this morning let my attitude be one of compassion and kindness.

(Evening)
God, let me rest in your love as I reflect on my day.

O Divine Spirit, it all comes down to love—why you came, how you lived, what you offer, what you want from us. It is love, so simple and yet so demanding. There seems to be no formula to follow, no rules that cover all the bases. But it is in my daily living, in my relation to you, and to those around me and the world, that I must carve what it means to be loving. Forgive me when I try to make it complicated and find it easy to discount loving as a possible answer. Forgive me when I think I have it all figured out. Thank you for your forgiving grace.

(Morning)
As I have been forgiven, bring to mind those persons who need my forgiveness.
(Prayers of Intercession)

(Evening)
Help me to review my day with your loving Spirit as my guide.
(Prayers of Intercession)

Drink deep of the love of God, that you might be empowered to offer love in action to a needy world.

(Morning)
Powerful Creator, your love turned the world upside down. Let me be so bold as to risk loving this day. In your powerful name. Amen.

(Evening)
Bind my day in your love, and let me rest in peace. Amen.

SUNDAY, DECEMBER 28
(Read Psalm 148 and 1 Samuel 2:18–20)
(Reading from Luke 2:41–52)

(Morning)
God, let me come this morning to sit at your feet and receive all you have for me.

(Evening)
God, as part of the body of Christ, let this worship be pleasing in your sight.

You were an ordinary kid, and the last place Mary and Joseph thought to look for you was in the temple. For at least three days, they searched for you. But there you were, making your presence known, making a place for yourself, quietly going about the work for which you had been sent. When I search for you today, often the church is the last place I look. For in a time when the church should be leading the way toward justice, equality, and peace, too often it is lagging far behind, taking its lead from the world. Yet you are still there, quietly and sometimes not so quietly going about your work. Give me patience and boldness to confront the church to be your body.

(Morning)
Transforming Spirit, let me celebrate those places where I see you at work in my life and in our world. Show me how I can join in your activity this day.
(Prayers of Intercession)

(Evening)
Loving God, you dream divine dreams for your world. This night as I rest, let me have visions of my mission with you.
(Prayers of Intercession)

Thank you for your active presence at work in base communities in Central America, in small villages in Africa, in community gatherings in Russia.

(Morning)
Let me be an active part of your transforming work in our world. Amen.

(Evening)
Divine Dreamer, let me rest in your peace, that I might be empowered to fulfill all that you dream for me. Amen.

Contributors

Lavon Bayler is conference minister of the Fox Valley Association, Illinois Conference of the United Church of Christ.

John Biegert is pastor of First Congregational Church in LaGrange, Illinois.

John E. Biersdorf is dean of Ecumenical Theological Seminary in Detroit, Michigan.

Gennifer Benjamin Brooks is pastor of Asbury United Methodist Church in Croton-on-Hudson, New York.

Margrethe B. J. Brown is a retired pastor in the Presbyterian Church USA.

Norval I. Brown is pastor of Gammon Memorial United Methodist Church in Chicago, Illinois.

LaTaunya M. Bynum, an ordained minister in the Christian Church (Disciples of Christ), is currently interim pastor of Bethany Christian Church in Lincoln, Nebraska.

Elizabeth Francis Caldwell is professor of educational ministry at McCormick Theological Seminary and a member of the Presbyterian Church.

Felix Carrion is associate for church empowerment, Office of Church in Society, United Church of Christ.

Martin Copenhaver is pastor of Wellesley Congregational Church in Wellesley, Massachusetts.

Kenneth A. Corr is pastor of First Baptist Church in Memphis, Tennessee.

Melva Costen is Helmar Emil Nielsen Professor of Worship and Music at the Interdenominational Theological Center. She is a member of the Presbyterian Church.

Hilda R. Davis is an editor at the United Methodist Publishing House.

Thomas Dipko is executive vice president of the United Church Board for Homeland Ministries, United Church of Christ.

Barbara Dumke is pastor of Trinity Episcopal Church in Anoka, Minnesota.

Barbara J. Essex is an ordained United Church of Christ minister and a private consultant.

Melbalenia D. Evans is minister of evangelism for local church renewal, United Church Board for Homeland Ministries, United Church of Christ.

Dorothy Ashman Fackre is currently a minister for pastoral and group counseling at South Congregational Church, UCC, in Centerville, Massachusetts.

Sidney D. Fowler is curriculum editor, United Church Board for Homeland Ministries, United Church of Christ.

Kathleen Gallas is a Benedictine sister.

Mary Susan Gast is executive director of the Coordinating Center for Women, United Church of Christ.

J. Denise Honeycutt is an ordained minister in the United Methodist Church. A professor of theology and New Testament at Banyam Theological Seminary, she is currently serving as a United Methodist Missionary in Nigeria.

Bernice Powell Jackson is executive director of the Commission for Racial Justice, United Church of Christ.

Carole Keim is the former Southwest Conference Minister, United Church of Christ.

James Richard Lahman is senior pastor of Salem United Church of Christ in Rochester, New York.

Dorothy M. Lester is minister for church life and leadership in the Office for Church Life and Leadership, United Church of Christ.

David T. Lyon is pastor of Saint Luke's United Church of Christ in Independence, Missouri.

Martha McMane is co-pastor of Saugatuck Congregational Church in Westport, Connecticut.

Lydia Waring Meyer is a pastoral intern at Lakeshore Community Church in Grand Haven, Michigan.

Mary Ann Neevel is pastor of Plymouth United Church of Christ in Milwaukee, Wisconsin.

Nell M. Payne is a retired teacher and former missionary in the United Methodist Church.

F. Allison Phillips is general secretary of the Division of the American Missionary Association, United Church Board for Homeland Ministries, United Church of Christ.

George Polk is interim pastor of Douglas Memorial Community Church in Baltimore, Maryland.

Morgan Ponder is professor of chemistry at Samford University in Birmingham, Alabama. He is a member of the Church of God in Christ.

Jan Richardson is associate pastor of St. Luke's Methodist Church in Orlando, Florida.

Anthony B. Robinson is senior pastor of Plymouth Congregational Church in Seattle, Washington.

Charles Shelby Rooks is the former executive vice president of the United Church Board for Homeland Ministries, United Church of Christ.

Paul H. Sadler Sr. is minister of evangelism for African American and Native American Indian church development, United Church Board for Homeland Ministries, United Church of Christ.

Susan M. Sanders is minister for volunteer services in the Division of American Missionary Association, United Church Board for Homeland Ministries, United Church of Christ.

G. Charles Satterwhite is senior pastor of North Gadsden Church of God and adjunct professor at Lee College in Cleveland, Tennessee.

Donna E. Schaper is area minister of the Massachusetts Conference, United Church of Christ.

Lisa Schoenwetter is the pastor of Immanuel United Church of Christ in Beverly, Massachusetts.

Don C. Skinner is a retired United Church of Christ minister and chaplain emeritus at Allegheny College in Meadville, Pennsylvania.

Susan K. Smith is pastor of Advent United Church of Christ in Columbus, Ohio.

Grant K. Sontag is minister for biblical and theological foundations in education for the United Church Board for Homeland Ministries, United Church of Christ.

Howard Stearns, a retired United Church of Christ minister, is currently interim pastor of the First Congregational Church in St. Albans, Vermont.

Jack Sullivan Jr. is senior pastor of United Christian Church in Detroit, Michigan.

Leslie Carole Taylor is minister for planning and constituency relations for the United Church Board for Homeland Ministries, United Church of Christ.

James A. Todhunter is senior pastor of Christ Congregational Church in Silver Spring, Maryland.

Frederick Trost is conference minister of the Wisconsin Conference, United Church of Christ.

Alan Weatherly is pastor of First United Methodist Church in Piedmont, Alabama.

Barbara Brown Zikmund is the president and a professor of American religious history at Hartford Seminary in Hartford, Connecticut.